Pictorial History of
SHIPS

J H Martin &
Geoffrey Bennett

octopus

Contents

First published 1977 by
Octopus Books Limited
59 Grosvenor Street
London W1

© 1977 Octopus Books Limited

ISBN 0 7064 0625 7

Produced by Mandarin Publishers Limited
22a Westlands Road
Quarry Bay, Hong Kong

Printed in Hong Kong

The Age of Fighting Sail

ON 17 NOVEMBER 1665, when the English and Dutch were at each other's throats, Samuel Pepys went to bed later than usual. As Clerk of the Acts, one of the four principal officers of the Navy Board, he had been writing a long letter to the Duke of York, the Lord High Admiral, about 'the ill condition of the Navy' and its need of money 'before it be too late'. That need was already a familiar theme in English naval history.

Just over 60 years earlier King James I had inherited from Queen Elizabeth a maritime fighting force which was to set a standard in ship design for more than two centuries, until the coming of steam. The English believed in the 'round' ship. With its ability to face heavy weather and to carry stores for a long voyage, it had served them well, and under Sir John Hawkins they had learnt to reduce its limitations as a vessel of war. By increasing its length in proportion to its breadth, they made it less 'round' and clumsy. It also looked less top-heavy and was better rigged, with a larger and more effective sail area.

From the time that Henry VIII, Elizabeth's father, introduced the broadside, the Navy was no longer seen as merely a fleet of vessels carrying armed men in 'castles' fore and aft. The 'great guns' on their carriages revolutionized the structure of the ships, as well as their purpose and the warfare in which they engaged. Weapons so big and heavy obviously had to be placed below, on the main cargo-deck. When one of Henry's shipwrights took the alarming step of cutting holes in the sides for the guns to fire through, the navy of the future was born. If the first vessel to have gunports was indeed the *Mary Rose* (with the *Great Harry*, or *Henry Grâce à Dieu*, the second), we may some day look upon the pioneer herself, put together from the remains lying off Spithead.

In making the old lofty upperworks unnecessary, the guns removed much of the dangerous top-weight. The less exaggerated forecastles which remained were set well back from the stem, and the awkward stern constructions were replaced by a quarter-deck and poop (or half-deck, quarter-deck and poop), each of them shorter than the one below. All the ships had the square tuck, or transom stern.

These improvements were accompanied by changes in rig. In the fleet which met the Spanish Armada, ten of the largest vessels had four masts and nearly all the others three. The fourth mast, the bonaventure mizzen – the second or outer mizzen, stepped well aft – grew in favour until it was driven out by the use, from 1618, of square topsails on the mizzen-mast. With the discovery that sail power could be better obtained in this way, the shipwrights let the bonaventure mizzen disappear; by 1640 it had gone from the English Navy.

Between 1611 and 1618, in King James's reign, a sprit-sail topsail was added, on a mast at the forward end of the bowsprit, where it remained, despite the exposed position, as late as the middle of the eighteenth century. The early Stuart period also brought in the general use of topgallants, developed from Hawkins's idea of topmasts which could be easily struck and sent down to the deck. They were standard equipment for the larger men-of-war by 1600, but the smaller vessels were still without them; these craft, of which little is known, had a rig of six sails: spritsail, fore course, fore topsail, main course, main topsail and lateen mizzen.

Links with the past inevitably remained. The fleet which confronted the Armada was still, in composition, the 'Old Navy of England'. Of the 197 vessels under Howard and Drake only 34 were 'Queen's ships'; the others, all 163 of them, belonged to private persons. The Elizabethans had not broken away completely from the medieval conception of the Navy as an emergency force composed of any ships that could take fighting men to sea. We feel very close to feudal times when we learn that the *Revenge* carried longbows and sheaves of arrows, together with harquebuses and hackbuts fired from forked rests or laid over the bulwarks. (There were 1,540 soldiers among the 15,925 men who waited for the Armada; on the Spanish side more than half the total were soldiers – 18,973 out of 30,656.)

Let us consider the *Revenge* for a moment. That famous man-of-war, Drake's flagship in the fateful summer of 1588, earned a place in naval history at the time of her completion for John Hawkins's fleet eleven years before the Armada. Two shipwrights of superlative ability, Matthew Baker and Peter Pett, built her as a new kind of warship, a floating gun-platform. She has a strong claim to be called the first sailing ship-of-the-line.

She carried 34 guns: 22 demi-cannon, cannon-perriers, culverins and demi-culverins on a single gundeck, and a dozen sakers, long five-pounders. Demi-cannon threw a 32lb shot, cannon-perriers a 24lb, culverins an 18lb and demi-culverins a 9lb.

We find the *Revenge* described as a fast, handy vessel of 500 tons measuring 92ft along the keel with a beam of 32ft, and lying 'low and snug' in the water. Besides being well-gunned, she could stay at sea for long periods and was easy to manoeuvre in close action. She was a four-master, with topmasts that could be struck in accordance with the new method adopted by Hawkins and welcomed as 'a wonderful ease to great ships'.

Her normal complement was 250: 150 sailors, 24 gunners and 76 soldiers. The light for them was poor even in daytime. At night, when most of them slept on the bare boards of the gun-deck wrapped in blankets and coats, they had the help of the 'purser's dip', a candle in a horn lantern.

England was proud of the *Revenge* and proud too of all the ships which had defeated the Armada. When Elizabeth died in 1603 she left James a fleet containing no more than 29 vessels of 100 tons and over; but those 29 represented the nucleus of a Navy which had destroyed the ambitions of the most powerful monarch on earth. 'I protest before God and as my soul shall answer for it that there were never in any place in the world worthier ships than these are': the words are the Lord Admiral's but they might have been her own.

Her successor was determined on a friendly settlement with Spain. After the war had ended, the Navy fell into neglect while its affairs were administered by incompetent and dishonest officials. From the highest of motives, the peace-loving James put an end to the letters of marque sanctioning the private capture by merchant-men of enemy ships and merchandise 'as reprisals'. Thereafter corsairs and privateers became so daring round the shores of Britain that seamen could not leave port without the risk of spending the rest of their lives as galley slaves. Any merchant captain who retaliated could be hanged from his own yardarm as a pirate. Landing at places in Cornwall, Devon and Ireland, 'Turks' from North Africa carried off young people to join the enslaved crews on the Barbary coast. Between 1609 and 1616 they captured nearly 500 English vessels. The 'Dun-kirkers' even levied a toll on ships using the Thames.

With the Narrow Seas full of terror, England's maritime trade declined appallingly. Seamen without employment at home went to work for the Dutch, and in the Medway noble ships rotted at their moorings, the Navy lacking the revenue from licensed privateering which had provided funds in Elizabeth's day. If Sir Walter Raleigh had written his projected treatise on sea power for Prince Henry, any part of it concerned with the Navy of his own time would have been melancholy indeed; but the Prince died, and in 1618 the King sent Raleigh to the block.

Among the few new men-of-war launched in James's reign was the *Prince Royal* of 1610, the largest ship which had yet been built. Some historians describe her as the first three-decker in the English Navy and others as the first two-decker: she had two full batteries and an armed upper deck. What first caught the eye was her decoration, the rich painting and gilding, the badges and coats of arms, the great carved lions' heads for the round gunports. The warships of Henry VIII and Elizabeth had been gaily coloured above their hulls, which were treated with a mixture of oil, turpentine and resin and left unpainted. Panels, arches and pillars, and geometrical designs were painted in bright contrasting colours on the upperworks. The *Revenge*, for instance, displayed the Tudor colours, green and white. Red was also favoured. On Elizabeth's ships yellow and purple, and occasionally blue, were seen. The sterns bore the Royal Arms, which may have been carved as well as painted, and there was an elaborately carved figurehead; but the *Prince Royal* introduced a completely new style. She looked so much a work of art that Phineas Pett who designed her was accused of making a showpiece rather than a man-of-war.

In 1637, working with his son Peter, he added the *Sovereign of the Seas* to the Navy of Charles I, who had succeeded James twelve years before. This historic three-decker, often referred to as the *Sovereign* or *Royal Sovereign*, was laid down at Woolwich on 16 January 1636 in the presence of the King and was launched in October of the following year. At the time of her building she displaced about 1,500 tons and was 232ft in length overall (with a keel of 127ft) and 46.5ft in beam, with a draught of 22.2ft.

She was a three-master, the bonaventure mizzen having vanished almost completely by that date. A well-known engraving by John Payne shows her with royals on the fore and main masts and a topgallant sail on the mizzen. These details, once questioned, are confirmed by a manuscript Navy list for 1640 at the Science Museum in London. Critics of the engraving – a copy of which Samuel Pepys hung in his green chamber – accepted that the 'Maintop Royal' and 'Foretop Royal' of the *Royal Sovereign* had been peculiar to that ship. At the end of the eighteenth century they came back into use as 'royals'.

Until the Restoration the *Sovereign* was the only English warship of 100 guns. In size and design the Navy's first true three-decker marked such an advance on any earlier vessel that she was hailed as 'this Britain's *Argo*', the eighth wonder of the world. To the ordinary person she was splendour afloat. Gerard Christmas, the royal master-carver, had ornamented her after drawings by Van Dyck, and at her prow a glittering equestrian figure, Edgar the Peaceful,

Above: Peter Pett with the splendid Sovereign of the Seas *which was designed by Phineas Pett, his father. The* Sovereign, *or* Royal Sovereign, *as she came to be known, was built at Woolwich under Peter Pett's supervision. After surviving half-a-dozen battles and the many hazards of nearly 60 years, she was accidentally burnt at Chatham in 1696.*

Right: Abraham Storck's painting of the Four Days' Battle in June 1666 during the Second Anglo–Dutch War. The Dutch struck three fine medals to commemorate their victory. The battle began on June 1, when the Duke of Albemarle had only 54 warships against the 84 commanded by de Ruyter.

trampled on seven conquered kings. She cost in all £40,833, to which £24,753 was added for the guns: the £6,691 spent on the inside and outside joining and the painting and carving would have paid for a 40-gun ship complete.

To the Dutch 'the eighth wonder of the world' was the Golden, or Gilded, Devil. She took part in the St James's Day Battle of 1666, the year of the Great Fire of London, and she was also in action against the Dutch at the Kentish Knock (1652), Solebay (1672) and the Texel (1673). By the time of her last battles, Beachy Head in 1690 and Barfleur in 1692, she was no longer a devil to the Hollanders; they had become the allies of England against the French. In the end the enemy which destroyed her was fire: after 60 years she caught alight accidentally at Chatham.

She was the queen of the Ship Money Fleet, her construction and lavish embellishment paid for out of the hated levy which helped bring about the Civil War in England. The King's decision to revive the Elizabethan naval tax and extend it so that it included inland communities as well as seaports and coastal counties, was itself thoroughly sound. It offered England a permanent force at sea, maintained by the people, in place of the old ramshackle arrangement of a temporary fleet provided by the monarch. Ultimately the nation accepted it; but the person who made it acceptable was Oliver Cromwell.

Under him the home waters were cleared of pirates, the maritime trade improved dramatically, and the Navy entered a new era of efficiency and strength. Money was no longer spent on exuberant decoration: indeed at one time, before the rules were eased, the ships appeared in

puritan black. Among other changes, the height of the hull above water was reduced and the length of the keel increased. Vessels became steadier and more weatherly; but no big improvements were made to the sails and rigging, and the sail area remained small in relation to tonnage.

Under the Commonwealth, the seamen were given a fairer deal – prompt and correct pay (at first), better care ashore when they were sick or wounded, and more opportunities for advancement.

The Cromwellian zest for organization extended from the Articles of War, which became the basis of all subsequent naval law and discipline, to the sailors' food – two pounds of beef or pork daily (or one-and-a-half pounds of fish on certain days) and one-and-a-half pounds of bread (really biscuit) and a gallon of beer; and from the food to a code of tactics governing the ships in battle. Fighting Instructions set out the manner of attack, with an agreed use of gun-and-flag signals. To take full advantage of the broadsides, the ships fought in line-ahead formation, as ordained by Blake, Deane and Monk (later Duke of Albemarle) on 29 March 1653, four months before Monk defeated the Dutch off Scheveningen.

When the Civil War began in 1642, the Navy had 34 vessels of between 300 and 850 tons, as well as the *Sovereign* and *Prince*, handsome first-rates. In the eleven years of Cromwell's rule it acquired, under the Navy Commissioners who had replaced the Navy Board, no fewer than 207, of which 121 were still on the active list at the Restoration. By the end of 1651 more than 20 ships suitable for the line of battle had been added, and at the beginning of the First Dutch

War in the spring of 1652 another ten were launched or on the stocks. Twenty-two new men-of-war entered the water in 1654 alone.

In May 1652 the Dutch could muster about 115 warships and the English 85; but Cromwell's vessels were superior in power. Eighteen of them mounted over 40 guns, whereas most of the Dutch had between 20 and 30. Tromp's flagship, the *Brederode*, stood out from all the rest with 59, the next most formidable carrying 48; the Hollanders possessed nothing to set against the *Sovereign*. Having to provide for the coastal waters and the river estuaries, their shipbuilders had evolved a man-of-war with a shallow draught and two gun-decks.

Off Portland Bill in 1653 Tromp lost twelve warships and 43 of the merchantmen which they had been convoying. Only one of Blake's ships, the 32-gun *Sansom*, was sunk. The Dutch also lost about 5,500 men killed, wounded or taken prisoner compared with 1,200 on the English side.

Ironically, the Parliamentarians left Charles II an impressive fleet of 154 vessels when he took over in 1660. As a further irony, Charles introduced the title 'Royal Navy' although the finance was still raised on the Cromwellian system of national taxation. He returned to England from Holland in the *Naseby*, renamed the *Royal Charles*. Three years later a jubilant crowd burnt her figurehead, which depicted Cromwell on horseback trampling on six nations. To replace it with a carving of Neptune cost Charles £100.

The King could ill afford to spend money on a figurehead or a new coat of arms (preserved at the Rijksmuseum in Amsterdam) for the stern. Parliament had fallen into debt; despite its good intentions, the seamen were owed nearly

made happily for the taverns.

Again and again such men as these saved England. One of the Royal Navy's great advantages in the wars with the Dutch was its superior morale. We can detect the sheer zest of the English sailors in the journals kept by Edward Barlow, the Prestwick farmhand's son who had never seen a ship until he walked from Manchester to London and was puzzled by the strange objects floating in the Thames. His vessels included the *Naseby* (or *Royal Charles*), the *Augustine*, one of the men-of-war sent against the Barbary pirates at Algiers, the frigate *Monck* and the *Royal Sovereign*.

The *Monck* served in the Battle of St James's Day in the Second Dutch War, which began in March 1665 after an expedition sent to America by the King's brother, the Duke of York (later James II), had captured New Amsterdam, which immediately became New York City, together with New Netherland. At the beginning of hostilities the English had about 160 ships, 5,000 guns and 25,000 men to oppose about

Left: A drawing by Van de Velde the Elder of the ornamentation on the stern of the Royal Charles. *In the Second Dutch War she was the flagship of the Duke of York. Admiral Sir William Penn, whose Quaker son founded Pennsylvania, was Great Captain Commander. The Dutch towed her off during their raid on the Medway.*

£400,000 just before the Restoration; some of them had not been paid for three or four years. With a fine Navy, the King also inherited a large debt. Shipbuilding declined and the old abuses came back.

Fortunately for England, the King, in reviving the Navy Board, appointed Samuel Pepys as Clerk. At the age of 27 Pepys entered upon his duties with intelligence and vigour. Through the administration which he set up as Clerk of the Acts and later as Secretary to the Lord High Admiral, this highly capable young man, son of a tailor and a washmaid, and at the same time a kinsman of Lord Sandwich, made himself, in Sir Arthur Bryant's words, the 'saviour of the Navy'.

Pepys's great difficulty was the old one of cash. From the diary that he wrote we learn of his distress at the 'lamentable moan of the poor seamen that be starving in the streets'. Naval service was not continuous: in peacetime the sailor was paid off, to find other work, or to beg, until the next emergency. When it occurred, there was no overwhelming rush of volunteers. Needing men in large numbers, the press gangs descended on coastal towns and villages, grabbing recruits left and right. Merchant seamen, tailors, ploughboys, men with the palsy, lads who could speak only Welsh – they were all the same to the 'press'. Some had never seen a ship before.

At sea the men lived between the guns. Kegs and sea chests formed their seats; any shelves or cupboards which they fixed in place had to be jettisoned when battle was imminent. On shore, free for a while from the stench, the unspeakable food on a long voyage, the iron discipline with its terrifying punishments (a third of the 39 Articles of War carried the death penalty), they

135 ships and a slightly smaller number of guns and sailors than their own. The Duke of York commanded the battle fleet as Lord High Admiral.

In June of the following year, after a Dutch victory in the Four Days' Fight and an English victory in the St James's Day fight which followed it, de Ruyter dealt his enemies a shattering humiliation by sailing up the Medway, past all the alleged defences and obstacles, raiding Sheppey, destroying the fort at Sheerness, and burning and sinking the 70-gun *Royal James*, the 90-gun *Loyal London* and the 76-gun *Royal Oak*. Many smaller vessels were also sunk, blocking the channel. To crown this breath-

Above: 'The True Portraicture of His Ma.ties Royall Ship The Soveraigne of the Seas.'

taking impudence, the Dutch carried off the *Royal Charles*. Her carved and gilded stern may be seen in Amsterdam today.

The Dutch Wars brought a higher degree of order into sea fighting. Fleets had grown so large and unwieldy that they were arranged in three divisions, each of them under an admiral flying a distinguishing flag; the Admiral of the Fleet a red flag in the centre, the Vice-Admiral a white flag in the van, and the Rear-Admiral, commanding the rear squadron, a blue flag. It was eventually realized that vessels in the line of battle should not be mixed, the weak with the strong. The powerful became the true 'ships of the line'; the rest were allotted other duties. All were rated according to the number of guns they carried.

Above: John Paul Jones, commanding the Bonhomme Richard, *attacks the* Serapis, *a frigate of 44 guns, off Flamborough Head in Yorkshire on 23 September 1779. The duel was one of the fiercest naval actions in history. Early in 1976 plans were announced for an international attempt at raising the* Bonhomme Richard *which went down with her unconquered flag flying.*

Right: The Shannon *and the* Chesapeake *in desperate combat off Cape Anne, near Boston, on 1 June 1813. The* Shannon *was the victor.*

Much of our knowledge of Restoration warships derives from the drawings and paintings of the Van de Veldes, the father and son who left their home in Holland and served as marine artists to Charles II. They are known to have set up their easels in the Queen's House at Greenwich, now the central part of the National Maritime Museum, which has 1,450 of their pictures. Anyone studying the Royal Navy of that period should visit Greenwich and also the great Rijksmuseum in the Dutch capital. The Van de Veldes saw the ships of war in action.

Another source of information is the Pepys Library at Magdalene College, Cambridge. The collection left by Mr Secretary Pepys includes Sir Anthony Deane's *Doctrine of Naval Architecture*, which contains a series of draughts and a set of masts and rigging plans for each of the six rates composing the fleet. From the draughts and the Van de Velde drawings we are able to see that since Elizabethan times the sterns have

become rounded.

For knowledge of the later Stuart vessels we depend largely on the scale models built, as a new practice, when the ships were laid down. There were no great changes in design. Projecting galleries built along each quarter in Elizabeth's reign, primarily as latrines for the officers (the men used a deck of gratings – the 'heads' – at the fore end), were embellished and later covered in completely (the *Sovereign* provides an example). In the *Royal Prince* of 1610 they were carried round the stern, to form a stern-gallery, or stern-walk, a fashion which then died out for some 80 years.

The most important change in rig was the introduction of staysails and jibs. By 1690 studding sails, said to have been invented by Raleigh in Armada year, were regularly employed. In a Van de Velde picture of the Battle of Solebay a line of reef points – short ropes for securing the sail when it had been reefed – can be seen across the upper part of the main and fore topsails. The men-of-war at the end of the century had much the same rig as their successors at Trafalgar.

In building the *Royal James* Anthony Deane experimented with the use of iron standards (upright posts between decks) and knees (angle pieces). We do not know if the idea was successful; the *Royal James*, flagship of the Earl of Sandwich, was set ablaze by a fireship at the Battle of Southwold Bay a year after her launching. Iron standards and knees solved a problem after the Napoleonic Wars when good bent timber was hard to find.

Deane also tried out a new form of sheathing, employing milled lead instead of wood to hold in place the layer of tar, hair, sulphur and tallow covering the underwater part of the hull. It served for about ten years before it was abandoned because of the corrosion caused by electrolytic action with iron and lead together in sea water. A better process, brought in after the Restoration, was studding: the use of broad-headed nails hammered close together over the bottom and covered with a mixture of tallow and resin. Corrosion again occurred when a frigate was given a full set of copper plates underwater in 1758.

Eight years after Deane had made his name with the *Rupert* and the *Resolution*, both laid down at Harwich, he went to Portsmouth as Commissioner and built the *Harwich*, one of the fastest vessels in the fleet and the forerunner of ten others like her. She had been copied from the 70-gun *Superbe* which visited the Thames with other French ships in 1673. The English were beginning to take a great interest in French men-of-war. Shipwrights across the Channel had discovered science: the proportions of a hull, the forces acting upon a mast – these and other subjects relating to naval architecture were

studied by French mathematicians, and theory was put into practice.

No one knew how much interest the French and their warships would soon command. In the winter of 1688 a fleet set out from the Scheldt bound for England: William of Orange was on his way to claim the throne of his father-in-law. He landed safely at Brixham in Devon while James's ships, which had assembled at Thamesmouth, were held back by ill winds. After escaping unhindered to France, James reached Ireland with French support, was defeated at the Battle of the Boyne, and embarked for France again. England and Holland, the two great Protestant maritime nations, now found themselves united against Louis XIV. The curtain was rising on a bloody drama that would continue, with intermissions, until 1815.

In 1690, the year of the Boyne, England had 100 ships of the line in a total of 173, and her ally 69 in a total of 102. Against these the French could muster 221 vessels, of which 93 were ships of the line. It was the age of great admirals. For generations to come men would speak with pride of Benbow off Jamaica directing the attack with his right leg shattered; of Hawke at Quiberon Bay, throwing formal tactics to the winds, and of Old Dreadnought Boscawen off Lagos; of Rodney at the Saints, off Dominica; of Howe and 'the Glorious First of June', the famous victory in 1794; of Jervis off Cape St Vincent, where Nelson in the 74-gun *Captain* left the hallowed line and fought the Spaniards for a short time alone.

Yet the English ships were inferior to the French. The vessels of the enemy had longer keels, finer underwater lines, a better proportion of length to breadth, deep holds, longer gundecks, and lower-tier gunports far enough above the water for the guns to be employed in rough weather when the corresponding ports in the English vessels had to be closed. The English men-of-war pitched, tossed and heeled alarmingly, emphasizing the lowness of the ports. They also lacked sound timbers, largely because suitable oak was increasingly hard to obtain, and they were over-gunned. In the dockyards conservative rule-of-thumb methods fitted

Pages 16 and 17: 'The Constitution *and* Guerrière *dropping Astern' by Thomas Birch. Before the* Guerrière *sank, Americans and British worked together transferring the wounded to the* Constitution – *which is afloat at Boston today.*

comfortably into a background of sloth and ignorance, fraud and neglect. A long-overdue visitation ordered by Admiral George Anson in 1749 was not repeated for another 20 years.

In the course of making improvements, Anson clarified the rating of ships by laying down that those fit to stand in the line were first-rates, three-deckers of 100 guns or more; second-rates, three-deckers of 90 guns; and third-rates, two-deckers of 74 or 64. The others were 'cruisers': the fourth-rates, two-deckers of 50 guns (occasionally 60); the fifth-rates, frigates of 36 guns; and the sixth-rates, frigates carrying from 28 to 32. At the middle of the eighteenth century the 74-gun ship became the standard medium class of third-rate, and the frigate – a word which had been given at least half a dozen meanings – acquired firm definition as the 'eyes of the fleet', a fast cruiser for scouting and raiding, with its guns on a single flush deck.

Improvements continued throughout the eighteenth century. During the first decade the steering wheel superseded the whipstaff – a vertical lever pivoted to the deck and able to

were yellow, crossed by black spars. Blue could be seen here and there, particularly on the stern-works, and scarlet was employed for relief. The painters liked to be as generous as they could with gilt. All in all, the vessels were brighter, better ventilated, healthier and more seaworthy than they had ever been before.

Well before 1800, a new navy came into existence on the other side of the Atlantic. Ships had taken the first English colonists to the New World, ships maintained their links with the home country, and craft of various kinds handled a good deal of the transport within America itself. The Thirteen Colonies could therefore call upon their own maritime resources when the trouble with the Crown grew acute.

Early in 1775 the Continental Congress bought and armed two merchant ships of about 450 tons, the *Black Prince*, renamed the *Alfred*, and the *Sally*, renamed the *Columbus*. It also obtained six brigs or brigantines, three schooners and five sloops, to which Washington's army added four schooners in Massachusetts and a sloop and two schooners on Lake Champlain.

throw the tiller sideways, though not far. We can sum up the progress in sail power by describing the man-of-war at the end of the period as a full-rigged ship.

About 1720 the hulls were light brown or deep cream in colour, an improvement on the nondescript tarry look produced by earlier economies. In the second half of the period they were coated with black or yellow, as the captains preferred. The familiar pattern of black divided into bands by yellow along the sides of the gun-decks, with the black port-lids on the yellow creating a chequerboard effect, was generally adopted in the 1790s. Ochre (a cheap colour) replaced the dark red of the gun-decks themselves. Masts

In these craft the Continental Navy had its beginnings.

At the end of 1775 the Congress ordered thirteen brand-new vessels, to be built by the following spring: the *Hancock, Raleigh, Randolph, Warren* and *Washington*, of 32 guns; the *Congress, Effingham, Providence, Trumbell* and *Virginia*, of 28; and the *Boston, Delaware* and *Montgomery*, of 24. Four were laid down at Philadelphia, two each at Newburyport, Poughkeepsie and Providence, Rhode Island, and one each at Baltimore, Chatham in Connecticut and Portsmouth in New Hampshire.

A private yard had launched a fourth-rate, the *Falkland*, in 1690, and some other men-of-war

had followed her – enough to establish a tradition of naval shipbuilding. It also helped the colonists that their shipwrights were especially skilled at constructing fast, cheap vessels, craft which could be employed against pirates, smugglers and others who gave trouble, besides serving the ordinary needs of small communities. For half a century before the Revolution the fast schooner was so much in evidence that the New Englanders believed they had invented it, at Gloucester, Massachusetts, in 1713.

With the coming of war the Americans were able to design and build some of the finest men-of-war afloat. Other ships were obtained from abroad. The *Bonhomme Richard* lost in battle

with HMS *Serapis* off Flamborough Head, Yorkshire, was an old French East Indiaman, the *Duc de Duras*, renamed in honour of *Poor Richard's Almanac* and its originator, the astonishing Benjamin Franklin who was mainly responsible for bringing France into the war on the side of the colonists.

Important to the general course of events was the Battle of Chesapeake Bay, or the Virginian Capes, fought on 5 September 1781 between the British fleet ('British' since the Union of England and Scotland in May 1707), under Rear-Admiral Thomas Graves, and two combined French fleets, with 36 ships of the line, under the Comte de Grasse. Victory went to the French and the

American Revolution was saved. 'It was the Battle of Chesapeake Bay', declared Sir Geoffrey Callender, the maritime historian, 'which decided the final issue of the war.'

After the Revolution the Americans disposed of their army and navy and for a time were without any defence forces apart from the local militia companies. Meanwhile they built up a large merchant marine. Their ships traded across the oceans, and when they were preyed upon in the Mediterranean by Barbary corsairs the President and Congress authorized, in March 1794, the construction of six frigates. Three of them were 44s: the *United States* laid down at Philadelphia, the *Constitution* at Boston

and the *President* at New York. Although the other three – the *Constellation* at Baltimore, the *Congress* at Portsmouth, New Hampshire and the *Chesapeake* at Gosport, the naval yard at Norfolk, Virginia – were supposed to be 36s, the War Office re-rated them as 38s before they had been completed.

Early in 1797, the year when the *Constitution*, *Constellation* and *United States* were launched, Sir John Jervis with fifteen ships of the line attacked a Spanish fleet twice as strong in size and fire power and won a victory which assured the British that if the French tried to invade their shores they would not have any naval help from the government at Madrid. During the battle,

Above: The Battle of Trafalgar. 'Now, gentlemen, let us do something today that the world may talk of hereafter,' said Collingwood off Cape Trafalgar. Many years later Alfred Thayer Mahan, the American naval historian wrote: 'It was those far-distant storm-beaten ships, upon which the Grand Army never looked, which stood between it and the dominion of the world.'

off Cape St Vincent 100 miles south east of Trafalgar, Horatio Nelson sailed his two-decker, *Captain*, across the path of the *Santísima Trinidad*, the flagship of Juan de Cordova and the biggest war vessel afloat. After engaging her, he attacked the *San Josef* of 112 guns and the *San Nicolas* of 80.

Greater glory lay ahead for the sailor from Norfolk. In 1798 he became a national hero with his victory at the Nile. Jervis had defeated the Spaniards at Cape St Vincent, Adam Duncan had destroyed the Dutch at Camperdown, a few miles off their coast, and now Napoleon's army in the Egyptian desert was cut off from home through the ruin of its fleet. So hard fought was the battle that when, towards midnight, the fighting slackened, men fell asleep in utter exhaustion beside their guns. About two hours earlier, the flagship *Orient* had blown up. The British did not lose a single ship.

Seven years later, when the Royal Navy consisted of 88 ships of the line, 125 frigates and about 140,000 seamen, the victor of the Nile went into battle again with the French, this time off Cape Trafalgar. His flagship, HMS *Victory*, a three-decker of 100 guns and 2,162 tons burden, was already 40 years old, if allowance is made for 'middling repairs' between 1783 and 1792 and a rebuilding between 1800 and 1803. She measured 151ft along the keel, 186ft along the gun-deck, and 226ft overall, with a beam of 52ft, and she set 31 sails, not including the studding or steering sails used when the wind was light. Her main topsail was 60ft on each side, 55ft along the head and 90ft along the foot. The mainmast, with topsail and topgallant, rose 175ft above her deck, and the main yard was 110ft long. Her guns needed a range of less than half a mile to be really effective, and at close quarters they could pierce five feet of solid oak – with the round shot brought to white heat if any attempt was being made to set the enemy ship on fire.

The first-rate had a complement of 633. Those on board her a few days before Trafalgar, at the last muster, included one African, 22 Americans, one Bengali, two Danes, seven Dutchmen, three Frenchmen, four Italians, two North Germans from Hamburg, one seaman from Madras, four Maltese, three Norwegians, two Portuguese, one Prussian, one Russian, six Swedes, two Swiss and nine from the West Indies.

Nelson had decided to attack the Franco-Spanish force, which was stronger than his own, at two separate points. While he bore slowly down upon the enemy line supported by the *Téméraire* and *Neptune*, both of 98 guns, Collingwood led the southern column in the *Royal Sovereign* with the *Belleisle* astern. In the silence, the tense windless hush, the *Victory* made a signal which would be remembered when all the details of the fighting were forgotten: 253 269 863 261 471 958 220 370 4 21 19 24 – 'England

Expects That Every Man Will Do His Duty'. (There was nothing in the code book for 'duty' and so it had to be spelt out: 4, 21, 19, 24.) By the end of that day the Emperor Napoleon, though still ten years from final defeat, had no chance of invading Britain unless he built himself another fleet.

Nelson had admired the American naval force in the Mediterranean. 'There is in the handling of those transatlantic ships', he said, 'a nucleus of trouble for the Navy of Great Britain.' He was right. Seven years after his victory and death at Trafalgar the young United States boldly took up arms over Britain's claim to have the right of searching neutral ships for deserters. Inevitably, with the ocean between, the war itself had a strong naval character. The Americans were known to possess only a small navy, seven frigates and eight sloops; but three of the frigates, the *Constitution*, *President* and *United States*, were in fact ships of the line called the 'pocket battleships'.

The War of 1812 produced several American naval heroes and some famous sea-fights – above all the duel between the *Constitution* and the *Guerrière*, off Cape Race on 19 August in the first year of hostilities (for the War of 1812 lasted until the end of 1814). After the *Guerrière* had been turned into a blazing hulk, the British accepted defeat, and victors and vanquished joined in helping the wounded. On 30 August the *Constitution* entered Boston in triumph, to report the first surrender of a British captain in a single ship action since 1803, two years before Trafalgar. The American victory made Captain Samuel Hull a national hero and gave a great boost to morale, especially in New England where opinion had been strongly opposed to 'Mr Madison's War'.

While the British were still shocked by the news of 'HM late ship *Guerrière*', further American successes added to their dismay. On 25 October 1812 Captain John Carden of HMS *Macedonian* offered his sword in surrender to Captain Stephen Decatur of the *United States* after an engagement in which one hundred of his men were lost, more than a third of all on board. Only then did he learn about the *Constitution* and the *Guerrière* and discover that he was not, as he had supposed, the first Briton to haul down his colours to an American.

On the first day of June the following year, the American frigate *Chesapeake* under James Lawrence lost her brief and furious battle with the *Shannon* off Cape Anne. For Americans the defeat was eased by the conduct of the wounded Lawrence. His own refusal to admit defeat – 'We have met the enemy and they are ours' – gained him the final victory of the war after two British ships, *Detroit* and *Queen Charlotte*, collided while he was defending Detroit at the western end of Lake Erie.

The age of fighting sail did not end with the war of 1812. British warships were improved by two Surveyors of the Navy. Between 1813 and 1832 Sir Robert Seppings introduced a complete system of diagonal framing, together with round sterns and bows; and then Captain William Symonds, his successor, concentrated on making the vessels faster. He gave them well-rounded midship sections and finer underwater bodies, and completely closed in the opening at the waist to create a continuous upper deck.

In 1827, a fleet of British, French and Russian ships went into battle against a Turkish force in the Bay of Navarino where the Athenians had forced the Spartans to surrender in 425 BC. It was the last battle fought under sail, and a very important one in that it secured the independence of Greece. While the British lost 75 killed, the

24

French 43 and the Russians 59, the Turks were estimated to have had over 1,000 killed and 3,000 wounded.

Preserved sailing warships can still be seen today. At Portsmouth, almost one hundred years after the Battle of Navarino, Nelson's flagship *Victory* was being restored to its original condition. At about the same time, USS *Constitution*, also known as 'Old Ironsides', was similarly preserved at Boston, Massachusetts, with the help of public subscription.

As long as some of the old battleships endure, they will remind us of the age of fighting sail, of the men-of-war Turner painted, of the vessels which inspired Ruskin to say:

Take it all in all, a Ship of the Line is the most honourable thing that man, as a gregarious animal, has ever produced. By himself, un-helped, he can do better things than ships of the line; he can make poems and pictures, and other such concentrations of what is best in him. But as a being living in flocks, and hammering out, with alternate strokes and mutual agreement, what is necessary for him in those flocks, to get or produce, the ship of the line is his first work. Into that he has put as much of his human patience, common sense, forethought, experimental philosophy, self-control, habits of order and obedience, thoroughly wrought handwork, defiance of brute elements, careless courage, careful patriotism, and calm expectation of the judgment of God, as can well be put into a space of 300 feet long by 80 broad. And I am thankful to have lived in an age when I could see this thing so done.

Below: John Clevely, Senior, a shipwright at Deptford on the Thames, painted this picture about 1750. It shows the launch of a 74-gun ship at Deptford yard. The larger ship is probably the Culloden, *of 74 guns, launched there in 1747, and the smaller, still on the stocks, the* Rochester *of 50 guns, launched in 1749.*

Modern Warships

NELSON WAS AWARE of steam power. The ships which he commanded seem closer to the age of Drake than to the Industrial Revolution, so remote do they look from anything suggestive of boilers, cylinders, pistons and condensers. It may therefore surprise us to realize that a steam engine, Thomas Newcomen's, had worked successfully more than half a century before Nelson was born. Nelson showed an interest in the *Charlotte Dundas*, of Chapter II, yet nearly 20 years passed before the Royal Navy had its first steam craft, the 212-ton *Monkey*, a tug built at Rotherhithe on the Thames with an 80 horsepower engine. In 1882 the Admiralty added the paddle steamer *Comet*, launched at Deptford; she displaced 238 tons, was propelled at four to five knots by an engine of 80 horsepower and carried four nine-pounder guns.

Britain was mistress of the seas. So long as the Navy remained as it was, all would be well: any radical alteration – and nothing could be more radical than the abandonment of sail – carried the risk that it might be a change for the worse; and it was sure to be vastly expensive. Their lordships of the Admiralty had no wish to desert the old familiar ways in favour of strange and dangerous paths, mysterious to themselves and to the Service. They had a good deal of clear fact to support them. Before we condemn them outright as obstinate diehards, we must understand that the steam power which they saw at work was the steam power of that time, a heavy and cumbrous assembly of boilers, engines and paddle wheels. Boilers had a tendency to blow up and engines a tendency to break down – a failure that in battle could be calamitous – while paddle wheels had the double disadvantage of preventing the ship from firing a proper broadside and at the same time offering the enemy a hard-to-miss target. If the power unit had been far less awkward for a ship at sea, the paddle wheels would still have been a huge drawback. The unit itself, vertical and well above the waterline, was equally

vulnerable. 'Mr Speaker,' Lord Napier told Parliament, 'when we enter His Majesty's naval service and face the chances of war, we go prepared to be hacked to pieces by cutlasses, to be riddled with bullets, or to be blown to bits by shell and shot; but, Mr Speaker, we do not go prepared to be boiled alive'.

For the Royal Navy steam power continued to mean a few little tugs useful for towing sailing vessels in and out of harbour. No great change was made until the introduction of the screw propeller, pioneered in its adopted form by John Ericsson, a retired Swedish naval officer, and Francis Pettit Smith, an English farmer. The screw, unlike the paddle wheel, was completely out of the way, with the engines well down inside the hull. It seemed the perfect solution to a difficulty which had appeared insurmountable; but the Admiralty still held back. When Ericsson built a steam launch with twin screws, and towed Admiralty officials along the Thames in a barge at fully ten knots, their lordships raised the objection that a vessel could not be accurately steered when its driving force was at the stern.

Fortunately for Ericsson, the trial had impressed two Americans, Francis B. Ogden – an engineer who had been the United States Consul at Liverpool – and Captain Robert Field Stockton, an influential naval officer. Stockton enticed Ericsson to America.

The United States were ahead of Britain in the adoption of steam naval vessels. In 1814 Adam and Noah Browne of New York built the first steam warship, Robert Fulton's *Demologos*. She was an extraordinary craft, with two hulls joined at bow and stern. Between the hulls, and protected by them, was a paddle wheel. Besides carrying a battery of 32-pounders intended to fire red-hot shot from behind wooden walls five feet thick, she had submarine guns which could shoot 100-pound projectiles from below the waterline. A great hose from a steam pump was to play on the enemy decks, washing off

Opposite previous page: *The 27,300-ton French aircraft-carrier* Clemenceau, *which was laid down in 1955, launched in 1957 and completed in 1961. She normally carries three squadrons of Crusader, Breguet and Etandard IV aircraft, numbering 40 in all. The crew of 1,228 men includes 65 officers.*

Above: The Great Britain *seen from another steamship.*

sailors and drenching the guns so that they could not be used.

Fulton built the *Demologos*, or *Fulton the First*, for the defence of New York in the War of 1812, but hostilities ended before she was ready, and her engine (of 120 nominal horsepower) had still not been installed when he died in February 1815; her guns sounded for his funeral.

The first screw warship was also American, the ten-gun sloop *Princeton*, built at the Philadelphia Navy Yard under the supervision of Robert Stockton and launched in 1843 as a vessel displacing 954 tons, with a deck length of 164ft and a beam of 30.5ft. Her 400-hp engine by Merrick and Towne of Philadelphia could

drive her at thirteen knots, owing to the use of a six-bladed screw of the Ericsson pattern. She was to mount twelve carronades and two twelve-inch wrought-iron guns, one designed by Ericsson and the other by Stockton. When the two were tried out on the quarterdeck, Stockton's burst and killed several people, among them the Secretary of State, the Secretary of the Navy and two Congressmen.

The first British steam warship was the 428-ton *Rising Star*, a wooden paddle ship constructed to the order of Thomas Cochrane, liberator of several nations and a champion of steam in the Royal Navy. In a picture of 1821 she is shown with two funnels and three masts. She was

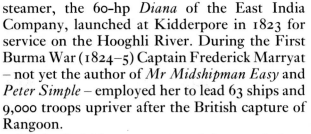

steamer, the 60-hp *Diana* of the East India Company, launched at Kidderpore in 1823 for service on the Hooghli River. During the First Burma War (1824–5) Captain Frederick Marryat – not yet the author of *Mr Midshipman Easy* and *Peter Simple* – employed her to lead 63 ships and 9,000 troops upriver after the British capture of Rangoon.

Pettit Smith's screw proved its worth in a series of experiments conducted by the Navy in the steam sloop *Rattler* after Brunel's *Great Britain* had been given screw propulsion. To the great excitement of the Royal Navy and the shipbuilding world, the *Rattler*, a screwship, raced the *Alecto*, a naval paddle sloop of equal horsepower. She beat her opponent three times over – the third time by 40 minutes, on a 60-mile course dead into wind and sea. When the friends of HMS *Alecto* maintained that their favourite was nevertheless the better ship for towing duties, the Navy secured the two together, stern to stern, with a pair of cables, and called for full steam ahead as soon as the cables had tautened. After an interval in which neither ship seemed to

intended to go into battle against the Spanish in Chile, but by the time of her arrival at Valparaiso in April 1822 the Chilean revolution was over. For the remainder of her career, until she was wrecked in 1830, she ran as a privately-owned vessel; but she has a place in naval history as the first steam-propelled British warship to be launched (on 5 February 1821), as the first steamer to make a westerly crossing of the Atlantic – however much she may have depended on her sails – and as the first steamer to range the Pacific.

The one distinction which she missed, the Chilean revolt against Spain having already succeeded, came the way of another paddle

move, the *Alecto* was towed backwards, her paddles thrashing to no effect, at a speed of about two knots.

Convinced at last, the Admiralty ordered the frigate *Amphion*, then on the stocks, to be fitted with a screw. She was not launched until 1846. In that year the *Rifleman*, the first screw ship built in dry dock at Portsmouth, was taken to the Thames for her engines to be installed. Even then the Navy regarded the wind as the normal and desirable form of power. The captain liked to know that when he had a chance to use his sails he could order the screw to be lifted clean out of the water.

The first British ship of the line to have screw

Above: Guns at Jutland. At 5 pm on 30 May 1916, the British Admiralty partly decoded a German signal suggesting that an important naval operation was about to begin. Before midnight Britain's Grand Fleet was at sea, heading eastwards. In the morning the British and German warships steamed towards each other; and at 3.45 pm, off Denmark, the Battle of Jutland began.

machinery from the outset was the 91-gun *Agamemnon* of 1852, Admiral Sir Edward Lyons' 'superb *Agamemnon*' who distinguished herself at the bombardment of Sebastopol in the Crimean War. She was, in effect, a steam-powered sailing ship.

The first Royal Naval vessel designed to fight under full steam seems to have been the screw ship *Dauntless* of 1844. The *Arrogant*, laid down at the same time, had only auxiliary engines.

Although the *Dauntless* was propelled by a 580-hp engine, she proved slower than many paddle vessels. Screw machinery could not work at its best in a ship which had a wooden hull and a bluff stern; as John Scott Russell told a meeting of fellow naval architects in 1864, 'bits of wood kept together with bits of metal cannot stand the continuous day-after-day wear and tear of the wriggle of a 1,000-horsepower screw in the tail of a ship'.

Richard Trevithick and Robert Dickenson had taken out a patent for iron-ship construction as early as 1809, and in 1822 Sir Charles Napier had sponsored the paddle steamer *Aaron Manby*, which had a hull constructed of iron plates a quarter of an inch thick, with a wood lining 'to prevent heat being communicated to the cargo'. The Admiralty showed little or no interest in so

revolutionary a craft; but in 1840 it acquired a small iron packet ship, the *Dover*, and three years later it invited a number of shipbuilders to submit plans for 'iron vessels capable of carrying heavy armaments'. John Laird laid down the frigate *Vulcan*, soon afterwards named the *Birkenhead* after the Mersey port where she was built. In all, eleven shipyards went to work on a programme embracing no fewer than 33 iron vessels, of which about half a dozen were fighting ships and the rest auxiliaries.

Not long before, in 1840, the 170ft *Nemesis*, one of four gunboats built by Laird for the East India Company, had advertised the value of iron

(and also of watertight bulkheads) by remaining intact when she ran aground off the Scillies, and then, in the First Opium War, by repelling everything fired at her by the Chinese, who called her the Devil Ship and offered a reward of $50,000 for her capture. Resolutely unimpressed, the enemies of floating iron replied that the accident in the Scillies had occurred because the compass of the *Nemesis* had been affected by the metal. To them an iron ship was almost as much of a monster as the *Nemesis* had been to the Chinese. They insisted that enemy shot would easily penetrate the thin metal, shattering itself and the target alike and causing deadly splinters; that a hole in metal could not be repaired, unlike a hole in timber, by ordinary members of the crew, using simple tools, anywhere in the world; and that an iron vessel which had been holed

Left : The paddle sloop Alecto. *She lost her famous tug-of-war with the screw-driven* Rattler *in May 1845.*

Above : HMS Falcon, *one of the six fast torpedo-boats built on the Clyde by Fairfield from 1896 to 1900. She was sunk in a collision in 1918.*

Below : La Gloire *of 1859, from a painting by Le Breton.*

badly would go straight to the bottom instead of lying for a time on the surface, or floating half-submerged.

At Portsmouth in 1845 HMS *Excellent* fired for two days on the *Ruby*, a small iron steamer, and reduced her to scrap worth £20. The test was not a fair one, but it persuaded Sir Robert Peel, the Prime Minister, to desist from the folly of building iron frigates. Sir Charles Napier, having deserted his old cause of steam, warned the House of Commons that if the *Birkenhead* were unfit to fight she was also unfit to carry troops (the duty which took her to her terrible end off the foot of South Africa in 1852).

Eventually the French took the lead by constructing *La Gloire*, a wooden three-master of 5,600 tons displacement which had been given a belt of iron 4¾ inches thick along both sides.

Above: HMS Colossus, *the first dreadnought built on the Clyde. As Rear-Admiral E.F.A. Gaunt's flagship at Jutland, she sank a destroyer at 7.05 pm and opened fire on the leading German battle-cruiser at 7.12 pm before she was hit, without serious damage, at 7.16 pm.*

Below: Launch of the Fulton the First, *or* Demologos, *at New York on 29 October 1814. She was the first steam warship in history. Robert Fulton intended her for service in the War of 1812.*

Britain's answer to Napoleon III and Dupuy de Lôme, his *directeur de matériel*, was the famous *Warrior*, laid down at Blackwall in the summer of 1859. Her lines paid tribute to the graceful clippers pioneered in the United States, but she was twice as long as a contemporary clipper (420ft overall; 380ft 2in. between perpendiculars) and between her fore and main masts she had two telescopic funnels. For about five-eights of her length she was protected by wrought-iron plates 4½ inches thick bolted to an eighteen-inch teak backing. She displaced 9,210 tons. On her trials she made over fourteen knots, a speed not achieved by any other warship afloat.

Her gunnery lieutenant, the Jacky Fisher who one day would give his name to a naval era, wrote of her that 'it certainly was not appreciated then that this, our first armour-clad ship of war, would cause a fundamental change in what had been in vogue for something like a thousand years'. The historic vessel ended her seagoing career in 1884, became part of the *Vernon* torpedo school in 1900, and in 1923 was sold, to serve as an oil pontoon at Pembroke Dock in South Wales where she was visited by the Duke of Edinburgh just before he founded the Maritime Trust.

By the middle of the nineteenth century even the most passionate defender of Britain's wooden walls saw that they could not withstand the assault of the cylindrical shells fired by the new rifled guns which were being developed. Any remaining doubts were swept away when news

Historic Ships

THE 'REVENGE'

'Sink me the ship, Master Gunner – sink her, split her in twain!
Fall into the hands of God, not into the hands of Spain.'

Students of naval history excepted, how many people remember the name of the ship in which Britain's King Henry VIII first caused 'great guns' to be mounted, firing through square ports cut in her sides? Yet the *Henry Grâce à Dieu*, of 1,500 tons and the largest warship of her time, has her place in history as the fore-runner of the ships-of-the-line with which so many wars were fought at sea in the seventeenth and eighteenth centuries. Again, how many people recall the ship in which, in the time of Queen Elizabeth I, Lord Howard of Effingham hoisted his flag as Lord High Admiral? Yet the *Ark*, of 800 tons, led the British fleet which, in 1588, harried the Duke of Medina Sidonia's great Spanish Armada so effectively as it passed up the English Channel.

In sharp contrast there must be few – at least in Britain – who do not remember the 'little *Revenge*', of only 500 tons, because at school they would probably have learned one of the most stirring poems in the English language, which begins with the classic line: *'At Flores in the Azores Sir Richard Grenville lay'*.

But if one puts Tennyson's poetic imagery aside, what is the *Revenge*'s claim to be numbered among the world's most famous ships? Built in 1577 she entered the pages of history in 1591. In her Sir Francis Drake led a fleet of more than 100 vessels carrying 11,000 soldiers who seized and burned the Spanish port of Corunna, and made an abortive attempt to do likewise with Lisbon.

There followed the *Revenge*'s finest hour. Later in the same year, now the flagship of Sir Richard Grenville, she went to the Azores with Lord Thomas Howard's squadron of seven ships, intent on capturing vessels bringing treasure

Opposite: 'The Resolution *in a Gale' by Willem Van de Velde the Younger.*

from the Americas to fill the coffers of King Philip II of Spain. And there they stayed for some six months until, on 31 August, a pinnace brought news of an approaching enemy fleet numbering 53 ships under Don Alonso.

Howard, in the *Foresight*, immediately weighed anchor. Five other British ships followed him out of Flores Bay to avoid being overwhelmed by a much stronger force. Grenville delayed to embark the sick members of his crew who were on shore at the time, with the consequence that he was surrounded. Since an adverse wind foiled Howard's efforts to come to her assistance, the *Revenge* faced odds of 53 to one.

And Sir Richard said again: 'We be all good English men.
Let us bang these dogs of Seville, the children of the devil,
For I never turned my back upon Don or devil yet.'

'The little Revenge *ran on sheer into the heart of the foe'*, and fought them for all of fifteen hours. At one time she was simultaneously laid aboard by five large Spanish vessels, including the *San Felipe* of 1,500 tons. And at no time was she in hot action with less than two of the enemy. As one Spaniard withdrew disabled, another took her place; more than fifteen ships engaged her, some of which she sank.

Soon after the fight began at 3.0 pm, Grenville was injured, but not until 11.0 that night did he agree to go below to have his wounds dressed.

And the sun went down, and the stars came out far over the summer sea,
But never a moment ceased the fight of the one and the fifty-three

until well into the middle watch. By that time all of the *Revenge*'s best men had been killed or wounded, the ship had suffered so much damage that she was unmanageable, and her last barrel of powder had been spent. She had six feet of water in her hold, none of her masts remained standing, and only some 60 men were still alive out of a crew of more than 200. For Grenville

Sir Richard Grenville's 'little Revenge'.

there was no alternative but to sink his helpless ship. But his surviving officers would not agree to such a drastic step which would cost them their lives. So the *Revenge* surrendered to the Spaniards on the understanding that all on board would be spared.

The wounded Grenville was carried, with every mark of respect, on board the Spanish flagship. Two days later:

... he rose upon their decks, and he cried:
'I have fought for Queen and Faith like a valiant
man and true;
I have only done my duty as a man is bound to do:
With a joyful spirit I Sir Richard Grenville die!'
And he fell upon their decks and he died.

Three days more and Don Alonso's fleet encountered a gale off St Michael's in which it lost 15 of its men-of-war. And in that gale, with 200 Spaniards on board:

... the little Revenge *herself went down by the*
island crags
To be lost evermore in the main.

THE 'VICTORY'

From Japan in the east to America in the west no fighting ship is better known than HMS *Victory*. Laid down in Britain's Chatham dockyard in 1759, she was launched six years later. With a hull of seasoned oak, copper-sheathed below the waterline as a protection against the destructive toredo worm, and with masts and yards of Scandinavian and Russian pine, she was a first-rate ship-of-the-line of 2,162 tons burthen (in modern terminology, she displaced approximately 3,500 tons). On a length of 186 feet (double that of a lawn tennis court), a beam of 52 feet and a draught of $21\frac{1}{2}$ feet, and with her main truck 205 feet above the water, she mounted 100 guns, half on each broadside – thirty 32-pounders on her lower deck, twenty-eight 24-pounders on her middle deck, and forty-two smaller weapons on her upper deck, forecastle and poop. Manned by nearly 750 officers and men (of many nationalities: in 1805 this figure included 22 American citizens), there was no larger warship in the Royal Navy.

With the outbreak of the War of American Independence (also known as the War of the American Revolution) in 1775, the *Victory* was chosen to be flagship of the Channel fleet. In her the 43-year-old Admiral Keppel led 30 ships-of-the-line against the French Comte d'Orvillier's 32 sail at the battle of Ushant fought on 27 July 1778. The result for Britain was disappointingly inconclusive, with the political consequence that Keppel and his second-in-command, Admiral Palliser, faced courts martial. Keppel was honourably acquitted but Palliser was officially censured and came near to being lynched by a London mob.

By 1781 Keppel had been succeeded in the *Victory* by the 63-year-old Admiral Kempenfelt, who was noted for devising the first effective system of flag signalling used by the Royal Navy, and who perished a year later on board the 100-gun *Royal George* when she suddenly capsized and sank at her moorings at Spithead.

Next, the 56-year-old Admiral Lord Howe hoisted his flag in the *Victory* in command of a fleet with which he carried much-needed reinforcements and supplies to Gibraltar, through a blockade that had been maintained for more than a year by a stronger Franco-Spanish force.

At the outbreak of the French Revolutionary War in 1793, the *Victory* went out to the Mediterranean flying the flag of the 69-year-old Admiral Lord Hood, whose successful operations included a five months' occupation of Toulon and, two years later, the conquest of Corsica.

The *Victory* was next the flagship of Admiral Man, second-in-command to the 59-year-old Admiral Hotham, who succeeded Hood. In this role she led the van in the unsatisfactory action with the French Admiral Martin's force out of Toulon fought off Hyères on 13 July 1795.

At the end of that year, the 60-year-old Admiral Jervis, on succeeding Hotham, hoisted his flag in the *Victory*. So it was in her, at the head of a fleet of only 15 British ships-of-the-line, that on 14 February 1797 he determined to do battle with the Spanish Admiral de Cordova's much stronger force of 27. Notwithstanding the disparity between the two fleets, and largely due to the initiative of the 39-year-old Commodore Nelson in HMS *Captain*, Jervis managed to capture four of his opponent's ships before the remainder could seek the safety of Cadiz, a victory for which he was created Earl St Vincent, and Nelson gained a knighthood.

The *Victory*'s greatest days came shortly after the turn of the century, forty years after her launch. On the outbreak of the Napoleonic War in 1803, she was again ordered out to the Mediterranean, this time flying Nelson's flag; Nelson was now 45, a vice-admiral, and famed for his victories of the Nile (1798) and Copenhagen (1801). In her he maintained an effective blockade of Toulon for more than eighteen months. Not until March 1805 did the French Admiral Villeneuve elude him, link up with the Spanish Admiral Gravina's ships out of Cadiz, and head for the West Indies as part of Napoleon's grandiose plans for invading England. But Nelson was soon in pursuit and, but for false intelligence, would have found his quarry in the Caribbean.

The *Victory*'s arrival there at the head of a British fleet of only ten ships-of-the-line persuaded Villeneuve, whose Combined Fleets numbered 17, to curtail his operations in those waters and to return to Europe. Again Nelson went after him. Off Cape Finisterre on 22 July, Villeneuve was intercepted and brought to action by a fleet under the command of Vice-Admiral Calder. Tactically this was indecisive but the strategic consequences were memorable. Instead of linking up with the French Brest fleet, to gain command of the English Channel so that Napoleon's army might cross it safely, Villeneuve took his Combined Fleets south to Cadiz, which delayed France's invasion plans until Napoleon was compelled to use his Grande Armée to counter a serious Austrian threat to his eastern frontiers.

Not until 19 October did the Combined Fleets leave Cadiz, intending to slip through the Straits of Gibraltar and return to Toulon. Their way was barred by Nelson with 27 ships-of-the-line against 33. On 21 October 1805, off Cape Trafalgar, the *Victory* broke the enemy's line at the start of a battle in which, before darkness fell, the British fleet destroyed or captured 18 enemy ships-of-the-line and put the rest to flight.

But this decisive victory was not gained without loss. In close action with Villeneuve's *Bucentaure* and the *Redoutable*, the *Victory* was crippled and had to be towed to Gibraltar for repairs. More important, at the height of the battle, while directing the fight from the *Victory*'s quarterdeck, Nelson was shot by a French sharpshooter and nearly two hours later he died in the darkness of her cockpit. One month after this the *Victory* carried his body home to England for burial in St Paul's Cathedral.

This was not, however, the end of the *Victory*'s service. In 1808 she headed the fleet with which the 51-year-old Admiral Saumarez operated successfully in the Baltic against the fleets of the Northern Powers. And after the Congress of Vienna closed the Napoleonic War in 1815, when much of the British fleet was paid off, she remained in commission as an accommodation ship at Portsmouth, and as flagship of the Commander-in-Chief.

In this humble role she swung round a buoy off Portsmouth dockyard throughout the transformation of the British fleet from wooden-hulled sailing ships-of-the-line to the steam-driven, armoured dreadnoughts of the twentieth century. But this episode in her life ended in January 1922 when it was suddenly discovered that her timbers were so rotten that she was in danger of sinking.

She was moved into Portsmouth's smallest dry dock, which had been built to the order of Henry VII, and steps were quickly taken to preserve her for posterity. Her rotten timbers replaced, she was restored to her Trafalgar appearance and raised on concrete blocks so that she could be seen as if waterborne. There she rests today, open to the public and welcoming aboard every year many thousands of visitors for whom Britain's greatest admiral and his finest victory have lasting fascination.

THE 'ORIENT'

Built in the latter part of the eighteenth century, the *Orient* was one of the largest men-of-war in the French navy. A first rate ship-of-the-line, she mounted as many as 120 guns, and in 1798 she was the flagship of Vice-Admiral Brueys.

In March of that year the French Directory agreed that their most successful general, the 28-year-old Bonaparte, should take command of an Armée d'Orient, which was to seize Egypt and 'make England tremble for the safety of India'. To this end 30,000 troops embarked in 300 transports which sailed from Toulon on 19 May, escorted by 13 ships-of-the-line, headed by the *Orient*, in which Bonaparte accompanied Brueys, and by four frigates.

This armada called first at Malta on 9 June and asked for water. When the Grand Master of the Knights refused to supply this vital need on the grounds that it contravened the island's neutrality in France's war with England, an angry Bonaparte determined to occupy Valletta. He expected to have to besiege this great fortress, but the Knights of that time lacked the tenacity which had enabled their forbears to hold out for so long against the Turks in the Great Siege. Rather than be bombarded into submission, they capitulated to Bonaparte as soon as 12 June. Seven days later Brueys's armada sailed into the eastern Mediterranean, after landing a garrison of 4,000 troops to hold Valletta.

Just over a fortnight later, on 1 July, the French arrived off Alexandria, where Bonaparte's Armée d'Orient disembarked and marched south across 150 miles of waterless desert. On 13 July and the 21st he overcame attacks by Mameluke forces and two days later he entered Cairo in triumph. Nine more and he received news which ended his hopes of going on to India.

Because the entrance to Alexandria harbour was too narrow for the *Orient* to berth inside it, Brueys had taken his battle fleet 15 miles to the east, to Aboukir Bay by one of the mouths of the Nile. There he anchored his ships-of-the-line on 8 July across the bay, with the head of their line under the guns of the citadel on Aboukir Island,

and with his lightly armed frigates inshore of them. From on board the *Orient* in the centre of the line, he was confident that his fleet, thus berthed, could repulse an attack by any likely British force.

He counted without Horatio Nelson. On receiving news that the French were preparing to embark a large army at Toulon in the spring of 1798, the British Admiralty ordered Lord St Vincent, whose fleet was blockading Cadiz, to send a force of 13 ships-of-the-line under the command of the 39-year-old Rear-Admiral Nelson, with his flag in the 74-gun *Vanguard*, into the Mediterranean to counter any move by Brueys. Driven away from Toulon by a storm, Nelson did not learn that the French had sailed on 19 May until the 28th, when he headed south in pursuit. News of Bonaparte's occupation of Malta persuaded him that the French must be going to Egypt but on arrival off Alexandria on 28 June he found that harbour empty.

Not knowing the reason, that the British fleet had passed Brueys's armada during the hours of darkness and arrived too early, Nelson promptly returned to Sicily for fresh intelligence of his enemy. When he failed to gain it there, he decided that his first appreciation must have been right after all and headed back to Alexandria, a round 600 miles. And at noon on 1 August his look-out ships discovered Brueys's fleet.

Nelson promptly made two vital decisions: to attack the French ships as soon as he could come up with them, before Brueys could weigh anchor and gain the advantage of the open sea; and to concentrate on first destroying the enemy's van by sending some of his ships round the head of his line, risking the danger of stranding them on the shoals off Aboukir, so that his fleet might open fire simultaneously on both sides of the enemy. These tactics were wholly successful. Captain Hood's *Zealous* found a safe way round the bows of Captain Trullet's *Guerrier* and as darkness fell around 6.0 pm the battle began. The rest of Nelson's fleet was soon in a furious action which only ended when all but two of the French ships-of-the-line and two frigates had been destroyed or captured.

Captain Casabianca's *Orient*, flying Brueys's flag, was first engaged by Captain Darby's *Bellerophon*, which lost all her masts; then by Captain Ball's *Alexander* and by Captain Hallowell's *Swiftsure*. Twice wounded, Brueys was almost cut in two by a round shot at 8.0 pm. When his men tried to take him below, he rebuked them: '*Un amiral français doit mourir sur son banc de quart.*'

By 9.0 pm the *Orient*, in which Casabianca had also been mortally wounded, caught fire. Fanned by the wind, the flames spread along her decks and leaped up her rigging. At 10.0 the blaze reached her magazines and shell lockers, and the darkness was rent by the brilliant flash and shattering roar of an explosion that threw burning fragments over the *Alexander* and *Swiftsure* and set these ships on fire. Almost all the *Orient*'s crew perished, but not quite all of their ship. Captain Hallowell salvaged part of her mainmast, and out of it had fashioned the coffin in which the victor of this battle of the Nile was destined to be buried eight years later.

Nelson's annihilating triumph impelled Austria, Russia and Turkey to join the war against Revolutionary France. It also secured for Britain control of the Mediterranean, so that neither supplies nor reinforcements could reach the Armée d'Orient, which obliged it to surrender.

The *Orient*'s niche in history is secure, not only for her catastrophic destruction at the height of this battle but also because the few who survived included Captain Casabianca's son, a child who inspired Mrs Felicity Hemans to write one of the best-known poems in the English language, her much parodied:

> *The boy stood on the burning deck,*
> *Whence all but he had fled,* ...
> *Casabianca.*

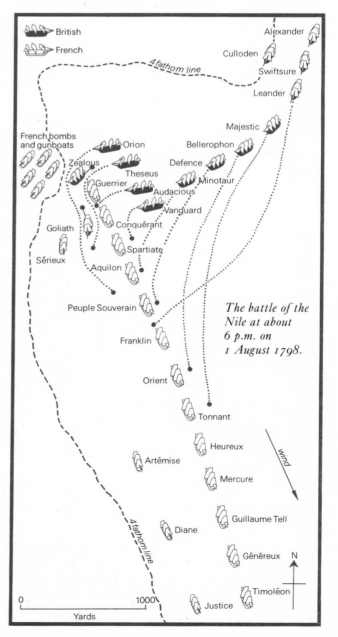

The battle of the Nile at about 6 p.m. on 1 August 1798.

THE 'CONSTITUTION'

Notwithstanding the damage inflicted on British shipping during the War of American Independence by a handful of stout-hearted American privateers, notably Paul Jones, the fledgling United States emerged from this revolution in 1783 with, in effect, no navy. The need for vessels to protect her maritime trade, especially in the Mediterranean against attacks by pirates from the Barbary States (Algiers, Morocco, Tripoli and Tunis) during the next decade, persuaded Congress to authorize the construction of their first six warships in 1794. The young nation's fragile economy was one of several reasons why these were not ships-of-the-line; they built instead larger and more powerfully armed frigates than those of such established naval powers as Britain and France.

One of these was the *Constitution*. Completed at Boston, Mass., in 1797, she displaced 2,200 tons and was designed to mount 44 guns, though she later carried more than this; in 1812, for example, thirty 24-pounders, twenty-four 32-pounder carronades and an 18-pounder bow chaser, a total of 55. Needing a crew of 450 officers and men to sail and fight her, she often made good more than 13 knots in a fair wind.

The *Constitution* and her sisters first protected American trade down their country's Atlantic coast against interference by French cruisers during the Revolutionary War. Four years later they were required to go overseas. The Barbary pirates were not content with seizing American vessels: their rulers demanded increased ransoms for them and their crews. Finally, in May 1801, the Pasha of Tripoli not only required a sum in excess of a million dollars, but cut down the flagstaff in front of the U.S. consulate – an insult to the Stars and Stripes that began a war which lasted for the next four years.

For two of these, the U.S. Navy was content with an ineffective blockade of Tripoli; but the arrival of Commodore Preble in 1803 heralded a more vigorous policy. Unhappily, on 31 October, while chasing an enemy cruiser, the frigate *Philadelphia* ran ashore where, surrounded by Tripolitan gunboats, Captain Bainbridge had no alternative but to surrender. Refloated by her captors she was taken into Tripoli harbour – but not for very long. In his cabin on board the *Constitution*, Preble planned to deprive the enemy of their captured vessel. On the night of 16 February 1804, Lieutenant Decatur led a party of 73 volunteers who boldly sailed a captured ketch into Tripoli. Running alongside the *Philadelphia* and boarding her, cutlasses in hand, they surprised and overwhelmed her sleeping crew. They could not, however, sail her out to sea: she was anchored too close under the guns of the castle. They could do no more than burn her down to the waterline, before making their escape.

Preble's squadron subsequently bombarded Tripoli for the best part of a month until he was succeeded in the *Constitution* by Commodore Barron. By continuing a vigorous blockade, the latter persuaded the Pasha to sue for peace at the end of 1804. Six months later Commodore Rodgers sailed the *Constitution* into Tunis and compelled the Bey to make peace. But before he could settle with the other Barbary States, growing differences between the U.S.A. and Britain over neutral rights required Washington to recall his ships for service nearer home.

Britain's persistence in seizing seamen from American ships for impressment in her own navy was just one of those 'differences' which so outraged public opinion in the United States that, in 1812, America found itself at war with Britain. Locked in conflict with Napoleonic France, the latter could not, initially, spare ships-of-the-line to cross the Atlantic – nor did she think it necessary to send them when the U.S. navy counted only 17 vessels. So, at sea, much of this war comprised brisk actions between frigates in which the Americans showed their superiority, as the number of White Ensigns hanging to this day in the Annapolis Naval Museum is mute testimony.

In July Captain Hull in the *Constitution* was sighted by a British squadron off the coast of New Jersey. Captain Dacres in HMS *Guerrière*, 38 guns, led a long chase after her but the wind proved too light for a decisive action. After two days of manœuvring, the *Constitution* eluded her opponents and escaped into Boston.

On 19 August, off the Gulf of St Lawrence, the *Constitution* again sighted the *Guerrière*, this time on her own. Both captains held their fire until they had closed well within 2,000 yards. Hull's more powerful broadsides then came near to dismasting and wrecking the British vessel, whose shots appeared to have such little effect against the *Constitution* that one of her crew is reputed to have cried: 'Huzza! Her sides are made of iron!', whereby the ship gained her renowned nickname of 'Old Ironsides'. When the *Guerrière*'s bowsprit fouled her opponent's rigging, both sides tried to board, but their ships were rolling too heavily for this to be possible. By the time they separated again, after an engagement lasting only 40 minutes, the British ship was in such a helpless condition that Dacres struck her colours. His casualties were 78 killed and wounded against only 14 Americans.

Less than five months later, on 29 December 1812, Commodore Bainbridge, who now commanded the *Constitution*, won a similar victory off Brazil. Superior American gunnery wrecked the British 38-gun frigate *Java* which, by the time she surrendered, had 161 killed or wounded, the former including her Captain Lambert, whereas the American vessel suffered only 34 casualties.

The *Constitution* then returned to Boston for a thorough refit. And before she was again ready for sea, towards the end of 1814, the British navy reasserted its supremacy, not only by sending a fleet of ships-of-the-line to blockade the American coast, but by fighting successful frigate actions, such as that in which Captain Broke in the *Shannon* took Captain Lawrence's *Chesapeake* on 1 June 1813. The Peace of Ghent, signed in December 1814, ended this 'unnecessary war', as it has been called, but before this could take effect the *Constitution* had her last fight. Sighting the British 22-gun frigate *Cyane* and the sloop *Levant* off Madeira, Captain Stewart fought both until they surrendered and he could take them back to the United States in prize.

Thereafter the *Constitution* was laid up in reserve until 1830 when she was condemned to be broken up. Public feeling was, however, so much aroused by this that enough money was raised to meet the cost of rebuilding her. Through the next twenty years she made numerous voyages, including one around the world in 1844–45 under Captain Percival. After the American Civil War she was for several years attached to the U.S. Naval Academy as a training ship. In 1871 she was again rebuilt, and seven years later made her last trip overseas, taking an American delegation to the Universal Exposition in Paris. Not until 1881 was her long active career finally ended when she became an accommodation ship in Boston harbour.

By 1905 it had become apparent that, as happened with the *Victory*, her timbers were rotting away. Partial restoration in that year was followed by a more thorough one in the 1920s. On completion she carried out a tour of American seaports so that those who had contributed towards her preservation might see her. Since then she has been berthed in Boston Navy Yard, as flagship of the Commandant of the U.S. First Naval District, open daily to an American public to whom she is a source of pride and inspiration.

Exceptionally, this grand 'old lady of the sea' still voyages as far as Boston's outer harbour, the last occasion being of unique historic significance. In July 1976 she was there to salute the British Royal Yacht *Britannia*, when she arrived with Queen Elizabeth II on board for the Bicentennial celebrations of America's Declaration of Independence from the rule of her forbear, King George III.

THE 'MIKASA'

It was not until the last decade of Queen Victoria's reign, in the heyday of the Pax Britannica, that Britain evolved a standard design of steel-hulled, armoured, steam-driven battleship, which was copied by other navies, and which formed the hard core of the world's principal fleets for the next fifteen years. Typical of these vessels was the Japanese *Mikasa*. Built in Britain by Vickers (because although bent on becoming the dominant power in the Far East, Japan had yet to develop her own shipyards), she was completed in 1902 with a displacement of 15,200 tons. Fourteen inches of armour protected her magazines, and coal-fired boilers and reciprocating engines gave her a best speed of 18 knots. Her armament comprised four 12-inch guns mounted in twin turrets forward and aft, plus two broadside batteries each of seven 6-inch.

Soon after the *Mikasa* reached Japanese waters she became the flagship of her country's battle fleet. Two years later a reckless Tsar allowed his country to be drawn into a war with Japan which was destined to be fought in Korea and Manchuria, and in the adjacent seas, all of which were so far from St Petersburg and Moscow that Russia could not hope to win. For the redoubtable Admiral Togo, born in 1847, partly educated in England where he became a keen student of Nelson's meteoric career, and now flying his flag in the *Mikasa*, this was his golden hour. And it is because his name and that of his flagship are inseparably linked, that the *Mikasa* ranks high in any list of historic ships.

Without waiting for a declaration of war Togo took the offensive. On 8 February 1904 he launched a surprise attack on the Russian fleet in Port Arthur as a prelude to establishing a blockade of that port. A month later Admiral Makarov began a series of sorties intended to break this blockade which, on 13 April, ended in disaster. The Russian flagship *Petropavlovsk* struck a mine and sank with all on board. Thereafter the Russian fleet stayed in harbour, while the Japanese landed an army on the Liaotung Peninsula which ringed Port Arthur so that it was isolated both by land and sea.

Minefields laid by both sides also proved expensive for the Japanese. By mid-June Togo's battleship strength had been cut to four, which encouraged Admiral Vitgeft to attempt a sortie on 23 June. But the mere sight of Togo's waiting fleet was enough to persuade him to return to harbour. Six weeks later the Tsar ordered Vitgeft to break out and make for Vladivostok. There followed the battle of the Yellow Sea, fought on 10 August, in which effective Japanese gunnery did more than compensate Togo for having only four battleships to the Russians' six. After an hour and a half of fierce fighting in which both sides suffered damage, Vitgeft was killed. The Russian fleet promptly fled back to Port Arthur, where it stayed until the port surrendered to the investing Japanese army on 2 January 1905. By that time most of its ships had been sunk by Japanese artillery from the heights commanding the city.

With no Russian warships left in the Far East to challenge Japan's control of the sea, on which her armies depended for their supplies and reinforcements, Togo was able to take home the

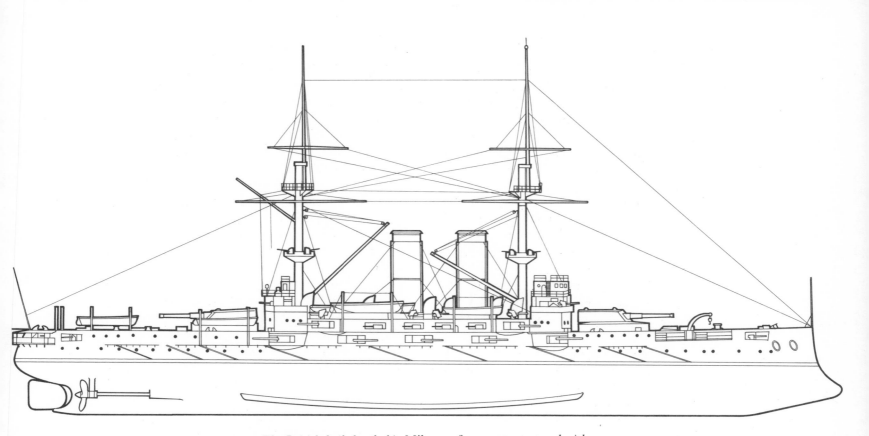

The British-built battleship Mikasa, *of 15,200 tons, armed with four 12-inch guns, in which Admiral Togo flew his flag throughout the Russo-Japanese War, notably at the battle of Tsushima in 1905.*

Mikasa and the rest of his fleet for refit and repair, before it faced a new challenge. The Tsar had ordered Admiral Rozhdestvensky's force out from the Baltic to the Far East.

His long voyage, almost half-way around the world, was beset with difficulties and misfortunes. A night attack on an innocent fishing fleet near the Dogger Bank in the North Sea, under the misguided impression that they were Japanese torpedo boats, came near to bringing Britain into the war. So many countries closed their ports to his belligerent ships that he was obliged to coal and replenish them from supply vessels in out-of-the-way anchorages. By the time Rozhdestvensky's eight battleships, eight cruisers and nine destroyers left their last port of call, in French Indo-China on 14 May 1905, and headed north, they were so ill-manned and so much in need of repairs that they were no match for Togo's fleet of four battleships and eight cruisers, but with the advantage of 60 torpedo boats.

With his ships unable to carry enough coal to go round to the east of Japan, whereby he might have evaded the enemy, Rozhdestvensky was obliged to take the direct route to Vladivostok, through the Strait of Tsushima into the Sea of Japan. And in that strait Togo intercepted him on 27 May. The *Mikasa* led the Japanese fleet across their opponents' 'T', and opened a devastating fire on the Russian flagship, *Suvorov*, at a range of 6,400 yards. And in less than two hours, by brilliantly manœuvring his smaller but faster force around the Russian ships, Togo put two battleships and a cruiser out of action.

By nightfall the Russian admiral had been wounded, three of his battleships had been sunk, and the survivors were fleeing north in confusion. Togo sent his armoured cruisers and torpedo boats to harry them throughout the hours of darkness. Next day he completed his virtual annihilation of the enemy. For the loss of only three torpedo boats, he had sunk or captured almost the whole of Rozhdestvensky's fleet. Only one cruiser and a handful of destroyers escaped to Vladivostok, or to internment in a neutral port.

For the *Mikasa* this great victory (which compelled the Russians to sign the peace Treaty of Portsmouth, U.S.A., in September 1905) was unhappily followed by a near disaster. In that month she was sunk by the accidental explosion of a magazine while lying in Sasebo harbour. The damage was not, however, enough to prevent her salvage, repair and return to duty.

Throughout the First World War the *Mikasa* was employed in Japanese home waters. In 1921 she was off Vladivostok supporting Japanese operations in the War of Intervention against Bolshevik Russia. The Naval Limitation Treaty signed at Washington, D.C., at the end of that year required the *Mikasa* to be stricken from the active list. She was not, however, scrapped. The Japanese decided to preserve her for posterity at Yokosuka. Damaged by American aircraft during the Second World War, she was subsequently repaired and to this day may be seen there, a lasting memorial to Togo and Tsushima, and the only remaining example anywhere of the standard pre-dreadnought type of capital ship.

THE 'TITANIC'

Of the score or more of very large liners designed by Britain, France, Germany and the United States for the trans-Atlantic passenger run between the years 1900 and 1960 – with names such as *Olympic, Mauretania, Bremen, Normandie, Queen Mary*, and *United States* – none is better remembered than the *Titanic*, for the most tragic of reasons.

Of 46,328 tons and 882 feet long, with a best speed of 25 knots, she was the largest ship afloat when she was completed by the Belfast yard of Harland and Wolff early in 1912. Long before she steamed round to Southampton at the beginning of April of that year, under the command of the 59-year-old Captain Edward Smith, her lavish accommodation had been much publicized. More importantly, she was labelled unsinkable, because she was subdivided by 15 transverse bulkheads into 17 major watertight compartments. If any two of these should be flooded, she would remain afloat, and no one could envisage an accident that would do greater damage – for which reason no one was concerned to know that, in accordance with the then current Board of Trade regulations, her lifeboats would carry only half her complement of passengers and crew.

On 10 April Smith took the *Titanic* out of Southampton for her maiden voyage to New York with 1,316 passengers, most of them British and American, and a crew of 891, in all 2,207 souls. They included Mr Thomas Andrews, managing director of Harland and Wolff, her designers and builders, who was naturally interested in their great new ship proving a successful addition to the White Star fleet.

The *Titanic* was scheduled to reach New York on 17 April. For three days she made such good progress that by Sunday the 14th she was 300 miles to the south-east of Newfoundland. As that day dawned calm and clear other ships in the area were heard radioing reports of ice. But none was sighted from the *Titanic*'s bridge, so Smith saw no reason to reduce speed, even when shortly after dark the temperature fell sharply by as much as five degrees Celcius.

By 11.30 pm, with the liner still steaming westwards at 24 knots, most of her passengers had retired to their cabins. Ten minutes later disaster struck. As the crow's-nest lookout reported, 'Iceberg right ahead', First Officer Murdoch on the bridge glimpsed a glistening white shape through the darkness and ordered, 'Hard-a-starboard' and, 'Full speed astern'. But he was too late to avoid the berg; as the *Titanic*'s bow swung to port it scraped down her starboard side and, like a giant tin-opener, sliced a gash for almost a third of her length.

Hurrying up to the bridge and ordering all watertight doors to be closed, Captain Smith soon learned that not just two compartments had been holed, but six. But to know the full implications of this he had to await a report from Thomas Andrews. Because the transverse bulkheads extended only up to D or E decks – to have built them higher would have interfered with her first-class passengers' comfort – the flooding could not be confined to the forward compartments. As the ship trimmed by the bow, the sea

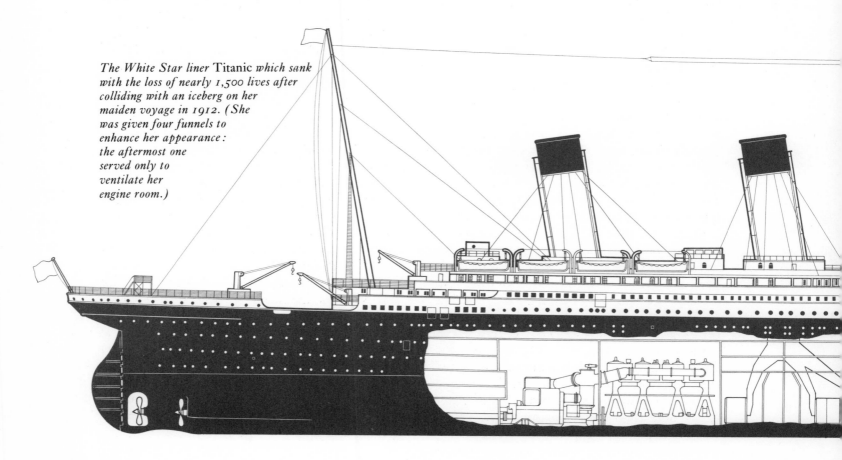

The White Star liner Titanic *which sank with the loss of nearly 1,500 lives after colliding with an iceberg on her maiden voyage in 1912. (She was given four funnels to enhance her appearance: the aftermost one served only to ventilate her engine room.)*

would flow over the bulkheads into compartments further aft. In short, the *Titanic* could not be saved: she must sink.

Shortly after midnight, Smith instructed his radio officer to send out a distress call and another officer to fire distress rockets, and gave the order to clear away the lifeboats. Half an hour later these were being loaded at their davits with women and children. By then, too, several ships had answered the *Titanic*'s radio call. But the nearest of these, Captain Arthur Rostron's *Carpathian*, could not reach the stricken ship in much less than four hours. And well before that time she would have sunk in a sea whose temperature was so near to freezing point that no one could hope to survive who had not found a place in one of the boats.

It was, therefore, with a heavy heart that, just an hour after the collision, Smith ordered the boats to be lowered and to pull away from a ship that was now much down by the bows. Because many of the passengers could not believe that this great new vessel could sink, Smith's officers had great difficulty in persuading them to fill the boats to capacity. It was nearly 2.0 pm by the time that the last of them was got away.

'Shortly after two o'clock,' wrote an eye-witness in one of the boats, 'we observed the *Titanic* settling very rapidly, with the bows and bridge completely under water. She slowly tilted straight on end with the stern vertically upwards. The lights in the cabins and saloons went out. We watched at least 150 feet of the *Titanic* towering above the sea, black against the sky. Then, with a quick dive, she disappeared, and there fell on our ears the cries of hundreds of our fellow beings struggling in the icy water, cries for help which we knew could not be answered.'

It was soon after half-past two when the *Titanic* actually disappeared. True to the traditions of the sea, Captain Smith remained on the bridge of his great command until the last and was not seen again. An hour later the survivors, who did not include Andrews, sighted the *Carpathian* coming to their rescue. She was followed by the *Californian*, a smaller liner that had been much closer to the scene of the disaster, but knew nothing of it until after 4.0 am, because she carried only one radio operator who was, quite properly, off watch when the *Titanic* sent out her distress calls, and because her Captain Lord believed a liner's rockets to be no more significant than recognition signals to another vessel of the same company, for which he was severely criticized. Between them these two ships rescued 713 passengers and crew from the greatest of all peace-time maritime disasters.

Three steps were soon taken to prevent anything like it from happening again. British Board of Trade regulations were amended to require ships to carry boats sufficient for their whole complement. An International Ice Patrol was established to keep ice in the north-west Atlantic under observation, and to broadcast warnings to shipping so that vessels could be routed clear of danger. And for ships that did not carry enough radio operators to maintain a 24-hour watch, an automatic alarm was devised which responded to a distress call by ringing a bell on the bridge.

THE 'EMDEN'

Of all the ships with which the Imperial German Navy fought the First World War, none created more havoc than the *Emden*. Completed at Danzig (now Gdansk) dockyard in 1908, she was a light cruiser of 3,650 tons, armed with ten 4.1-inch guns and two torpedo tubes, and with a best speed of 24½ knots. By 1914 she was stationed in the Far East as a unit of Vice-Admiral Graf von Spee's East Asiatic squadron based on Tsingtau, her crew of 360 officers and men under the command of the 41-year-old Captain Karl von Müller.

As Germany threatened war in Europe against Russia, France and Britain early in July, most of von Spee's force was cruising in the Pacific. Only the *Emden* was left in Chinese waters. Three weeks later von Müller was ordered to join von Spee at Ponapé. Successfully avoiding the Allied ships which were heading for Tsingtau, the *Emden* arrived at this island shortly after the war was declared at the beginning of August. From there von Spee detached her to act as a lone wolf in the Indian Ocean, while the rest of his force headed east across the Pacific.

Having coaled from two tenders in various isolated anchorages in the Netherlands East Indies (now Indonesia), where she narrowly escaped discovery by HMS *Hampshire*, the *Emden* began her marauding career in the Bay of Bengal on 10 September. 'During the next few days,' wrote her first lieutenant, 'our business flourished. As soon as a steamer came our way she was stopped, boarded, and made ready to be sunk. Then another masthead appeared on the horizon. At times we had five or six vessels collected at one spot.'

Von Müller had rightly judged this to be the best area in which he could carry on cruiser warfare against the Allies' maritime trade. Not until 14 September did the British Admiralty learn that he was there, when all traffic in the Bay of Bengal and on the Colombo–Singapore route was stopped, and Admiral Jerram sent every available British, French, Russian and Japanese warship after this dangerous foe.

Forewarned by intercepted radio messages, von Müller, with characteristic boldness, headed for Madras. Arriving off this port well after dark on 22 September, he spent half an hour bombarding the docks area, setting two of the Burmah Oil Company's tanks ablaze, before disappearing again into the night. He next intended a similar assault on Colombo, but was warned off by sweeping searchlights indicating that the coast defence batteries were on the alert. Instead, he headed for Minikoi, a focal point on the trade route to the west of Ceylon (now Sri Lanka) where he disposed of six of his enemies' merchant ships before the alarm was raised. And by the time Jerram's ships could reach this area, von Müller had withdrawn to the Maldive Islands.

Von Müller was scrupulously careful to ensure that his attacks on enemy shipping caused no loss of life. Every now and again he refrained from sinking an intercepted vessel: instead he allowed her to make for the nearest port loaded with the crews and passengers whom he had taken off earlier prizes. So, too, did he sometimes refrain from sinking a ship until he had coaled the *Emden* from her.

He next headed south for the Chagos Archipelago. Finding no prey there, he stayed ten days at Diego Garcia overhauling his ship's engines, before again descending on Minikoi. This time, between 16 and 19 October, the *Emden* sank seven merchant ships, and totally disrupted trade on the Aden–Colombo route, before von Müller judged that Allied warships were in hot pursuit. Indeed, only a chance rain squall saved him from being sighted by HMS *Empress of Asia* early on the 21st.

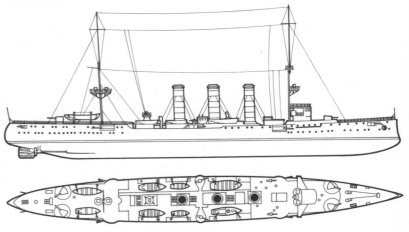

The German light cruiser Emden *which preyed so successfully on Allied merchant shipping in the Indian Ocean in 1914.*

Now heading east, back across the Bay of Bengal, von Müller was bent on his most audacious exploit. Disguising his ship with a dummy funnel of canvas to look like a British cruiser, he closed the port of Penang at dawn on 28 October. Unsuspected, the *Emden* steamed into the harbour to surprise and sink the Russian cruiser *Zemchug*. Having stirred a hornet's nest, von Müller sped for the open sea, with the French destroyer *Mousquet* in pursuit. Commander Theroinne's vessel put up a gallant fight but, inevitably, was soon overpowered and sunk. With characteristic chivalry, von Müller stopped to rescue her crew.

For his next objective he chose the Cocos Islands, intending to destroy the Eastern Telegraph Company's cable and wireless station. He 'hoped to create the impression that the *Emden* was about to harry the steamer traffic south and west of Australia, and so withdraw from the Indian Ocean some of the English cruisers that were hunting her there before I made for Socotra and the steamer route between Aden and Bombay.'

Jerram had, however, wisely instructed the Cocos cable station to radio an immediate report of any attack on the island. This the superintendent promptly did when he sighted the *Emden* at dawn on the morning of 9 November, before her landing party could destroy the company's equipment. And, unluckily for von Müller, there was then an Allied convoy, carrying Australian and New Zealand troops to Europe, only 55 miles away.

The 5,400 tons Australian cruiser *Sydney*, Captain M. L. Silver, was immediately detached from the convoy's escort. Proceeding at her full speed of $25\frac{1}{2}$ knots, she sighted the *Emden* at 9.15 am, and half an hour later opened fire with her eight 6-inch guns. The duel between the two ships lasted for the best part of ninety minutes, but the result was never in doubt. Although the *Emden* tried to flee from her more powerful opponent, the *Sydney*'s heavier weapons wrought so much destruction that by 11.0 the German's guns had been silenced.

'Since it was now impossible for me to do further damage to my opponent,' wrote von Müller, 'I decided to wreck my badly damaged ship on North Keeling Island, rather than sacrifice needlessly the lives of those who still survived.' There the stranded *Emden* hauled down her ensign, and the *Sydney* embarked 202 members of her crew. Except for the small party landed to destroy the cable station (who, after an adventurous voyage, managed to return to Germany), the rest of the *Emden*'s company had perished. In sharp contrast the *Sydney*'s casualties numbered only three killed and 11 wounded.

Wrote the London *Daily Telegraph*: 'It is almost in our heart to regret that the *Emden* has been destroyed. Von Müller has been enterprising, cool and daring in making war on our shipping. There is not a survivor who does not speak well of this young German. The war at sea will lose something of its interest now that the *Emden* has gone.' Von Müller spent the rest of the First World War as a prisoner of war in Malta. His compensation was a richly deserved Iron Cross First Class.

THE 'AURORA'

For tourists who now visit Leningrad, once Imperial Russia's capital St Petersburg, renamed Petrograd in 1914, the inescapable sights include an evidently obsolete three-funnelled warship berthed in the River Neva, not far from the high-spired Peter and Paul fortress whose cathedral contains the tombs of the Tsars. This is the *Aurora*, a typical protected cruiser of the decade immediately before the dreadnought era. Completed in 1902, she mounted eight 6-inch guns on a displacement of 6,630 tons, and had a best speed of 19 knots. Assigned to the Baltic fleet, she sailed under Admiral Rozhdestvensky to the Far East, and was one of the very few Russian vessels

to escape from the disastrous battle of Tsushima to neutral Manila, from where she returned to the Baltic in 1906.

The outbreak of the First World War in 1914 aroused as much patriotic fervour among the crews of the Baltic fleet as it did in the Russian army and among the Russian people. The *Aurora* was first based at Abo (Turku) with other units to guard the entrance to the Gulf of Finland, until the German army's advance on land compelled their withdrawal inside the Gulf. Then, in November 1916, the *Aurora* was ordered to the Franco-Russian Shipbuilding Works, at the mouth of the Neva, for a routine refit.

By this time all enthusiasm for the war had ebbed away from the bulk of the people in Petrograd. The defeats inflicted on Russia's ill-equipped armies, and the breakdown of food supplies, especially bread, to the city had brought them near to revolt. This was especially true of the workers in the factories and shipyards, so it was not long before a spirit of unrest infected the *Aurora*'s crew.

Since the Neva was icebound during the winter months, the ship was still under repair in February 1917 when disturbances broke out in Petrograd on a scale that became the first Russian Revolution. The Tsar was compelled to abdicate, and his autocratic powers passed to the Provisional Government of the *Duma* (elected parliament) and the Petrograd *Soviet* (council) of Workers and Soldiers' Deputies, which was dominated by the Bolsheviks. The evening of 27 February (according to the 'old-style' calendar then used in Russia) brought news of a mutiny on board the Petrograd naval depot ship, which inspired a sympathetic demonstration by the *Aurora*'s crew, who seized their ship, killing her Captain Nikolsky and seriously wounding her second-in-command.

All repair work on the ship was now stopped. Controlled by her mutinous crew, she remained in her berth until October 1917. Kerensky's Provisional Government then had good reason to fear a serious revolt in the capital. Knowing that Bolshevik influence on board the *Aurora*, the only warship of any significance in the Neva, was strong, they ordered her to join the rest of the Baltic fleet at Helsingfors. Her Soviet agreed that she should sail on 25 October.

Before this, however, on the morning of the 24th, the Military Revolutionary Committee of the Petrograd Soviet called a meeting of delegates from all naval and military units in the city, with the consequence that later in the day 20,000 garrison troops began occupying strategically important points, such as the telephone exchange, central telegraph office, railway termini and power plants. But when they tried to seize the Neva bridges, these were held by cadets from the Petrograd Engineering School and a women's battalion, which remained loyal to the Provisional Government. To overcome this obstacle the Military Committee instructed the *Aurora* to move up the Neva and to threaten the defenders of the first bridge, the Nikolaevsky, with her guns.

With red flags flying and her searchlights piercing the darkness, the cruiser began moving up the river in the early hours of 25 October, and this had the desired effect upon the stubborn defenders of the bridges. They withdrew soon after the warship anchored just below the Nikolaevsky Bridge at 3.30 am, so that she was not required to open fire.

The Military Committee then agreed plans for seizing the last significant position held by the Provisional Government. A red light would be hoisted after dark by the Peter and Paul fortress. This was to be the signal for the *Aurora* to fire several blank rounds. Clearly audible throughout the city, these would synchronize a concerted attack on the Winter Palace by all forces opposed to the Provisional Government.

The light was seen by the *Aurora*'s crew at 9.40 pm. Her forecastle gun promptly fired a single blank round – no more than this. The only artillery support for the assault was provided by the guns of the Peter and Paul fortress, which hit the Winter Palace just twice before, at 2.0 am on 26 October, the Provisional Government surrendered to the Bolsheviks.

According to the official history of the Soviet Communist Party: 'By the thunder of her guns directed on the Winter Palace the cruiser *Aurora* heralded the beginning of a new era, the era of the Great Socialist Revolution.' The truth, that she fired only a single blank round as a signal for the final assault on 25–26 October 1917 (celebrated annually, since the calendar was updated, on 7 November), is more accurately recorded on a brass plate affixed to her forecastle gun. The reality is that, by her chance presence in the river under the control of a crew who had been in open mutiny since February, the *Aurora* was a visible symbol of the Bolsheviks' ascendancy which enabled Lenin and Trotsky to complete the transformation of Imperial Russia into the U.S.S.R.

THE 'WARSPITE'

HMS *Dreadnought*, completed in 1906, with a displacement of 17,900 tons, was the world's first all-big-gun (ten 12-inch) battleship; the first, moreover, to have steam-turbine propulsion giving her a best speed of $21\frac{1}{2}$ knots. Her subsequent career was not, however, a notable one: she took no part in any of the naval battles of the First World War, and was one of the first ships to be scrapped after the Treaty of Versailles was signed in 1919.

In sharp contrast, one of the numerous progeny which she spawned, termed 'dread-noughts', in more than a dozen of the world's fleets, had the unique distinction of playing a more prominent role in both World Wars than any other warship of any navy.

In 1912 the British Admiralty, under Winston Churchill's dynamic leadership, decided to build the first *fast* battleships, forerunners of those which were the norm by the beginning of the Second World War. And one of the five of this 'Queen Elizabeth' class was christened *Warspite*. Completed by Devonport dockyard early in 1915, she displaced 27,500 tons, mounted eight 15-inch guns plus fourteen 6-inch, was protected by a 13-inch armour belt, and had a best speed of 24 knots.

By the end of May 1916, she and her sisters formed the Grand Fleet's Fifth Battle Squadron, which chanced to be at Rosyth when the Admiralty received radio intelligence that the German High Seas Fleet was about to sortie, and ordered Admirals Jellicoe and Beatty to intercept. The *Warspite* was thus with Beatty's battlecruisers when they clashed with Admiral Hipper's off Jutland on 31 May, when the stoutly armoured, heavily gunned Fifth Battle Squadron was instrumental in saving the day for Beatty's faster but too lightly protected 'greyhounds'.

A couple of hours later, as Jellicoe's battle fleet was deploying to engage Admiral Scheer's, a shell hit jammed the *Warspite*'s helm, so that she turned a complete, involuntary circle at what became known as 'Windy Corner', drawing the fire of the leading enemy battleships for a crucial ten minutes. This gave the British battle fleet a valuable breathing space while it was deploying into action in this the only major naval battle of the First World War, though the *Warspite* suffered so much damage that she had to be ordered back to Rosyth for repairs. Thereafter she stayed with the Grand Fleet until the end of hostilities.

Between the wars the *Warspite* served in either the Atlantic or Mediterranean fleets except for two extensive refits. From the first, 1924–26, she emerged with her two funnels trunked into one to allow space for larger bridges and control positions. In the second, 1934–37, she was modernized with new engines, with increased elevation and therefore range for her 15-inch guns, and with thicker deck armour and more anti-aircraft guns.

At the outbreak of the Second World War the *Warspite* was the flagship of the C.-in-C. Mediterranean, Admiral Cunningham. But when Italy decided to delay joining in on the Axis side, she was recalled, first to escort a Canadian troop convoy across the Atlantic, and then to join the Home Fleet, with which she played a notable role in the Norwegian campaign. At the second battle of Narvik, fought on 13 April 1940, she sank the eight large destroyers which remained off the town after bringing north the German troops that had earlier seized the port. Then, with Italy threatening war, the *Warspite* returned to the Mediterranean.

Soon after Mussolini finally declared his hand, she covered two convoys from Malta to Alexandria when, on 9 July, a single 15-inch shell hit from her long-range guns on the Italian battleship *Giulio Cesare* put to flight a faster, more powerful, Italian force in the battle of Calabria. In September 1940 Cunningham's ships, headed by the *Warspite*, bombarded Bardia and Fort Capuzzo in North Africa. And in her he led the force which included the aircraft-carrier *Illustrious*, whose planes attacked Taranto during the night of 11 November and effectively sank half the Italian battle fleet.

In March 1941 a large Italian force was sent to attack the convoys which the British were running from Alexandria to support their troops in Crete and Greece. Forewarned by radio intelligence, Cunningham, in the *Warspite*, took his fleet to sea to intercept. During the morning of 28 March his cruisers and carrier-borne aircraft harried the enemy to the south of Cape Matapan to an extent that persuaded them to retire from the scene. Not all of them were, however, to escape. During the afternoon a plane from the aircraft-carrier *Formidable* scored a torpedo hit on the Italian flagship *Vittorio Veneto* which came near to crippling her. More important, the 8-inch-gunned cruiser *Pola* was so seriously damaged that she was brought to a halt. And during the ensuing night the *Warspite*, accompanied by her sisters, *Barham* and *Valiant*, found not only this helpless ship, but also the 8-inch-gunned *Fiume* and *Zara* which were standing by her – with the consequence that all three were virtually blown out of the water.

There followed the battle to prevent German airborne forces seizing Crete during which the *Warspite* survived more than 400 bombs, all that is except for one. And this did enough damage for her to have to proceed by way of Singapore and Pearl Harbor to the U.S. Navy Yard at Bremerton, Seattle, for major repairs. These completed, she joined the Eastern Fleet which Britain established after Japan's entry into the war. And there she was Admiral Somerville's flagship during the operations in which he played the classic role of a 'fleet in being' so successfully while the main Japanese fleet attacked Ceylon, that it never again came into the Indian Ocean.

Early in 1943 the *Warspite* was recalled to join Admiral Willis's Force H in the eastern Mediterranean when this was reinforced to cover the Anglo-U.S. landings in Sicily in July, and at Salerno on the Italian mainland in September. Following the Italian armistice she had the well-earned distinction of leading the British squadron which accepted the surrender of the Italian fleet. Then, when a German army came near to throwing back into the sea the Allied troops landed at

Salerno, a hurriedly arranged bombardment by the *Warspite*'s heavy guns saved the day, and earned her this tribute from Cunningham: '. . . when the old lady lifts her skirts she can still run'.

Unhappily, a couple of days later, while still off the Salerno beach head, the *Warspite* was so badly crippled by a German radio-controlled bomb that she had to be towed back to Malta. Thence she returned to England under her own power for major repairs. Finally, on D-Day, 6 June 1944, she took her place among the bombarding ships whose guns supported the Allied landings in Normandy; and in November she performed the same service in support of the landings at Walcheren in the Scheldt estuary.

Not until after World War Two was won in 1945, by which time the *Warspite* had served in the British navy for all of 30 years, did the Admiralty decide that she should be scrapped. But such a fine 'old lady' had no intention of ending her career in this ignominious way. While under tow from Portsmouth to the shipbreaker's yard, she broke adrift and went so hard on to the rocks of Cornwall's Prussia Cove that she had to be broken up for scrap at this her last resting place.

THE 'BISMARCK'

In 1935 Nazi Germany repudiated the Treaty of Versailles and began to build up a modern balanced fleet. The largest vessel then laid down was the battleship *Bismarck*, of 41,700 tons, armed with eight 15-inch guns, with a $12\frac{3}{4}$-inch armoured belt and a best speed of 29 knots. Completed in 1941, this fine ship soon made her first sortie whose dramatic events ensured her a niche in history.

Admiral Lütjens, who had already made a successful sortie against Allied trade in the North Atlantic with the battlecruisers *Scharnhorst* and *Gneisenau*, was ordered to take the *Bismarck* and the 8-inch-gunned cruiser *Prinz Eugen* out of Gdynia on 18 May for a similar foray. Inevitably these ships' passage out of the Baltic, by way of the narrow passage between Denmark and Sweden, did not pass unnoticed by friends of the Allies. Two days later Coastal Command aircraft discovered them in Kors Fjord. Admiral Tovey, commanding Britain's Home Fleet, promptly sailed the 20-year-old

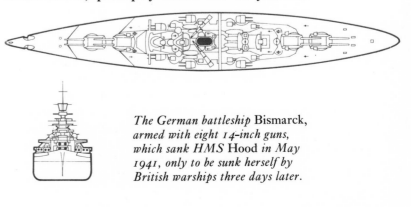

The German battleship Bismarck, *armed with eight 14-inch guns, which sank HMS* Hood *in May 1941, only to be sunk herself by British warships three days later.*

battlecruiser *Hood* – of 41,200 tons, the most handsome ship in the British navy which also mounted eight 15-inch guns and had a speed of 32 knots but which, because she was designed before the battle of Jutland, was insufficiently armoured – and the newly completed 35,000 tons fast battleship *Prince of Wales*, armed with ten 14-inch guns, to back up the two cruisers which were patrolling the Denmark Strait between Iceland and Greenland. Tovey subsequently left Scapa Flow with the rest of his fleet, headed by the 14-inch-gunned fast battleship *King George V*, when on the evening of the 22nd, a single Fleet Air Arm plane brought news that the German vessels had left their Norwegian fjord.

The *Bismarck* and *Prinz Eugen* were next sighted by the 8-inch-gunned cruisers *Norfolk* and *Suffolk*, while passing through the Denmark Strait late on the 23rd. And because these ships were fitted with radar, Lütjens was unable to shake them off before next morning when, shortly after dawn, he sighted the *Hood* and *Prince of Wales*. He promptly engaged them with such devastating accuracy that within ten minutes the British battlecruiser was struck by a salvo that penetrated her after magazines, and she blew up with the loss of Admiral Holland and almost all her crew. This German success was followed by hits on the *Prince of Wales* which put five of her 14-inch guns out of action, and impelled Captain Leach to break off the engagement.

The British ships had, however, scored three hits on the *Bismarck*, one of which produced a tell-tale leak from two of her fuel tanks, and contaminated the oil in others. Realizing that his flagship was therefore in no condition to continue her cruise, Lütjens detached the *Prinz Eugen* to operate alone, and turned for the safety of St Nazaire, the only port on the Atlantic coast of France with a dock large enough to take the *Bismarck*.

That night the German battleship was attacked by planes from the British aircraft-carrier *Victorious* which scored one torpedo hit. Later, however, she was lost by Tovey's shadowing cruisers, after which it seemed that she might escape through the net of ships which the Admiralty had ordered out to deal with her. Nor was she again found, this time by a Coastal Command plane, for more than 24 hours, by which time it seemed that she was too close to Brest for Tovey to catch her.

Unknown to Lütjens, however, Admiral Somerville's Force H barred the way. On 26 May, his aircraft-carrier, the *Ark Royal*, launched air strikes which scored two torpedo hits on the *Bismarck*, one of which jammed her rudder. Lütjens responded by signalling Berlin: 'Ship no longer manœuvrable. We fight to the last shell. Long live the *Führer*.'

That night the crippled vessel was attacked again and again by Captain Vian's destroyers.

These slowed her so much that, as day dawned on 27 May, Lütjens saw Tovey's flagship and the 16-inch-gunned battleship *Rodney* coming up over the horizon. At 8.40 am these opened fire at 25,000 yards. The *Bismarck* promptly replied and continued to fight her two opponents until by 10.0 all her guns were silent. The 8-inch-gunned cruiser *Dorsetshire* then closed the battered hulk and, with her torpedoes, sent the *Bismarck* to the bottom of the Bay of Biscay.

In his despatch on the battle of the Falkland Islands, written in December 1914, Admiral Sturdee paid a tribute to the 'bravery, skill and endurance' with which Admiral von Spee, his officers and men, fought their ships until they went down with their colours flying – only to have it deleted by the Admiralty before publication in the *London Gazette*. In retrospect, although one understands why this was done, such a denial of a victor's salute to a courageous foe after he had been vanquished in fair fight is to be regretted. So, also, with the chivalrous tribute which Tovey paid to Lütjens, his officers and men in his despatch on the sinking of the *Bismarck*; it, too, was deleted – because the first casualty in modern war is Truth.

THE 'RICHELIEU' AND 'JEAN BART'

In the mid-1930s the French began building their first battleships to be laid down since the First World War. Limited by the Washington Treaty to 35,000 tons, they were designed to mount eight 15-inch guns in two quadruple turrets, were to be protected by $13\frac{1}{2}$ inches of armour, and have a best speed of 30 knots. Named *Richelieu* and *Jean Bart*, no ships had a more unusual record than these in the chequered years of France's history during the Second World War.

One had only just been commissioned and the other was far from complete when the Germans overran France in 1940. Nonetheless, much to the credit of the French navy, both were got away before they could be seized by the enemy. In mid-June Admiral de Laborde, commanding at Brest, had just ten hours in which to get more than 150 warships and merchant vessels out of this great port. One of these was the newly completed *Richelieu* which headed for Dakar.

There followed operations to ensure that the French fleet did not fall into German hands. A few days after Admiral Somerville's Force H had bombarded Admiral Gensoul's ships berthed in Mers-el-Kebir (near Oran) at the beginning of July, a small British force closed Dakar. Depth charges dropped by a motorboat under the *Richelieu*'s stern failed to explode, but an aircraft torpedo rendered her unseaworthy for more than a year. In September, however, from her harbour berth where she suffered only slight damage, her heavy guns played a significant role in Admiral Lacroix's successful defeat of an ill-conceived

Anglo-Free French attempt to seize this West African port from those who chose to remain loyal to Marshal Pétain's Vichy Government.

Against this, the *Richelieu* made no attempt to interfere with the Anglo-U.S. landings in Vichy French North Africa in November 1942. Moreover, when these proved successful, her officers and men put aside their anglophobia engendered by the Royal Navy's attack on Mers-el-Kebir, and made common cause against Nazi Germany by joining Britain's Home Fleet.

As readily, after a refit in the U.S.A. in 1943, which included mounting radar and additional A.A. guns, did *Richelieu* sail for the Indian Ocean, where she became a unit of Admiral Somerville's now powerful Eastern Fleet. On 16 April 1944 she took part in a damaging attack on the Japanese naval base at Sabang in Sumatra. Thereafter she continued to carry out similar operations in those waters, thus playing her part in the defeat of Japan.

The *Jean Bart* was so far from completion in

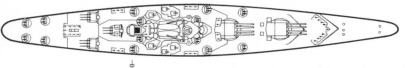

The French battleship Richelieu *which helped to defend Dakar in 1940 before joining the Allied navies in the war against Japan.*

June 1940 that it was only by almost superhuman endeavour that Captain Ronar'ch got her away from St Nazaire during the night of the 18th, almost in sight of the advancing German army. With only half her machinery available for use, and with only half her armament mounted and none of it able to fire, she fuelled from a tanker in the roads under German air attack, and set course for Casablanca where she arrived safely on the 22nd. There, notwithstanding the almost total lack of dockyard facilities and a grave shortage of materials, her forward 15-inch turret and a part of her secondary armament were made ready for action by the autumn of 1943, although her main machinery could not be completed.

When the American Admiral Hewitt's ships closed Casablanca and adjacent beaches in November, intending a surprise landing by General Patton's U.S. troops as a part of the Allied invasion of French North Africa, Admiral Michelier's ships put up a stout defence. The *Jean Bart* may not have been able to proceed to sea and engage the U.S. battleships *New York* and *Massachusetts*, but from her camouflaged harbour berth she used her forward turret to such effect that Hewitt ordered the aircraft-carrier *Ranger*'s planes 'to sink that damned yellow-painted ship' at all costs. They inflicted considerable damage, but failed to send her to the bottom before Michelier decided that honour

had been satisfied and ordered a cease fire, which allowed American troops to complete their landing without adding to the losses already suffered by both sides.

For the rest of the war the *Jean Bart* remained idle at Casablanca. Not until the war was over in Europe could she be brought back to France and the work of completing her undertaken. But when this was done, she and the *Richelieu* served as the principal units of France's post-war fleet until it was finally accepted that capital ships had had their day: that the period of more than four centuries through which ships-of-the-line and their battleship successors, mounting 'great guns', had been the queens on the maritime chess boards of the world were over; that maritime power now rested with carrier-borne aircraft and ships armed with guided missiles.

THE 'LEXINGTON'

The U.S.A.'s entry into the First World War on the side of the Allies in 1917 required her to expand her fleet. The many additional ships approved by Congress included six battlecruisers which were designed to displace 43,000 tons, to be armed with eight 16-inch guns and to have a best speed of 33 knots. But none had been completed by the time that the U.S.A. signed, with Britain, Japan, France and Italy, the Washington Treaty of 1921. By this act America agreed to abandon these great vessels; she was, however, allowed to convert the two which were most advanced into the U.S. navy's first aircraft-carriers (excluding the small and slow converted collier *Langley*). Completed in the late 1920s as the *Lexington* and *Saratoga*, these displaced 36,000 tons, had a speed in excess of 30 knots, were armed with eight 8-inch guns, and carried 72 planes.

In the years that followed, up to 1941, the *Lexington* and *Saratoga* served chiefly in the Pacific where, prior to the expiry of the Washington Treaty in 1935, they were joined only by the 14,500-ton *Ranger*. On 7 December 1941, when Admiral Yamamoto's Combined Fleets carried out a surprise attack on Pearl Harbor which crippled most of Admiral Kimmel's battleships, his three carriers, the *Lexington*, the recently completed *Enterprise* and the *Saratoga* were, most fortunately, absent from this Hawaiian base. The first two chanced to be delivering fighter reinforcements to the Pacific islands of Midway and Wake, and the other was away refitting on the American west coast. This allowed Kimmel's successor, Admiral Nimitz, to begin hitting back at the Japanese as soon as 1 February 1942, when the Marshall and Gilbert Islands were attacked by planes from the *Lexington*, *Yorktown* and *Enterprise*. These were followed two days later by raids on Wake.

Much more important, however, were the events of the first week of May. From radio intelligence Nimitz learned that the Japanese intended a landing on New Guinea, for which three separate forces were to enter the Solomon Sea, one of these under Admiral Takagi including the large carriers, *Shokaku* and *Zuikaku*, and another under Admiral Goto including the small carrier *Shoho*. To counter these Nimitz ordered the *Lexington*, flying the flag of Admiral Fitch, to rendezvous with the *Yorktown* in the Coral Sea where both carriers were supported by cruisers and destroyers.

The *Lexington* and the *Yorktown* met on 1 May. Two days later Fitch learned that Japanese troops had landed on the island of Tulagi, but although the carriers of both sides sometimes came as close as 70 miles during the next four days poor visibility prevented any sightings by their planes.

On 7 May Takagi ordered the *Shokaku* and *Zuikaku* to launch air strikes against an American carrier which they supposed that they had sighted but found, too late, to be only a replenishment oil tanker. A couple of hours later Fitch made a comparable mistake: he ordered the *Lexington* and *Yorktown* to send air strikes after a force which had been erroneously reported to contain Takagi's two big carriers. Instead they found and sank Goto's *Shoho*.

To avenge this loss, Takagi launched a large force of planes towards evening with orders to find and sink Fitch's carriers. Frustrated by dirty weather, these were compelled to jettison their bombs and torpedoes and head for 'home' through the gathering dusk. This chanced to take them over Fitch's radar-equipped force with the consequence that nine Japanese planes were shot down by American fighters, six were lost trying to land on the *Yorktown* in the belief that she was their own ship, and eleven more failed to return to 'base'.

Next morning, 8 May, each side had some 120 planes still serviceable. Because Takagi's carriers chanced to be covered by a belt of low rain-clouds while Fitch's were in bright sunshine, the first air strike launched by the *Lexington* and *Yorktown* failed to find the *Zuikaku*, and scored only three bomb hits on the *Shokaku*, for the loss of 33 U.S. planes to Japanese guns and fighters. The damage done to the *Shokaku* was, however, enough to prevent her operating aircraft, which

decided Takagi to order her back to Truk. Against this, the first Japanese air strike scored one damaging bomb hit on the *Yorktown*, and struck the *Lexington*, around noon, with two bombs and two torpedoes, at the cost of 30 planes to U.S. guns and fighters.

With several compartments holed and flooded, the *Lexington* listed over to port; but although she was also ablaze in four places from bomb hits, her power plant remained in service so that Captain Sherman expected to save her. Unhappily, shortly before 1.0 pm, leaking petrol fumes reached a motor generator room, and the *Lexington* was shaken by a violent explosion. More explosions followed, and the ship lost power so that the fires could no longer be fought. At 5.0 pm Sherman had to order 'abandon ship'; and at 8.0 the destroyer *Phelps* gave her the *coup de grâce* with five torpedoes, after all but 251 of her large ship's company had been rescued.

To whom then the victory? The U.S.A. lost the *Lexington* of 36,000 tons, the Japanese the *Shoho* of only 11,620. But although both Japan and the U.S.A. also had a large carrier damaged, they did not remain on this apparently equal footing for much longer. The *Yorktown* was repaired in time to take part in the crucial battle of Midway, fought on 4 June, whereas neither the *Shokaku* nor the *Zuikaku* was present, so that the American carrier force scored a decisive victory.

So, although she was lost so early in the war, the *Lexington* has her place in history for two reasons. She and the *Yorktown* had the distinction of taking part in the first naval battle of all history between two fleets at sea whose ships never sighted each other; which were, indeed, never within 50 miles of each other, and in which the chief weapon was not, as of old, the shell-firing gun, nor the more recently invented ship-launched torpedo, but carrier-borne planes armed with bombs and torpedoes. More importantly, perhaps, it was the experience gained with the *Lexington* and the *Saratoga* in the decade before the Second World War which laid the firmest of foundations for the great carrier task forces with which the U.S. and British Pacific Fleets destroyed Japanese sea power in 1944–45, and threatened such disaster to her island empire that she sued for the peace that ended hostilities in September 1945.

The U.S. aircraft-carrier Lexington *which was sunk by Japanese planes in 1942.*

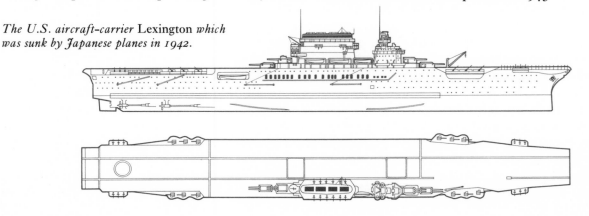

The Triumph of Steam

ON 14 OCTOBER 1788 young Robert Burns went for a trip in a steamboat. The vessel consisted of two hulls with a couple of paddle wheels in line between them. In one part was the boiler and in the other the engine, which had two vertical open-topped Newcomen cylinders of four in. diameter by about eighteen in. stroke. Chain gearing took the power to the paddle wheels which drove the craft at the rate of five miles an hour. Those on board with Robert Burns were William Symington, who had designed the engine, Patrick Miller who had commissioned Symington to design one, James Taylor, who had recommended the use of a steam engine in the first place and Alexander Nasmyth, inventor of the steam hammer. In the words of James Taylor, the steamboat 'answered Mr Miller's expectation fully and afforded great pleasure to the spectators present'. The engine still exists, preserved at the Science Museum in London.

Thirteen years after that experimental trip on Dalswinton Lake, near Dumfries, William Symington produced an engine for the *Charlotte Dundas*, a 56ft craft built of wood. The engine, which had a single horizontal cylinder, drove a paddle wheel housed in a recess at the stern. As governor of the Firth and Clyde Canal Company, Lord Dundas thought that steam tugs might be used instead of horses to tow vessels along the waterway. The *Charlotte Dundas*, when she was tried out in March 1802, gave an excellent performance, steaming confidently against a strong wind which held up all the other traffic; but fears that the wash from her paddle would damage the banks led to her rejection.

The next important person to be impressed by a steamboat was none other than Napoleon. Working together in France, the Americans Robert Fulton and Robert R. Livingston had leased a steam engine of eight horsepower from the inventor, and had fitted it in a hull 70ft long with paddle wheels 12ft diameter. Fulton informed Napoleon of his plans, and the Emperor was attracted by the picture of invasion barges towed by steam tugs on a windless day when the British fleet could not stir.

However, the steamboat broke and sank under the weight of the machinery. Fulton raised her, working himself ill, and rebuilt her completely. 'During the past two or three months,' said the *Journal des Débats* on 9 August 1803, 'there has been seen at the end of the Quai Chaillot a boat of strange appearance, equipped with two large wheels mounted on an axle like a cart, while behind these wheels was a kind of large stove with a pipe as if some sort of fire engine were intended to operate the wheels of the boat.' At six o'clock in the evening the vessel began towing two other craft. For an hour and a half the spectators witnessed 'the strange spectacle of a boat moved by wheels like a cart, these wheels being provided with paddles or flat plates and being moved by a fire engine'.

The *Journal* continued: 'As we followed it along the quay, the speed against the current of the Seine seemed to be about that of a rapid pedestrian, that is, about 2,400 toises an hour [2.9 miles]; while going down stream it was more rapid.' Fulton was disappointed, having expected about sixteen miles an hour, and so was Napoleon. Clearly, Fulton's steamboat could not cross the English Channel, with or without an invasion fleet.

Back home in 1807 the inventor completed a steamboat at Paulus Hook on the Hudson. Before the vessel had moved, the local boatmen reacted violently, fearing that their livelihood was threatened, and Fulton had to post a guard at his workshop. The new vessel was 133 feet in length and thirteen feet in breadth, with a displacement of 100 tons. Her two paddle wheels, placed at the sides, were fifteen feet in diameter and carried radial floats four feet long and two feet wide.

On 17 August 1807 the *American Citizen*

Great Men of the Sea

DRAKE

'Drake he was a Devon man.'

There is no need to quote more of Sir Henry Newbolt's well-known ballad. This sentence alone is the key to how, in the time of Queen Elizabeth I, England so successfully challenged the great power of Spain. The west country, chiefly Devon, produced a plenitude of distinguished fighting seamen, of whom the greatest was Francis Drake. His adventurous life has been much embellished by legend, notably concerning the game of bowls on Plymouth Hoe which he is said to have insisted on finishing before sailing to deal with the approaching Spanish Armada, but this chapter will keep to the facts.

Drake was born near the Devon town of Tavistock during the reign of Henry VIII – possibly in 1543, the date is uncertain. Because his father became a preacher at Chatham, he served his apprenticeship in the Thames coastal trade before making a voyage to West Africa. Through his cousin John Hawkins of Plymouth, he obtained his first command, of the 50-ton *Judith*. In 1567 she was one of only two ships to return from a slave-trading voyage to the Gulf of Mexico – the Spanish Main. Believing the attack by which the Spaniards destroyed the rest of the squadron to have been a treacherous one, Drake was filled with a burning desire for revenge.

By now something of a swashbuckler, Drake, who was small in stature and had a neatly trimmed red beard, spent the next few years as a privateer, that is, as captain of his own ship authorized by the Crown to attack Spanish trade in the Caribbean whenever and wherever he might find it. Most notably he raided the port of Nombre de Dios in 1572, seizing a large haul of silver carried by mules across the Isthmus of Panama from Panama on the Pacific side. He brought back treasure to enrich the coffers of Queen Elizabeth I estimated to be worth half a

Opposite: Sir Francis Drake (c. 1543–1596).

million pounds sterling, for which he was rewarded with a knighthood.

Having made his home at Buckland Abbey, near Plymouth, Drake was next given command, in 1585, of a combined operation sent to the Caribbean 'to humble' the insufferably arrogant King Phillip II of Spain, upon whom Elizabeth had recently declared war. Descending successively upon San Domingo, Cartagena and St Augustine in Florida, he sacked all three. Two years later Drake did as much to the Spanish port of Cadiz where a part of the Armada was already assembling, an operation which he described as 'singeing the King of Spain's beard'.

When this Armada, of 130 ships under the Duke of Medina Sidonia, finally sailed in 1588 from Lisbon for the Netherlands to embark the Prince of Parma's army for the invasion of England, Drake was appointed vice-admiral of the fleet under Lord Howard of Effingham which sailed from Plymouth on 19 July to oppose it. With his flag in the *Revenge*, Drake led the ships that attacked the Spanish force in its crescent-shaped formation during the night off this west-country port and captured the galleon *Rosario*. He played as prominent a part in the British fleet's week-long chase after the Armada as it sailed up the Channel.

When Medina Sidonia anchored his ships off Calais on 27 July to collect Parma's troops, Drake suggested a fireship attack on them during the following night. This inflicted so much damage that the enemy cut their cables and fled to the north. Drake also played a leading role in the battle fought off Gravelines on 29 July. And he continued the chase until 2 August, by which time the Armada had reached the latitude of the Firth of Forth and had become too scattered to make further pursuit worthwhile. Thereafter, having sailed round the north of Scotland, much of it was stranded by Atlantic gales on that country's rocky west coasts, including the Hebrides, and on the west coast of Ireland. In the end only 67 out of its 130 ships regained the

81

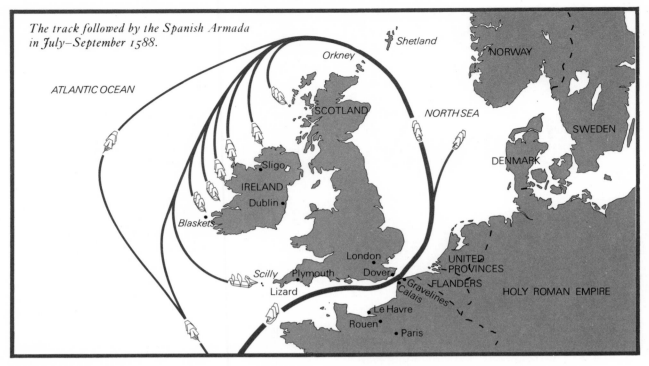

The track followed by the Spanish Armada in July–September 1588.

safety of their home ports – without landing a single man on English soil, apart from the few who survived from the ships that were wrecked.

Drake's success against the Armada gained him as great a reputation as a tactician as he had already achieved as a privateer. Boastful and ruthless he may have been, but there is no denying the style with which he led his men. He was also generous to those who suffered adversity, which ironically was now to be his own lot.

In 1589 Drake was given command of an expedition to destroy the remnants of the Armada lying in Spain's northern ports. But he and Sir John Norreys, who commanded the troops, achieved little before their men were decimated by disease and were obliged to return to England. An imperious Queen vented her displeasure by denying Drake further employment for five years, during which his only compensations were the mayoralty of Plymouth and election to Parliament.

Not until 1595 did Elizabeth so far forgive Drake as to appoint him, and his cousin Hawkins, to command another expedition 'to annoy' King Philip of Spain. But this descent upon the Indies proved fatal for them both. Hawkins died of dysentery shortly before a vain attempt to sack Puerto Rico, and not long afterwards yellow fever claimed Drake who was buried at sea off this Spanish port in January 1596.

Although Drake's last years were disappointing ones, his place in history is secure as the admiral who was chiefly responsible for the defeat of the Spanish Armada. He was, moreover, the true founder of the traditions which did so much to ensure the greatness of the Royal Navy (so termed by King Charles II) in the course of the next three centuries – traditions which, although that Navy no longer reigns supreme, are still very much alive.

DE RUYTER AND TROMP

Not many years elapsed after the British navy gained supremacy over the Spanish fleet before it was, in its turn, challenged by another, chiefly for control of the Narrow Seas that separate England from the rest of Europe. The Royal Navy had, indeed, to fight three wars between 1652 and 1678 before the issue was decided, because the Dutch fleet had the advantage of being led by two exceptionally distinguished seamen.

Marten Hapertszoon Tromp was born near Rotterdam in 1597 and went to sea in his father's ship so early that he was present at the action fought in Gibraltar Bay on 25 April 1607 in which Jacob van Heemskerk's fleet destroyed a sizeable Spanish force. He spent a long time suppressing piracy in the Mediterranean before formally joining his country's navy in 1622. No sooner had he been promoted captain in 1624 than he was outspokenly critical of the way in which that navy was being administered, with the consequence that he was relieved of his command and not employed again until 1637 when he achieved flag rank.

On 18 September in that year, with a much inferior fleet, Tromp gained a significant victory over Don Quenato's Spanish fleet off the Downs. The need for reforms in the Dutch navy was now so apparent, and Tromp's moral courage as much appreciated as his physical bravery and fighting skill, that he was next employed remedying its weaknesses and abuses; his concern for the well-being of officers and men earned him the sobriquet of 'Father'. But, for world renown, he had to wait another 15 years until the outbreak of the First Anglo-Dutch War in 1652.

Long before this Michiel Adrienszoon de Ruyter was born at Flushing – only ten years after Tromp – to begin his maritime career as a boatswain's boy. From the merchant service he transferred to the navy in which he showed himself to be such a splendid seaman and a born leader of men that he gained flag rank at the early age of 34. He was appointed rear-admiral in command of a fleet of 15 ships sent to support Portugal against Spain in 1641, when he displayed the bravery and determination that were to gain him a firm place in history's pages. But that was not before he had returned to the merchant service for a further ten years, until the outbreak of the First Anglo-Dutch War (1652–4) when he rejoined the navy.

One of the reasons for hostilities was the arrogant insistence of Oliver Cromwell's General-at-Sea Robert Blake that British ships should be saluted by foreign ones. Tromp, in command of the Dutch fleet, not only rejected this indignity but fought an inconclusive action in which he was worsted by Blake off Dover on 19 May. Tromp's subsequent failure to find Blake's fleet in order to reverse this setback led to his relief by the bellicose Admiral de With.

De Ruyter was more successful. Appointed in command of 29 sail, he was ordered to escort a convoy of merchant ships down the English Channel. His way was barred off the Channel Islands on 16 August by a comparable British force under Admiral Ayscue. De Ruyter so badly damaged Ayscue's ships that they were unable to pursue his convoy.

De Ruyter returned up Channel to join the Dutch main fleet under de With, and to lead the van in the battle of Kentish Knock fought in the southern part of the North Sea on 28 September. On this occasion a superior British fleet of 68 sail under Blake and William Penn engaged de With's 59 from 5.0 pm until dark, capturing two of them and badly damaging many others for very small loss. For this unsatisfactory result de With was, in his turn, relieved of a command which Tromp regained. So it was Tromp and de Ruyter together who, with a fleet of 80 ships, gained a decisive victory when they encountered Blake's force of half this size off Dungeness on 30 November.

This gave rise to the legend that Tromp hoisted a broom at his flagship's masthead as a symbol that he had swept the British from the sea. If there be any truth in this, events proved that he was over-confident. As soon as 18 February 1653, while escorting a homebound convoy, Tromp, with de Ruyter in the van of his 80 sail, met Blake's fleet of 70 off Portland. There followed a running fight lasting for three days by the end of which the Dutch had lost 17 warships and some 50 of the merchant vessels they were escorting.

Thirsting for revenge for this defeat, Tromp, again supported by de Ruyter, put to sea as soon as he could collect a fresh fleet. On 2 June, with 98 sail, he once more encountered the British, this time a fleet of 100 sail under Generals Richard Deane and George Monck. And in the ensuing battle of the Gabbard, the Dutch were not worsted until after the timely arrival of Blake with reinforcements.

This victory allowed the British to establish a close blockade of the Texel. To break it Tromp and de Ruyter sailed from the Maas with 80 sail on 24 July and, by skilful manoeuvring, evaded the enemy until they could join up with 25 more ships from the Texel under de With. A week later the combined Dutch fleets fought the bloody battle of Scheveningen against Monck's force. This was not only a sufficiently decisive British victory to persuade the Dutch to sue for peace but also the action in which the 1,600 Dutchmen killed included Tromp. Accorded a state funeral, he was buried at Delft.

During the peace that followed, de Ruyter returned to the Mediterranean before proceeding to the West Indies. There his attack on Barbados precipitated the outbreak of the Second Anglo-Dutch War in 1665. Successfully evading the British squadrons sent out to look for him, de Ruyter brought his ships back to the Texel later in the year. Almost a year later, on 1 June 1666, de Ruyter led a Dutch fleet of 80 sail into battle against Monck off the North Foreland. The latter made the mistake of detaching 25 of his ships under Prince Rupert to intercept a French squadron, which he mistakenly believed was coming to de Ruyter's support, before he made his first attack. The arrival of Dutch reinforcements next day obliged Monck to withdraw until Prince Rupert's squadron could rejoin him on 3 June. Next day, the last of this Four Days Battle, de Ruyter handled his fleet so well that Monck lost 20 ships and was obliged to retreat into the Thames, which the Dutch then proceeded to blockade.

Undaunted and as soon as his ships had been repaired, Monck broke this blockade, and brought de Ruyter to action off the North Foreland on 25 July. This time the British were the victors, in large measure because Tromp's son, Cornelius, failed to support his superior. Moreover, after the Dutch had lost 20 warships in this action, Monck proceeded to capture or destroy as many as 160 merchantmen anchored off the coast of Holland, which persuaded the Dutch to sue for peace.

Influenced by the disastrous effects upon London of the Great Plague of 1665 and the Great Fire of 1666, King Charles II promptly laid up the greater part of his fleet. This gave de Ruyter his chance to ensure that the peace terms were favourable ones. While they were still being negotiated in June 1667, he carried out a daring raid on the Thames and Medway, taking his fleet up both rivers to within 20 miles of London, burning 16 British warships and taking in tow back to Holland the pride of the Royal Navy, the *Royal Charles*. Not since the coming of William the Conqueror had Britain suffered such a humiliation; nor would she again until the wars of the twentieth century.

At the outbreak of the Third Dutch War in 1672, de Ruyter faced the combined fleets of Britain and France. Off Sole Bay on 28 May, with 75 ships, he surprised an enemy force of 98 under the Duke of York in an engagement from which the 35 French, under Admiral d'Estrées, rapidly withdrew. This allowed de Ruyter to mass his ships against a smaller British fleet which was badly mauled before the arrival of reinforcements impelled the Dutch to retire.

In March 1673, and again in May, de Ruyter repulsed attacks on his fleet at its coastal anchorage by a British fleet commanded by Prince Rupert which suffered heavy losses. In June he went over to the offensive, forcing Rupert to retire into the Thames. There followed, on 11 August, de Ruyter's most notable success. Ordered to escort a home-bound East Indies convoy, his way out of the Texel was barred by Prince Rupert's combined Anglo-French fleet against which he fought and gained a clear-cut tactical victory which allowed him to bring the convoy safely in.

In 1674 Britain dropped out of the war, but the French continued hostilities, and when Spain appealed for Dutch help, de Ruyter took a fleet out to the Mediterranean to recover Messina, in Sicily. In January 1676 he fought an indecisive battle against the French off the volcanic island of Stromboli, followed on 22 April by a victory over Admiral Duquesne off the east coast of Sicily. In this action, as with Tromp off Scheveningen, and as Nelson was to be off Cape Trafalgar more than a century later, de Ruyter was mortally wounded, and died seven days later almost in his hour of triumph. His body was brought home for burial in Amsterdam beneath a fitting marble memorial.

In sum, Marten Tromp was the 'Father' of the Dutch navy, the man who laid the firm foundations for Holland's importance as a naval power in the centuries to come. But de Ruyter was the man who, above all, built upon these foundations; who proved himself the most skilful tactician of his time; who, along with such British leaders as Blake and Monck, evolved the method of fighting a naval action as a gun duel between ships in formal line ahead as opposed to the confused mêlées with which such battles as those with the Spanish Armada had been fought a century before.

DE GRASSE AND DE SUFFREN

During the successive conflicts waged by France against Britain during more than a century, from the beginning of the War of the English Succession in 1689 to the final defeat of Napoleon in 1815, the French navy produced a number of distinguished seamen whose careers are of con-siderable interest. Two of these led their country's fleets during the conflict in which the French came all too near to depriving Britain of her naval supremacy, the War of American Independence.

François-Joseph Paul, Comte de Grasse was born in 1736 and joined the French navy in time to take part in several actions fought during the War of the Austrian Succession (1740–48), in which he was wounded and taken prisoner, and in the subsequent Seven Years War (1756–63). But despite so much valuable experience, he was not promoted to captain until he reached the then late age of 40. So, when France joined the War of American Independence in 1778, to gain revenge on Britain rather than out of concern for the rebellious colonists, he was no more than a commodore in command of the *Robuste*. However, the part which he played in the battle fought by a French fleet of 30 sail under Admiral Comte d'Orvilliers against a similar British one under Admirals Augustus Keppel and Hugh Palliser soon gained him further promotion. Early in 1781 he was selected for the important appointment of C.-in-C. of the French Atlantic fleet, with the rank of vice-admiral.

By 5 September de Grasse's 34 ships-of-the-line were anchored just inside America's Chesapeake Bay, where Yorktown, held by a British army under General Charles Cornwallis, was near to being starved into surrender by an investing Franco-American force. That morning Admiral Thomas Graves arrived off Chesapeake Bay with 19 sail-of-the-line escorting a convoy bearing supplies to relieve Yorktown. De Grasse promptly ordered his fleet to weigh and engage the British. But Graves handled his force so ineptly that the result was worse than an indecisive battle in which several of his ships were crippled: he was prevented from entering Chesapeake Bay. Moreover, for the next four days de Grasse, by skilful manœuvring, achieved as much without a further engagement. For want of water, Graves was then obliged to take his fleet, including the convoy carrying relief supplies for Yorktown, south to New York. Cornwallis was left with no alternative but to surrender, with the consequence that Chesapeake proved to be the decisive battle of the war. De Grasse's success in wresting control of the sea from Graves did more than anything else to ensure that the American colonies secured independence in 1783.

Before this, however, Britain determined on revenge, and did not do so in vain. When de Grasse took his fleet of 30 sail down to the Caribbean, in the winter of 1781, he came up against a British fleet of 36 sail under the redoubtable Admiral Sir George Rodney. And off The Saints on 12 April 1782, by breaking through the French line and throwing it into confusion, instead of fighting the formal line-ahead gun duel enjoined by the *Fighting Instructions* produced during the Anglo-Dutch Wars, Rodney not only gained a decisive victory which put the French to flight, but captured their flagship, the *Ville de Paris*, and took de Grasse prisoner.

From this disaster de Grasse was unable to exculpate himself after his return to France. He suffered banishment from court and retirement from the navy, and died in the year before the outbreak of the French Revolution. In his lifetime he earned the gratitude of George Washington; not until much later was his greatness appreciated by his own countrymen and recognized by others.

Of Pierre André de Suffren, Napoleon said: 'Had he been alive in my time, he would have been my Nelson.' Born in 1729 de Suffren became a midshipman in 1743, and four years later was taken prisoner by Admiral Edward Hawke, shortly before the end of the War of the Austrian Succession.

During the Seven Years War he was a lieutenant in the action fought off Minorca in 1756, for whose loss Admiral Byng was court martialled and shot '*pour encourager les autres*', and was again taken prisoner in 1759, this time by Admiral Edward Boscawen. During the ensuing peace he gained experience in suppressing piracy in the Mediterranean.

By the time that France joined the War of American Independence, de Suffren was a captain in command of a ship in Vice-Admiral d'Estaing's fleet, when he had the distinction of leading the line in the action off Grenada. But thereafter his career took an unusual turn. In 1781, instead of being appointed to one of France's main fleets, he was ordered to take a squadron of five ships to help the Dutch resist a possible British attack on the Cape of Good Hope, and subsequently to operate in the Indian Ocean under Admiral d'Orves. De Suffren caught the British squadron at anchor in the Cape Verde Islands and did enough damage to ensure that it did not complete its voyage to the Cape. He then went on to Mauritius, to learn that d'Orves had recently died, so that he, de Suffren, was in command of all eleven French ships-of-the-line in the Indian Ocean.

No believer in his navy's 'fleet-in-being' strategy, nor in its preferred tactics of an engagement at long range, he sought out his opponent, Admiral Sir Edward Hughes, whenever and wherever he could. Even when at a numerical disadvantage, he nonetheless pressed five actions during the next two years with such vigour that, although he failed to destroy his opponent, he invariably defeated him without losing a single ship. And he did this without a base in which to refit his fleet, in itself an outstanding achievement.

When he returned to France at the end of the war, de Suffren was without question his country's greatest admiral. And in 1788 he was chosen to command the Brest fleet. Unhappily, before he could take up this appointment (or show whether he would have supported or opposed the French Revolution), he died, officially of apoplexy but in all probability of an infected wound after duelling with the Prince de Mirepoix, whose sons he had refused to reinstate in the navy after they had been dismissed for misconduct. In this tragic way France lost an admiral who, one can be sure (just as Napoleon was), would have handled his fleet in action against the British during the Napoleonic Wars with greater success than, for example, Comte Honoré Ganteaume managed to do.

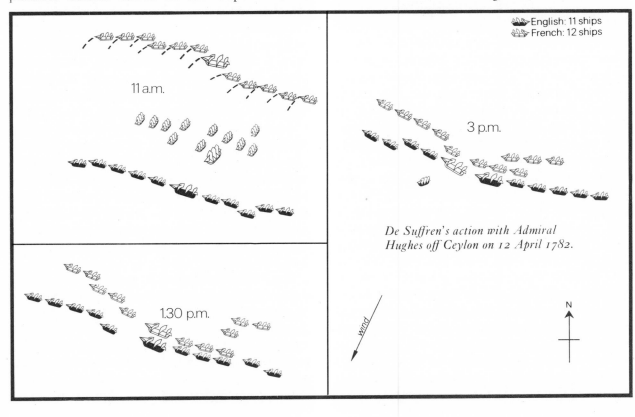

De Suffren's action with Admiral Hughes off Ceylon on 12 April 1782.

English: 11 ships
French: 12 ships

85

JOHN PAUL JONES

The great majority of seamen whose careers are told in this chapter happen to have achieved fame as admirals. To this rule, however, there is one notable exception, the U.S. navy's first major hero, John Paul Jones. Born a Scotsman at Kirkbean, Galloway, in 1747, Jones joined the British merchant marine in 1761 at the age of 14. In due time he achieved the status of master of ships that voyaged to the West Indies and to Britain's American colonies. But while visiting the island of Tobago in 1773 he had the misfortune to strike and kill a mutinous seaman. He could have pleaded self defence but he chose to avoid arrest by fleeing to Virginia to which his elder brother had emigrated. And he was still a fugitive from justice when the Thirteen Colonies revolted against British rule two years later.

Not surprisingly, when Congress decided to built a navy Jones applied to join it. His experience readily gained him a commission, and in 1777 he was promoted captain and appointed to command the new 18-gun sloop *Ranger*. Ordered to attack British trade in European waters, Jones first called at Nantes. Thence he headed the *Ranger* for the Irish Sea and, after capturing several small British coasters, raided the Cumbrian port of Whitehaven on the night of 22/23 April, destroying by fire a number of ships berthed in the harbour.

In the morning Jones landed on the southwest coast of Scotland, intending to abduct the Earl of Selkirk as a hostage for the release of American seamen held in British gaols. Unfortunately the Earl was away from home. To compensate for this disappointment, Jones's men seized a valuable collection of silver. To his credit, Jones returned this to its owner with a letter of apology for taking private property.

Next day, 24 April, the *Ranger* encountered off Belfast Lough the 20-gun British sloop *Drake*, Commander George Burdon, which was looking for him. The two well-matched vessels fought a stubborn duel for more than an hour before Burdon struck his colours. Jones towed his crippled prize to Brest whence her 200 prisoners were exchanged for Americans held in Britain.

Pleased with this success, Congress gave Jones a more important command in 1779, the 42-gun converted East Indiaman *Bonhomme Richard*, and sent her to European waters in company with the 32-gun frigate *Alliance*, the 30-gun *Pallas*, the 18-gun *Cerf* and the 12-gun *Vengeance*. But this squadron was soon in trouble. On leaving Lorient the *Alliance* collided with the *Bonhomme Richard* and both ships had to put back for repairs. Next, after taking two prizes off the Irish coast, the captains of the *Alliance* and *Cerf* decided to part company and operate on their own. After rounding the north of Scotland, Jones's squadron went south and, to the rising alarm of Britain, seized more than a dozen

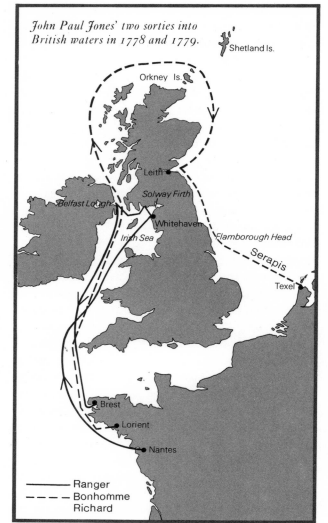

John Paul Jones' two sorties into British waters in 1778 and 1779.

Shetland Is.
Orkney Is.
Leith
Solway Firth
Belfast Lough
Whitehaven
Irish Sea
Flamborough Head
Serapis
Texel
Brest
Lorient
Nantes

—— Ranger
- - - Bonhomme Richard

merchant vessels off Flamborough Head before, on the morning 23 September, the *Alliance* rejoined. That same afternoon a British convoy of 44 vessels homeward bound from the Baltic was sighted, escorted by the 44-gun frigate *Serapis*, Captain Richard Pearson, and the 20-gun *Countess of Scarborough*.

The battle that followed was fought chiefly between the *Bonhomme Richard* and the *Serapis*. After a bitter muzzle-to-muzzle engagement lasting for all of two hours, the *Bonhomme Richard* was crippled. But Jones refused to strike his colours, and was well rewarded. The *Serapis*, which had so far gained the advantage, suddenly caught fire and blazed so fiercely that Pearson was obliged to strike. The American vessel's casualties numbered 150 killed and wounded, the British ship's 128. But Jones's ship was so badly damaged that, after his prize's flames had been extinguished, he was obliged to transfer the survivors of his crew to her. Two days later the *Bonhomme Richard* sank.

The whole Baltic convoy, however, succeeded in escaping and this battle ended Jones's marauding career. When the *Serapis*, and the rest of his squadron, sought refuge in the Texel, Holland's neutrality delayed their repairs. Only the *Alliance* was ready by the end of December when Jones sailed her to Corunna and back to Lorient. Thence he travelled to Paris in April 1780, to be welcomed as the hero of the year by the capital of a country that had recently joined the war on the side of the Colonies against Britain.

On returning to America, Jones was appointed to command Congress's first ship-of-the-line, the 74-gun *America*. He was not, however, destined to take her to sea: the Treaty of Versailles was signed before she finished building, and Congress, unwilling to maintain a navy in peace, gave her to France.

Finding that it was now impossible for a man of his achievements and ambitions to obtain further employment in America, Jones spent some time in Paris trying to join the French navy. When he failed in this, he went on to St Petersburg where he was more successful. Catherine the Great welcomed him to take command, as a rear-admiral, of the hotch-potch collection of vessels with which the Russians were trying to capture Ochakov, in the Black Sea, from the Turks. But the Empress's powerful Prince Potemkin objected to a foreign flag officer commanding a Russian squadron. Although Jones fought and won two battles in June 1788, Potemkin gave all the credit to his chief Russian subordinate. Comparable jealousy led to Jones being falsely accused of rape after his return to St Petersburg, with the consequence that he was denied command of Russia's Baltic fleet.

Jones then returned to France from where he wrote to every distinguished person whom he knew appealing for a naval or diplomatic post. He was finally rewarded in June 1792 when President Washington appointed him U.S. consul in Algiers. But before he could begin negotiations with the Dey for the release of American seamen taken prisoner by this Barbary State, Jones died of bronchial pneumonia on 18 July. The French Assembly gave him a state funeral before his burial in a Paris cemetery.

More than a century later, in 1905, Jones's coffin was exhumed and taken back to the United States on board an American cruiser to be met and saluted off Annapolis by a U.S. battle fleet. There, in the crypt of the beautiful chapel of the U.S. Naval Academy, he was finally laid to rest.

VILLENEUVE

The victorious career of Horatio Nelson, Vice-Admiral of the White, Viscount of the Nile and Duke of Brontë, the greatest naval commander of all time, is too well known to justify retelling in this chapter. Let us instead recall a distinguished French seaman whose name will always be linked with Nelson's, who came near to eluding his fleet when taking part in Napoleon's grand design to invade England in the summer of 1805, and who met his end in tragic circumstances less than a year after the battle in which Nelson was killed.

Pierre Charles Jean de Villeneuve was born in 1763, which made him five years younger than Nelson. Joining the French navy at 15, he first fought against Britain in the War of American Independence, when he became a close friend of Denis Decrès, who was destined to be Napoleon's Minister of Marine. Having declared his loyalty to the Republican Convention, Villeneuve was promoted to post-captain at the outset of the French Revolutionary War in 1793. And in 1796, after only three years in command of ships-of-the-line, he achieved flag rank, a reflection of Jacobin France's serious shortage of senior officers for her fleet.

Near the end of 1796, the 33-year-old Admiral Villeneuve was ordered to take a squadron out of Toulon, and to accompany Admiral Don Juan de Langara's Spanish fleet round to Brest. Helped by a gale he eluded Admiral John Jervis's ships which were watching the Straits of Gibraltar. But Admiral Lord Bridport's Channel fleet was keeping such a close watch on Brest that Villeneuve had to change his destination to Lorient. His ships could not, therefore, be included in the fleet with which Admiral Morard de Galles made an abortive attempt to land a French army in Ireland's Bantry Bay in December.

By the spring of 1797 Villeneuve was back at Toulon to join the fleet with which Admiral François Brueys escorted Napoleon Bonaparte's Armée d'Orient for its conquest of Egypt. His ships were at the leeward end of the French line anchored across the mouth of Aboukir Bay when Nelson's fleet appeared and attacked its windward and centre divisions on the evening of 1 August. For remaining at anchor during this battle of the Nile, instead of weighing and supporting the rest of the French fleet, Villeneuve was subjected to much criticism. But Bonaparte was more concerned to congratulate him on saving two ships-of-the-line and two frigates from Nelson's otherwise annihilating victory, and taking them to Malta, where Villeneuve stayed until the island's French garrison surrendered in September 1800.

His career during the next four years is veiled in decent obscurity. Not until August 1804 did Villeneuve again emerge into the limelight when, following the sudden death of Admiral Louis Latouche-Tréville, his friend Decrès chose him to command France's Toulon fleet. For the past year this had been held in port by Nelson's blockade which Villeneuve made no attempt to break until early in the next year.

On 17 January, in accordance with Napoleon's complex plan for gaining control of the English Channel with a superior fleet, so that his Grande Armée might cross it safely and invade Britain, Villeneuve left Toulon only to be driven back three days later by a storm in the Gulf of Lions, of which Nelson learned nothing until he had taken his fleet on a wild goose chase all the way to Alexandria and back.

Villeneuve sailed again on 30 March. His

orders were to lure Nelson's fleet across the Atlantic, then to return and join up with Admiral Honoré Ganteaume's Brest fleet, which would provide a sufficient force to wrest control of the Channel from Admiral William Cornwallis. This time he so successfully evaded the British ships watching Toulon that Nelson did not learn that he was out until 18 April. Nor until 5 May, when the British fleet anchored off Gibraltar, did its admiral know that Villeneuve's 12 ships-of-the-line had been reinforced by the Spanish Admiral Don Federico Gravina's six out of Cadiz, and that these Combined Fleets, numbering 18 sail, were steering for the Caribbean.

Having arrived in the West Indies near the end of May, Villeneuve carried out several successful operations. Specifically, on 2 June he recaptured the Diamond Rock, off Martinique, which, occupied by a British force, had been a sharp thorn in France's flesh for the past 18 months, and a week later he destroyed a homebound British sugar convoy off Antigua. On the same day, 8 June, Villeneuve heard that Nelson's fleet of 10 sail-of-the-line had arrived at Barbados after pursuing him across the Atlantic. Knowing that he had successfully fulfilled the first part of Napoleon's orders, Villeneuve promptly headed back for Europe intent on fulfilling the second, to join up with Ganteaume.

So far so good: all seemed set fair for Napoleon to launch his invasion of England in August. But thenceforward the British navy proved more than a match for the Emperor's plans. On hearing that Villeneuve had left the Caribbean, Nelson not only sailed after him, but sent a speedy brig, the *Curieux*, on ahead to England with news of the French Toulon fleet's coming.

To this Britain's First Lord, Admiral Lord Barham, reacted by ordering Cornwallis to send half his fleet under Admiral Sir Robert Calder to await Villeneuve's ships off Cape Finisterre, while he himself waited with the rest off Ushant. By 16 July Calder was on his allotted station with 15 ships-of-the-line. Four days later he sighted Villeneuve's and Gravina's Combined Fleets which now numbered 20. There followed a battle in which two of Villeneuve's ships were so badly damaged that they had to surrender. Thereafter, remembering Napoleon's orders that he was to do his best to avoid action before joining up with Ganteaume, Villeneuve successfully evaded Calder's half-hearted attempts to renew the battle and escaped into Vigo Bay.

Calder tried to blockade him there, but a gale drove his ships so far away from this Spanish haven that Villeneuve was able to sail round into Ferrol where his Combined Fleets were reinforced to a total of 29 ships-of-the-line. Supposing his fleet, reduced by damage to only nine sail, to be too small to counter such a large force, Calder rejoined Cornwallis off Ushant, just one day before Nelson's fleet arrived there from its vain pursuit across the Atlantic and back.

Napoleon then issued orders for Ganteaume and Villeneuve to rendezvous in the Bay of Biscay on 19 August, and from there to head up the Channel. But the mere sight of Cornwallis's 17 ships-of-the-line was enough to deter Ganteaume from leaving Brest with 21. And Villeneuve had already taken advantage of Calder's absence to leave Ferrol and head, not north, but south for the greater safety of Cadiz. And there Calder blockaded him again.

To these events Barham reacted by ordering Nelson, who was enjoying his first leave at Merton with Emma Hamilton for more than two years, to relieve Calder, who was to be sent home to face a court martial for failing to engage the Combined Fleets more effectively on 22 July. By 28 September Nelson was off Cadiz. Three weeks later Villeneuve learned that Admiral François Rosily was on his way from Paris to relieve him, because Napoleon held him to blame for failing to reach Brest, thereby aborting his plans for invading England.

Thereupon Villeneuve determined on an attempt to save his reputation. On 19 October, before Rosily could reach Cadiz, the Combined Fleets, numbering 33 ships-of-the-line, left Cadiz intent on entering the Mediterranean and making for Toulon from where they could support Napoleon in northern Italy. Two days later, before they had progressed as far as the Straits of Gibraltar, Nelson brought them to action off Cape Trafalgar. By dividing his weaker force of 27 sail into two divisions, one under his own leadership in the *Victory*, the other led by Admiral Cuthbert Collingwood in the *Royal Sovereign*, Nelson broke through his enemy's line in two places, cutting off its centre and rear from its van which was all too slow in turning to their support. By these masterly tactics, the British fleet destroyed or captured 18 French and Spanish ships before nightfall, which gave Britain effective control of the sea throughout the subsequent ten years of the Napoleonic War.

In this battle of Trafalgar the *Victory* was in close action with the *Redoutable*, from whose tops Nelson was mortally wounded by a shot fired by a French sharpshooter. He died some two hours later after he knew the extent of his greatest victory. The French flagship *Bucentaure* was so hotly engaged by HMS *Conqueror* that she lost all her masts and was virtually wrecked, which left Villeneuve with no alternative but to allow her captain to strike his colours.

Having surrendered his sword to the commander of HMS *Mars*, Villeneuve was taken to England, where he stayed as a prisoner of war until April 1806. Repatriated, he learned on landing at St Malo that Napoleon required him to wait further orders at Rennes. There he wrote, 'How fortunate that I have no child to bear the weight of my disgrace and of my dishonoured name', before, in Napoleon's heartless words, 'fearing to be convicted by a council of war of having disobeyed my orders, and having lost the fleet as a result, Villeneuve determined to end his own life. When they opened his room next morning they found him dead, a long pin through his heart. He should not have done this. He was a brave man, although he lacked talent' – a criticism with which few would now agree.

Fleet. And by 1914 his reputation was so high that he was appointed to command Germany's battlecruisers. He could not have asked for a better appointment in which to display his outstanding qualities.

When Germany's light forces suffered a considerable defeat in the battle of Heligoland Bight, fought as soon as 28 August 1914, the Kaiser's High Command decided that their

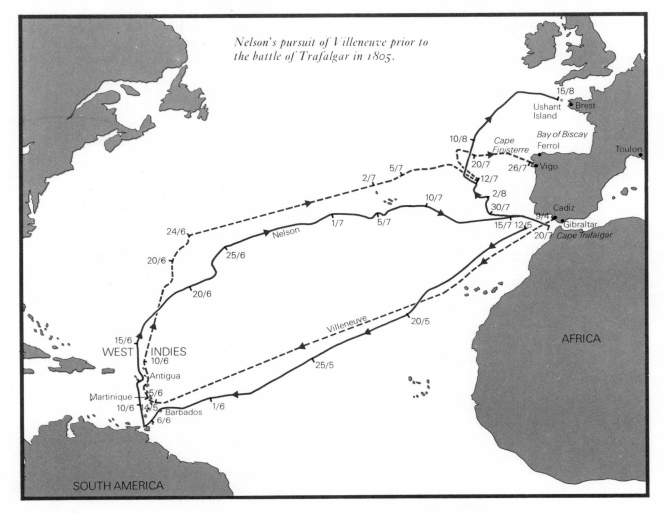

Nelson's pursuit of Villeneuve prior to the battle of Trafalgar in 1805.

HIPPER

There will always be diverse opinions as to which was the greater British admiral of the First World War: Sir John Jellicoe who commanded the Grand Fleet from August 1914, or Sir David Beatty who succeeded him in 1916. But the greatest German naval commander was indubitably Admiral von Hipper.

Born a Bavarian in 1863, Franz Ritter Hipper opted to join an embryo Imperial German Navy in 1881 on the strength of reading the works of Captain Marryat. His unassuming personality hampered his early progress, which included command of torpedoboats, navigating officer of the Kaiser's yacht *Hohenzollern*, and executive officer of the new armoured cruiser *Gneisenau*. But after promotion to captain in 1907, when he again served in torpedoboats, and was chief of staff in the Second Scouting Group of cruisers, he achieved flag rank as soon as 1913. He then once more returned to torpedoboats, this time in overall command of these craft in the High Seas

battleships should not risk destruction by Britain's more powerful Grand Fleet. But 'there is nothing to be said against an attempt by the battlecruisers to damage the enemy'. So, shortly after dawn on 3 November, the *Seydlitz*, flying Hipper's flag, accompanied by three more battlecruisers, briefly bombarded the port of Yarmouth, then turned for home before Commodore Reginald Tyrwhitt's Harwich Force could intercept them.

Notwithstanding British anger at such a raid on a defenceless town, Hipper was authorized to carry out another. Soon after dawn on 16 December, the *Seydlitz*, *Moltke* and *Blücher* bombarded the Yorkshire port of Hartlepool, while the *Derfflinger* and *Von der Tann* fired on the seaside resorts of Scarborough and Whitby. But when these ships turned for home they ran into Beatty's battlecruisers, supported by a battle squadron. Helped by bad visibility and a serious British signal error, Hipper was able to escape from this trap. And as soon as January 1915 he risked a further sortie: three of his battlecruisers, plus the heavy cruiser *Blücher*, went out to raid Britain's Dogger Bank fishing fleet.

This time, forewarned by radio intelligence, Beatty's five battlecruisers were waiting for him. The two forces clashed early on the 24th, when Hipper turned for home. There followed a long stern chase in which the British ships inflicted considerable damage on the *Blücher*, *Moltke* and *Seydlitz*, which would have been disastrous had not German gunfire suddenly crippled Beatty's flagship, the *Lion*. Temporarily deprived of his leadership, his other four battlecruisers delayed to sink the already crippled *Blücher*, which allowed the rest of Hipper's force to escape.

Hipper's force off the coast of Jutland. The latter immediately turned away, to lead his opponent towards Scheer's battle fleet. There followed a running fight in which the German battlecruisers sank the *Indefatigable* and *Queen Mary* before Britain's four fast battleships of the 'Queen Elizabeth' class could come to Beatty's support, when they threatened to turn the tables on their skilfully-handled opponents.

But before they could achieve this, Beatty sighted Scheer's battle fleet. He promptly turned north to lure it towards Jellicoe's, which was already hastening to support its battlecruisers. Hipper likewise turned north, ahead of the German battleships, and in his subsequent

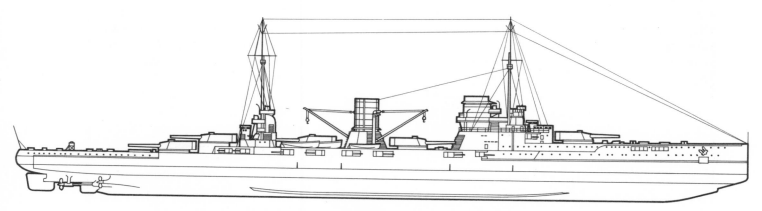

The Seydlitz, *one of Hipper's battlecruisers armed with ten 11-inch guns, which was seriously damaged and nearly sunk during the battle of Jutland on 31 May 1916.*

By 1916 the High Command was sufficiently disturbed by the effects of the Grand Fleet's blockade to authorize the High Seas Fleet to be more adventurous. Its C.in-C., Admiral Reinhard Scheer, planned a sortie designed to trap just a part of the Grand Fleet and thereby to weaken it. The first attempt, early in March, achieved nothing. For the second, on 25 April, when Hipper chanced to be away sick, his battlecruisers bombarded Lowestoft as a bait to draw a British force into the maw of Scheer's battle fleet. But harrassing attacks by Tyrwhitt's Harwich Force persuaded the German ships to retire before Beatty's battlecruisers, hurrying south from Rosyth, could reach the scene.

Scheer next decided to bombard Sunderland; but when this operation had to be delayed until the end of May, he chose instead the less hazardous venture of appearing off the Norwegian coast. On 30 May Hipper, in the *Lützow*, led his five battlecruisers out of the Jade and headed north, with Scheer's battleships following some 50 miles astern.

Radio intelligence gave the Admiralty warning of Hipper's sortie, but not of Scheer's. Nonetheless, Jellicoe's stronger battle fleet was ordered out of Scapa Flow, and Beatty's battlecruisers out of Rosyth. And at 2.30 pm on 31 May, before these two forces could join up, Beatty sighted

pursuit the *Lützow*, *Seydlitz* and *Derrflinger* were seriously damaged by British gunfire for the loss of a third of Beatty's too lightly armoured battlecruisers, HMS *Invincible*.

Around 6.0 pm, just as Beatty was surprised to see Scheer's battle fleet, so were Hipper and Scheer surprised by the British battle fleet, which Jellicoe deployed into action between the German ships and their base. After a brief engagement, Scheer managed to extricate his force by turning away to the west into a gathering mist, while Hipper's ships 'charged' dauntlessly towards their opponents, when the *Lützow* incurred so much damage that Hipper had to transfer his flag first to a destroyer and later to the *Moltke*.

Before darkness fell around 10.0 pm Scheer made two attempts to get back to the east of the Grand Fleet, both of which were frustrated by its heavy gunfire. After nightfall Jellicoe and Beatty steered a southerly course, knowing Scheer and Hipper to be to the west of them, and expecting to fight a decisive battle after dawn next day. But the German admirals proved too determined and too skilful: they forced a way through the British light forces which were stationed astern of Jellicoe's capital ships, and before dawn gained the safety of their own minefields for the loss of the *Lützow* and one battleship.

This battle of Jutland was so near to being tactically indecisive that both sides claimed a victory, for which much that was to Germany's credit goes to Hipper. But the Kaiser could not claim it to be a strategic victory because it did nothing to break the Grand Fleet's blockade. Moreover, Scheer was so disturbed by the damage done to his ships that, except for a fruitless sortie in mid-August 1916, he kept most of the High Seas Fleet within the safety of the Jade, while Germany concentrated its resources on unrestricted U-boat warfare which in 1917 came near to strangling Britain's maritime trade.

In July 1918 Scheer became Germany's Chief of Naval Staff, when von Hipper (as he had now been honourably styled) succeeded him in command of the High Seas Fleet. Three months later, recognizing that Germany's U-boat campaign had failed and that his country was near to losing the war, he planned an attack on the Thames estuary, covered by his battle fleet, which he hoped would draw the Grand Fleet south. But this 'death ride' was not put to the test. Von Hipper's quiet personality was unable to sustain the morale of his men after it had been undermined by inactivity and by socialist propaganda. When he ordered his ships to sail on 29 October, they hoisted the red flag of mutiny.

Germany's most distinguished admiral was not required to lead the High Seas Fleet into internment at Scapa Flow after the Armistice had been signed on 11 November 1918. This humbling task, and the ships' subsequent scuttling to avoid surrender in accordance with the peace treaty, was entrusted to a more junior admiral. And since this Treaty of Versailles left Germany with only a minuscule navy, von Hipper went into lonely retirement in Saxony. He died there in 1932, his distinctive place in history well assured, shortly before Hitler established the Nazi regime, with Admiral Erich Raeder, who had been on Hipper's staff at Jutland, at the head of the navy of the Third Reich.

KEYES

Most great men, having scaled the heights of fame, retire gracefully from public life. A few, like Nelson, are fated to die while still relatively young. As few, like Lord Barham, do not achieve greatness until they have passed the Biblical span of three score years and ten. Unhappily, there are also those who, having achieved fame, subsequently tarnish their reputations by some act of folly for which they tend to be remembered rather than for the deeds by which they deserve their place in history.

Among these few is Roger John Brownlow Keyes. Born in India in 1872, he joined HMS *Britannia* at the usual age of 13, and was appointed midshipman to the full-rigged frigate *Raleigh* on the Cape Station in 1887. There he saw active service in the suppression of the slave trade, and

in a punitive expedition against the Sultan of Witu, to the north of Zanzibar. After serving briefly in the Royal Yacht *Victoria and Albert*, in the sloop *Beagle* in South American waters, and in the corvette *Curacoa* at Devonport, he was appointed lieutenant-in-command of the destroyer *Fame* on the China Station.

In this small vessel of only 310 tons Keyes first made his name. During the 1900 Boxer Rising he captured four Chinese destroyers by boarding, then led a landing party which secured the key Chinese fort on the route by which an international force intended to proceed to the relief of the besieged foreign legations in Peking. But having contrived to join this force, he played a too dashing role in his determination to be among the first to reach the Chinese capital, for which he incurred his C.-in-C.'s wrath. It is a measure of his achievements that he was, nonetheless, promoted to commander at the end of 1900 at the early age of 28.

In this rank he commanded the Devonport destroyer flotilla, then worked in the Admiralty's Intelligence Department during the Russo-Japanese War, before being appointed naval attaché in Rome. While there he not only gained promotion to captain despite the unusual fact that he had never served in a battleship nor in a cruiser – a clear indication that he was in the Royal Navy's 'First Eleven' – but entered into matrimony and in time produced a family which was, inevitably, known as 'the Bunch of Keys'.

Command of the small cruiser *Venus* in the Atlantic Fleet was followed in 1910 by his selection to head Britain's submarine service from headquarters at Portsmouth. He did so much to develop these new-fangled craft that he was still in this appointment when the First World War erupted in August 1914. Keyes then transferred his headquarters to Harwich from where, in the destroyer *Lurcher*, he sortied to control his 'D'- and 'E'-class submarines operating in the Heligoland Bight. More importantly, he planned a sortie on 28 August into these waters by Commodore Tyrwhitt's light cruisers and destroyers, supported by Admiral Beatty's battle-cruisers, which resulted in a battle in which three German light cruisers were sunk. His subsequent plans for continuing the offensive in this area did not, however, meet with Admiralty approval.

In January 1915 Keyes became chief of staff to Admiral S. H. Carden in the Mediterranean and, later, to his successor, Admiral John de Robeck, with whom he played a substantial part in the Allied naval attempts to force the Dardanelles, notably those in March. When the subsequent Allied landings on the Gallipoli peninsula failed to make any substantial progress, he urged de Robeck to try again with his fleet. And, wholly in character, when de Robeck would not agree, Keyes obtained his permission to travel to London to argue his own plans for gaining entry to the Bosphorus. He was, however, unable to persuade the Admiralty to accept his belief that these had a reasonable chance of success.

Notwithstanding this difference of opinion with de Robeck, Keyes remained as his chief of staff until the middle of 1916, when he was appointed to command the battleship *Centurion* in the Grand Fleet. After fifteen uneventful months in this dreadnought, he was promoted in April 1917 and was immediately ordered to fly his flag as a rear-admiral in Admiral Sturdee's Fourth Battle Squadron. He did not, however, remain in the battleship *Colossus* for very long; at the end of September he was called to the Admiralty to be Director of Plans, where he so persuasively argued the need to block the Zeebrugge and Ostend entrances to the canals leading to the German U-boat and torpedoboat base at Bruges that, in January 1918, he was ordered to relieve Admiral Bacon in command of the Dover Patrol and to put his plans into execution.

On St George's Day, 23 April, a miscellaneous armada sailed from the Thames estuary, to divide a few hours later into two parts. One, under Keyes's direct command, headed for Zeebrugge. Three old cruisers largely filled with concrete were to be sunk in the entrance to that canal during the night. To make this possible the old cruiser *Vindictive* – whose captain replied to Keyes's signal, 'St George for England', with 'And may we give the dragon's tail a damn good twist' – went alongside the Zeebrugge mole and, through a hail of gunfire, landed Royal Marines and bluejackets who seized and held the batteries on the mole for the necessary few hours. At the same time a small submarine filled with explosives blew up the viaduct connecting the mole to the shore so that reinforcements could not reach its German defenders.

In truth this raid on Zeebrugge proved a failure: although two of the blockships gained the canal entrance, they sealed the fairway for very few days. Moreover, the other half of the operation, which was designed to block the Ostend canal, was even less successful, the two blockships being led astray by the removal of a navigational buoy. (Nor was a fresh attempt a couple of weeks later much more successful.) Nonetheless, the Zeebrugge raid was carried out with such spectacular dash and heroism, for which eight VCs were awarded, that it gave a much-needed boost to British morale, and did as much to depress Germany's, at a crucial stage of the war. And for this Keyes became the nation's hero of the hour for which he was rewarded with a baronetcy. But not everyone thought that he had earned this; a few thought his prowess to be exaggerated and that he lacked judgement.

In the immediate post-war years, Keyes, now a vice-admiral, commanded the Atlantic Fleet's Battlecruiser Squadron. Then, from the autumn of 1921, he was at the Admiralty as Deputy Chief of the Naval Staff. He left this office early in 1925 as a full admiral to take the prestigious command of the Mediterranean fleet, having been told that he would in due time return to fill the navy's highest post, that of First Sea Lord.

Unhappily, Keyes was far from being a successful C.-in-C. It became increasingly clear that he was more interested in Malta's social life and in playing polo than in maintaining his fleet's efficiency. And when he so far mishandled the '*Royal Oak* affair' (he used a sledge-hammer to crack the nut of a minor 'mutiny' by the captain and commander of this battleship against the tactless and bad-tempered Rear-Admiral Collard) that it attracted widespread publicity including major press coverage of two courts martial, much to the navy's discredit, the First Sea Lord decided that Keyes lacked the judgement required for the top Admiralty appointment. A Labour Government's belief that Keyes would not prove amenable to their intention to promote naval reductions at a forthcoming five-Power Conference in London made certain that Keyes would not attain his great ambition. He was appointed C.-in-C. Portsmouth instead.

His promotion to admiral of the fleet in 1930 was no consolation for this disappointment; he became a sour, embittered man, whose only outlet after his retirement in 1931 was as a Member of Parliament. Following the outbreak of the Second World War in 1939, he pressed the First Lord, Winston Churchill, to give him active employment in which he could assuage his thirst for action, notably during the Norwegian campaign when he proposed to lead an assault on Trondheim – but without result. Not until after Churchill became Prime Minister in the summer of 1940 did he find a suitable job for a very old friend: Keyes became the first Director of Combined Operations.

In this job, however, he spent too much of his time pressing the Admiralty to execute unrealistic operations: notably an assault on the Italian island of Pantelleria which even that great fighter Admiral Cunningham opposed, and in complaining to Churchill that the Sea Lords did nothing but frustrate his efforts towards winning the war. By October 1941 the Prime Minister had been driven to denying him the entrée to 10 Downing Street, and to appointing Lord Louis Mountbatten to succeed him.

For Keyes this was the last straw. He returned to the House of Commons to make speeches highly critical of Churchill until he was elevated to the Lords as a baron 'of Zeebrugge and Dover' in 1943. At the height of Lord Keyes's fame, Philip de Laszlo painted a portrait of a handsome, dashing hero, a 'verray parfait knight'. Alas, by the time that he died in 1945, it was as if he had been afflicted with a disease akin to that which destroyed Oscar Wilde's Dorian Gray. So let history, in the long run, forget his later years, and remember him as *Punch* did in a cartoon published shortly after the Zeebrugge raid, in which the ghost of Drake addresses Keyes with the words: 'Bravo, sir! Tradition holds. My men singed a king's beard, and yours have singed a kaiser's moustaches!'

CUNNINGHAM

There is no disputing who was Britain's finest fighting seaman in the Second World War. His is the only bust which has been accorded a place in London's Trafalgar Square, along with those of Admirals Jellicoe and Beatty, at the foot of Nelson's column.

Andrew Browne Cunningham, who was to become widely known as 'ABC', joined the *Britannia* training ship at Dartmouth in 1897 at the then usual age of 14. Just three years later he was on active service: by the chance that, as a midshipman, he was appointed to the cruiser *Doris* on the Cape station, he accompanied the naval brigade's advance on Pretoria during the first year of the South African War.

Cunningham's time as a lieutenant and, from mid-1915, as a commander was spent almost wholly in destroyers. Curiously he was never with the Grand Fleet during the First World War: after three years in the Mediterranean (including the Dardanelles campaign for which he was awarded the D.S.O.) where he learned much that was to be of value to him later, notably the Italian fleet's singular reluctance to face up to the Austrian fleet in the Adriatic, he got no nearer to Scapa Flow than the Dover Patrol. There his ship was several times in action with German destroyers for which he gained a bar to his D.S.O. Two years later he added a second bar for the exceptional way in which he coped with the complex problems that faced the ships of Admiral

Walter Cowan's force, which was sent into the Baltic shortly after the 1918 Armistice to help Finland, Latvia, Estonia and Lithuania gain their freedom from Bolshevik Russia.

Promoted to captain in 1920, Cunningham was first in charge of the Port Edgar base in the Firth of Forth; then flag captain to Cowan during his time as C.-in-C. of the America and West Indies station. In 1929 his exceptional qualities were recognized by command of the new battle-ship *Rodney* in the Atlantic fleet. In the same year he was married; wholly in character, he deferred this happy event until he was in his forty-sixth year. He completed his post-captain's time as Commodore of Chatham Barracks before being promoted to flag rank in September 1932.

In those peaceful days admirals often spent long periods on half-pay and Cunningham was no exception. More than a year elapsed before he returned to the craft he knew so well, when he went out to the Mediterranean as Rear-Admiral (Destroyers). During the difficult year that a much reinforced Mediterranean fleet awaited, at Alexandria, the possibility of war with Italy because of Mussolini's unprovoked aggression against Abyssinia, he brought his flotillas to a pitch of efficiency rarely, if ever, exceeded.

This appointment was followed by another period on half-pay, this time as a vice-admiral, until 1937 when Cunningham returned to the Mediterranean in command of the Battlecruiser squadron, with his flag in the Royal Navy's largest ship, HMS *Hood*. In her, as with so much of Britain's Mediterranean and Home fleets at this time, he was involved in the special problems presented by the Spanish Civil War, notably the patrols arranged by an international conference at Nyons to deter Fascist Italy from using her submarines to support General Franco by indiscriminately sinking merchant ships proceeding

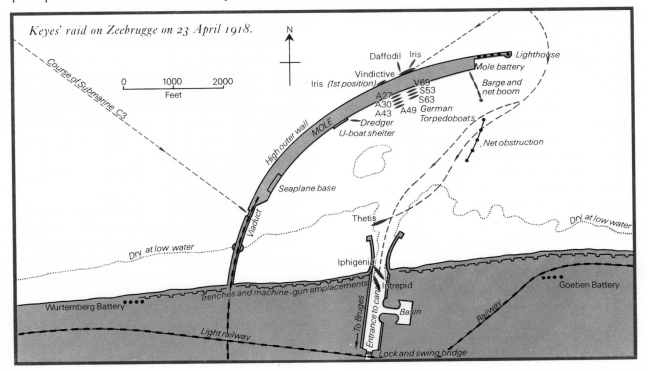

Keyes' raid on Zeebrugge on 23 April 1918.

to Spanish ports without regard for their flags.

At the end of 1938 Cunningham came home to serve, for the first time, in the Admiralty as Vice-Chief of the Naval Staff. He was not, however, to remain there for very long. Soon after he was knighted early in 1939, the First Sea Lord, Admiral Sir Roger Backhouse, died in harness, which required Admiral Sir Dudley Pound to return from the Mediterranean to succeed him. Cunningham was chosen to be the new C.-in-C. at Malta with the rank of acting admiral and his flag in the battleship *Warspite*.

In the difficult years that followed he showed that he shared many of Nelson's attributes. Though not as physically frail as Britain's epic hero, he was as conspicuously small. Cunningham might not have been the type of leader who inspired a 'band of brothers'; on the contrary, though greatly respected and admired, he was feared rather than loved – and by none more so than his country's enemies. But he was devoid of physical fear and, more important for a senior officer, he was never lacking in moral courage, even when (as too often happened in the Second World War) he was 'needled' by Prime Minister Winston Churchill.

Above all Cunningham was, like Nelson, imbued with the offensive spirit. He had to spend most of the first year of hostilities doing very little because Mussolini delayed honouring his pledge to support Hitler in 1939, and most of the Mediterranean fleet was deployed in other seas. But from the moment that Italy came into the war in June 1940, with a considerably more powerful fleet, and France had to ask for an armistice, Cunningham came into his own. By his tact and diplomacy the French squadron at Alexandria was immobilized without suffering the bloodshed inflicted by Admiral Sir James Somerville's Force H on the main French fleet at Mers-el-Kebir (near Oran). As soon as 9 July he put a stronger Italian force to flight at the battle of Calabria. On 11 November, he carried out a carrier-borne air attack on Taranto that sank half the Italian battle fleet, and earned for HMS *Illustrious* the accolade of the signal, 'Manœuvre well executed', flown by every ship of the Mediterranean fleet.

On 28 March 1941, after several bombardments of Italian-held ports in North Africa, Cunningham destroyed three 8-inch gunned Italian cruisers in a brilliantly fought night action off Cape Matapan, after putting their battle fleet to flight.

When Germany invaded Greece and later Crete that summer, his grim determination was responsible for safely evacuating most of the British, Commonwealth and Allied troops that had been sent to these places. Though his ships were bombed heavily by the *Luftwaffe* time and again, and so many were damaged and put out of action that his advisers counselled him against

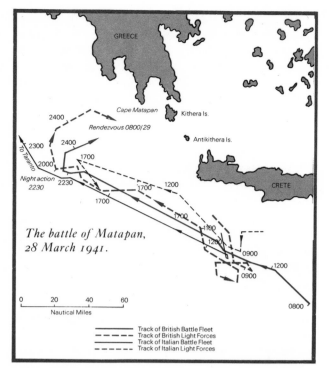

The battle of Matapan, 28 March 1941.

| 0 | 20 | 40 | 60 |
Nautical Miles

——————— Track of British Battle Fleet
– – – – – – Track of British Light Forces
———————— Track of Italian Battle Fleet
– – – – – – Track of Italian Light Forces

risking further losses, he answered: 'It takes three years to build a ship; but 300 to build a tradition. We cannot let the Army down!'

Nemesis struck his gallant ships, which had so effectively countered the Italian fleet, in the last months of 1941. First the battleship *Barham* was lost to a U-boat; then her sisters, the *Queen Elizabeth* and *Valiant*, were immobilized in Alexandria by a gallantly executed Italian two-man torpedo attack. Thereafter, Cunningham's operations were necessarily curtailed by his lack of a battle fleet in the eastern Mediterranean.

In mid-1942 he was honoured with a baronetcy and appointed to head the British Admiralty Delegation in Washington, D.C., but this was for less than six months. In November he was the naval commander of the Allied Expeditionary Force which invaded French North Africa, after which he resumed his position as C.-in-C. Mediterranean. His pre-eminent position, under the Supreme Commander, General Eisenhower, is well illustrated by this, possibly apocryphal, anecdote. An American G.I. sentry rebuked a British bluejacket for bathing from an unauthorized Mediterranean beach. To bowdlerize the sailor's reply: 'That there land may belong to your General Eisenhower, but this here sea is our Admiral Cunningham's.'

Early in 1943 Cunningham received the rare honour of promotion to admiral of the fleet while holding an active appointment. In this rank he was the naval commander for two major combined operations, the invasion of Sicily in July, and the landings at Salerno, near Naples, in September. And following the Italian armistice he had the supreme satisfaction of signalling the Admiralty: 'Be pleased to inform Their Lordships that the Italian battle fleet now lies at anchor under the guns of the fortress of Malta.'

In October, after the untimely death of

Admiral Pound, Cunningham was recalled to succeed him as First Sea Lord, for the good reason expressed by Admiral Sir Bruce Fraser, then in command of the Home fleet, who declined the post because, 'whilst I enjoy the confidence of my own fleet, Admiral Cunningham has the confidence of the whole Navy'.

Immediately after the war Cunningham was created a baron, and a year later was raised to the dignity of a viscount 'of Hyndhope and Matapan'. More significantly, on his retirement from the Admiralty in 1946, he received the rarest of Britain's honours, the Order of Merit. He died in 1963, at the age of 80, to be fittingly buried at sea, in the sure knowledge that he had gained a place among the greatest of Britain's sea kings.

HALSEY

The United States Navy's greatest admirals of the Second World War were indisputedly Ernest King and Chester Nimitz. But as Chief of Naval Operations the former managed his fleet's world-wide tasks from an office in the Pentagon, in Washington, D.C., while the latter as CinCPac controlled the Pacific Fleet as successfully from Hawaii's Pearl Harbor. It is not so easy to choose the greatest who fought the war *at sea*, but high on any list, and indubitably the most colourful personality, must be William Frederick Halsey who was widely known as 'Bull'.

Having graduated at the Annapolis Naval Academy in 1904 at the age of 22, Halsey spent most of his early career, including the First World War, in destroyers on whose handling he became a recognized authority. Then, in 1935, he qualified as a naval aviator so that, as a captain, he might command an aircraft-carrier, a type of ship whose importance in any future war he now recognized. But by 1941, already aged 59, he was no more than a rear-admiral commanding the U.S. Pacific Fleet's three carriers.

Fortunately for the U.S.A., and contrary to Japan's calculations, none of these was in Pearl Harbor on 7 December 1941, when the planes from Admiral Isoroku Yamamoto's fleet struck that base, without warning, and decimated America's battle fleet. Characteristically, Halsey came near to starting a shooting war up to ten days before this 'day of infamy'. Unlike Admiral H. E. Kimmel, then CinCPac, who was caught very much unawares and thereby lost his job to Nimitz, Halsey so far appreciated the dangerously strained relations between his country and Japan that, before sailing on 28 November, he issued orders to his force to shoot down any suspicious ships or planes which they might encounter, and 'ask questions afterwards'.

Less than two months after the débâcle of Pearl Harbor, America's carriers began to strike back, Halsey playing his spectacular part on 18 April. From the USS *Hornet* and *Enterprise* he launched 16 long-range B-25s, led by General Doolittle, which to Japan's alarm dropped their bombs on a surprised Tokyo. It was a raid which although it did little damage, thereafter pinned down a large part of Japan's fighter force to defend her capital, and gave a welcome boost to public morale in the U.S.A.

Shortly after this 'answer to Pearl Harbor', Halsey had to go into hospital, so that he took no part in the battle of the Coral Sea in May or of Midway in June. As soon as he was fit, in October, Nimitz ordered him to take charge of the south Pacific with his headquarters at Noumea. From there Halsey controlled the latter part of the hard-fought Guadalcanal campaign, including the battle of Santa Cruz, which was tactically indecisive, and of Guadalcanal itself, in which the U.S navy scored such a decisive victory that in February 1942 the Japanese gave up their tenuous hold on this Pacific island. Halsey thus played a major role in finally stopping the Japanese advance southwards across the Pacific, all too near to Australia and New Zealand.

Moreover, he immediately began to drive the Japanese back out of the Solomon Islands, a task which he continued to control until early in 1944, when Nimitz decided to reorganize his fleet to recapture the Philippines, and then, if necessary, to invade Japan. Realizing that with his ships almost continuously at sea – a feat achieved by replenishment of fuel, ammunition and stores while under way – one admiral and his staff could not simultaneously conduct an operation and plan the next, he arranged for two to be appointed. While one executed an operation, another in the quiet of a shore base, planned the next which he then executed. The same, by now vast, armada of ships was employed, being first referred to as the Third Fleet and, for the next operation, as the Fifth Fleet. And to command the Third Fleet, Halsey was Nimitz's, and King's choice.

In this capacity he was first involved in the amphibious operations designed to retake the Philippines. These began with a landing on the island of Leyte in mid-October 1944. A multitude of landing ships and craft, with air cover provided by three groups of escort carriers and bombardment support by a squadron of battleships, comprised the Seventh Fleet under Admiral Thomas Kincaid. Halsey's Third Fleet, of four groups of aircraft-carriers, supported by battleships, was ordered to protect this Seventh Fleet against Japanese attack. From Tokyo the Japanese C.-in-C., Admiral Soemu Toyoda, who by this time had no serviceable aircraft-carriers in his fleet, responded to news of the American landing on Leyte by ordering two forces of battleships and cruisers to launch a twin-pronged attack on the Seventh Fleet through the Philippines from the west, while a third group came down from the north to decoy the powerful Third Fleet away from the scene.

To cut short the long story of the battle of

Leyte, the largest naval action of the Second World War, Toyoda's plan came near to success because Halsey swallowed the bait. He went off to the north leaving the Seventh Fleet unprotected. Kincaid's ships were saved only by the magnificent gunnery of his bombardment squadron which, in a night action, destroyed one Japanese force, and by the skilful handling and dauntless courage of his escort carriers and their aircrews which, for small losses to kamikaze suicide planes, eluded annihilation by the other enemy force.

The situation was, nonetheless, so crucial at one stage that an anxious Nimitz signalled from Pearl Harbor: 'Where is Task Force 34?' (i.e. the Third Fleet's battleships). Through a decoding error this reached Halsey in the form: 'Where is Task Force 34. The world wonders.' A victim of his own mercurial temperament, he took this to be an insulting rebuke, and more than an hour elapsed before he so far overcame his wrath as to send one of his carrier groups south to help a hard-pressed Seventh Fleet. Halsey had the satisfaction of sinking most of the Japanese decoy force in what became known as the 'battle of Bull Run', but he also received a stern rebuke from Nimitz. The battle of Leyte was a major American victory but it came near to being a defeat and, had it been so, Halsey would have carried much of the blame.

As it was, he soon erased this stain by the way in which his carriers, operating in the South China Sea, provided air support for the Seventh Fleet, and for General Douglas McArthur's troops onshore as they fought hard to recover Luzon, the principal island in the Philippines, for more than four months. Not until 4 March 1945 did the capital, Manila, surrender when the

Third Fleet became the Fifth Fleet and its admiral and his staff retired from the scene.

Halsey was next back on the bridge at the end of May, with a fleet whose core again comprised a large force of aircraft-carriers, one group being provided by the British Pacific fleet. Its first task was to help the army and marines to complete their capture of Okinawa, at considerable cost to Japanese air attacks, much damage being done to its ships by kamikazes. Next, on 1 July, Halsey had the satisfaction of sortieing to attack Japan itself. His carrier-borne planes began raiding Tokyo and other cities, while his battleships bombarded important coastal targets. Replenishing at sea, his fleet operated continuously to the east of the Japanese mainland with such effect that the Emperor was near to surrender even before atomic bombs were dropped on Hiroshima and Nagasaki at the beginning of August. The Third Fleet was still there when the Japanese capitulated at the end of that month, and Halsey was able to lead his ships into Tokyo Bay and have the supreme satisfaction of seeing Japanese delegates sign the surrender document in the presence of Nimitz and McArthur, and of Britain's Admiral Sir Bruce Fraser, on board the battleship *Missouri*.

Like Nelson, Halsey was not only a strategic genius but inclined to vanity. If it be argued that his belief in Danton's words, *'L'audace, toujours l'audace'*, led him to a potentially fatal blunder at the battle of Leyte, so did they lead Nelson to make his disastrous attack on Santa Cruz. But, like Nelson, he was both an inspiring leader and generous to others. The five stars of a fleet admiral with which he ended his active career in 1947 were well earned. He died in 1959, his place secure among the U.S. Navy's immortals.

A typical World War Two aircraft-carrier, the USS Enterprise *of 19,900 tons which carried 100 planes.*

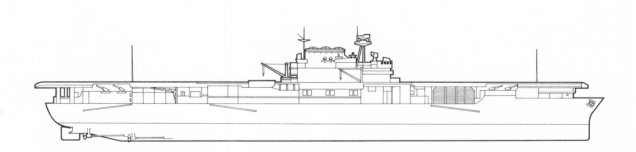

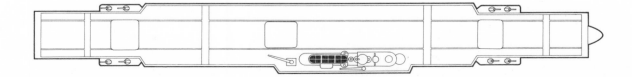

Great Ocean Liners

NO ONE CAN STUDY the life of colonial America without being impressed by the extent of the traffic between the New World and the Old. The little ship *Arbella*, taking across the leaders of the Massachusetts Bay colony in 1630, ten years after the *Mayflower* sailed, led a continuous migration.

Having settled in America, the immigrants relied upon ships from England for a great variety of merchandise – everything which they could not grow or make themselves – and some of them also kept a more personal contact with the homeland, crossing for business or pleasure, or sending their sons across to the universities of Oxford and Cambridge. By the eighteenth century the 'news of Virginia' was a familiar topic in the London coffee houses, and throughout the nineteenth century a strong Atlantic culture was in flower. Americans followed the Washington Irving trail to Stratford-upon-Avon, and Dickens went to America at Irving's invitation; Ralph Waldo Emerson called on Wordsworth in the Lake District; Fanny Kemble, the actress, was impressed by Niagara; Harriet Beecher Stowe, the author of *Uncle Tom's Cabin*, regretted that she could never again visit Sir Walter Scott's country for the *first* time. Yet even the best passages were grimly uncomfortable, at least by the standards of today. Until the 1830s the crowded ships were propelled by the same capricious power that had taken Sir Richard Grenville's colonists to Roanoke in 1585 and the *Susan Constant, Godspeed* and *Discovery* to the James River in 1607. Voyages were long and uncertain; a vessel might be weeks beating her way down Channel from the Thames or waiting for a favourable wind.

The Black Ball Line, founded at New York in 1816, brought the first big improvement by shortening the period of discomfort. It boasted an average passage of 40 days from Liverpool to New York and 23 days back to Liverpool.

Running in competition with the packets of the Swallow Tail Line, the Black Star, the Red Star, the Black X, the White Diamond and the Dramatic, the Black Ball vessels sailed on time whether they were packed or empty; one of them left New York for Liverpool on the first and sixteenth of every month.

When the ship berthed, none of the new arrivals was happier than those travelling steerage. While first-class passengers drank whisky and played cards like travellers in Mississippi and Ohio steamboats, poor emigrants huddled in semi-darkness, enduring frightful discomforts and miseries, and sometimes agonies too. Most of the passengers had no intention of returning, except perhaps on a visit when they had found their crock of gold. According to the official figures, over 2,300,000 immigrants crossed to America from the British Isles in the ten years from 1846 to 1855.

In 1838 two Nova Scotians, Judge Thomas Haliburton and Joseph Howe, were 20 days out of Halifax on a visit to England when their ship met the paddle steamer *Sirius*. The little steamship, said Howe, approached 'with the speed of a hunter, while we were moving with the rapidity of an ox-cart loaded with marsh mud'. It can hardly have been an accident that in November of that year another leading Haligonian, Samuel Cunard, a devout Quaker whose forebears had emigrated to Philadelphia in 1683, answered an Admiralty request for steamships capable of maintaining a monthly mail service across the Atlantic. After two of his tenders had been rejected, he left for England.

By an agreement made on 11 February 1839, he undertook to provide three steamships and to incorporate, during the continuance of the contract, 'any improvements in Steam Navigation' which the heads of the Admiralty might consider essential. He then called on James C. Melvill, Secretary of the East India Company for advice as to who could build the three ships. Without hesitation, Melvill recommended Robert Napier, a brilliant marine engineer who

Right: Reconstruction of the 1620 Mayflower *by Stuart Upham of Brixham in Devon to the plans of the American ship designer William Baker. In 1957 Alan Villiers sailed her from Plymouth, Devon, to Plymouth Rock, New England.*

Below: The P & O ship Britannia *of 1887. She was one of four 6,500-ton, 15-knot liners built by the company in 1887 and 1888 for the Australian route to celebrate the Golden Jubilee of Queen Victoria and the P & O. The other three were the* Victoria, Oceana *and* Arcadia. *For a short time they carried sails as well as using steam.*

designed and built the machinery for hulls constructed by his partner, John Wood.

In March 1839, Samuel Cunard and Robert Napier met for the first time. Out of that meeting grew the great and famous Cunard Steamship Company. The problem of finance was solved when Napier called in George Burns, owner of coastal steamships, and David McIver, his Liverpool agent. Within a few days 32 businessmen had subscribed £270,000, more than enough capital to build the three ships required by the Admiralty and another vessel as well, the head postmaster at Quebec having suggested that with four ships the service could have fixed departure days on both sides of the Atlantic. The line was first known as 'The British and North American Royal Mail Steam-Packet Company'.

Writing to Melvill about Cunard on 18 March, Napier had said: 'From the frank off-hand manner in which he contracted with me, I have given him the vessels cheap, and I am certain they will be good and very strong ships.' The four were the *Britannia* of 1840 and her sister ships, the *Acadia*, *Caledonia* and the *Columbia*.

At Liverpool the *Britannia* had to be swung out into midstream 'owing to her immense size'. She was 228ft long overall and 34.3ft in beam (56ft over the paddle boxes) with a mean draught of 16.8ft and a gross tonnage of 1,156. Two side-lever engines of 740 indicated horsepower turned her 28ft paddle wheels at sixteen revolutions a minute and gave her a normal speed of about 8.5 knots. Leaving Liverpool on 4 July 1840, she crossed to Halifax in eleven days four hours at a mean speed of ten knots and completed her run to Boston in fourteen days eight hours.

Her accommodation – the dining saloon and cabins for 115 on the main deck below – was described as luxurious.

When the *Britannia* was gripped by ice seven feet thick at Boston on 1 February 1844, residents cut a passage seven miles long and 100 feet wide to free her. She left on 3 February, only two days late, followed by cheering citizens in sleighs and 'sailing boats fitted up with long blades of iron like skates'. Bostonians were proud of the *Britannia*, and they did not want her to call at New York instead on the grounds that the sea there was less likely to freeze.

The Cunard company did not lack competitors. At the outset the Great Western Steamship Company at Bristol had expected to receive the mail contract as the owners of the only fully effective Atlantic steamship, Brunel's *Great Western*. When the Admiralty accepted Samuel Cunard's tender, Brunel began work on the *Great Britain*. But she took six years to build, and by the time she went into service the Cunard Line was firmly established. She did not remain long on the Atlantic.

Samuel Cunard met his first serious challenge when Edward Knight Collins from Cape Cod, after running the Dramatic Line of sailing packets, turned to steamships. He was not one to do things by halves. His first packet had been the *Shakespeare*, the largest merchant ship that had ever flown the American flag; and his *Atlantic* of 1849 was a beautiful wooden steamship of 2,860 tons which set new standards in comfort and speed. Contracting with the United States Government to operate a subsidized mail service between New York and Liverpool every two weeks for eight months of the year and monthly in the winter, he devoted himself to 'the absolute conquest of this man Cunard' by offering the Atlantic travellers a fast voyage in a ship which boasted such luxuries as steam heat, bathrooms (Cunard passengers were hosed down on request), ice, a barber's shop, a proper smoking room, and two main saloons panelled

Above left: The P & O Jubilee ship Victoria. *In later years she was often on the Bombay run. She was scrapped in 1909.*

Above: Inman's City of New York *passes* Bowling *on the Clyde.*

Right: P & O's Canberra, 45,000 tons. At the time of her launching in March 1960 she was the largest ship to have been built in Britain since the Queen Elizabeth. She was designed for 2,250 passengers.

Above far right: The France.

Below far right: The Oriana (41,923 tons) at Pago-Pago in Samoa. In December 1960 this luxury liner entered the P & O-Orient Lines service between London, Australia, New Zealand and California. Note her bulbous bow.

Below centre: Cunard's latest in 1976, the Countess.

Below: The Queen Mary leaving Southampton.

and *Constitution* of American Export Isbrandtsen Lines were with Atlantic Far East Lines, a subsidiary of the C. Y. Tung Group; and the *Rotterdam* was sailing under the flag of the Netherlands Antilles. In 1975 the *United States* was reported to be rusting away at Norfolk, Virginia, at a cost of $1 million a year.

While there were hopes that the *Michelangelo* and *Raffaello* of the Italia Line might be turned into hospital ships for cancer patients, a question mark still hovered above the graceful bows of the *France*. The decision of the French Government to withdraw her in October 1974 provoked her crew to stage a sit-in-at-sea; the astonishing scene was witnessed by trade unionists and rich Americans united in support of a luxury ship which had been costing the taxpayer huge sums. In 1972 she had circumnavigated the world in 88 days. Two ladies from Texas paid the equivalent of nearly £30,000 for four cabins.

In the mid-seventies the Red Flag seemed to to be taking the place of the Red Duster on the Atlantic passenger routes. Two impressive Soviet liners of 20,000 tons were sailing to North America three times a year from Tilbury on the Thames, with a call at Le Havre. It was announced early in 1976 that one of them, the *Alexander Pushkin*, would leave for Montreal on 9 May, 9 June and 29 September, and the other, the *Mikhail Lermontov*, for New York on 23 May, 15 September and 17 October. Poland also had a liner on the Atlantic run. The *Stefan Batory* sailed monthly from Gdynia to Montreal *via* Rotterdam and London, returning by way of Southampton and Rotterdam. Once a year when the St Lawrence is frozen she ends her outward voyage at New York instead of Montreal. She was formerly the Holland-America *Maasdam*, built in 1952.

Among all the sea changes the last great Cunarder continued to create her own legend. Something of the twenties spirit lived again in the *QE2*. We do not know what Samuel Cunard would have thought of the nine bars and the 200 different cocktails, the casino with its roulette and blackjack, the Theatre Bar and the Q4 night club where passengers might dance the hours and the miles away; but we can be sure that Dickens, the celebrated passenger in the *Britannia* of 1840, would have enjoyed describing it all for another volume of *American Notes*. Perhaps he would have ended with the question: 'Does anyone ever notice the sea?'

115

against the slavers. It also built some new vessels incorporating elements of the Baltimore design and altered older ones to embody these improvements as far as possible. William Symonds, the Secretary of the Navy, made a profitable study of the American hulls. But the Baltimore clippers fortune hunter had to go by ship round Cape Horn unless he were prepared to attempt the slow and dangerous journey overland. Clipper after clipper put out for California. The demand kept the shipbuilders busy and at the same time improved the design: some of the clippers were

Above: Donald McKay's Lightning. *On her maiden voyage from Boston to Liverpool in 1854, she logged 436 miles in 24 hours. 'It was 35 years before an ocean-going steamship exceeded that day's work,' wrote James A. Farrell, the steel tycoon whose father commanded the* Glory of the Seas. *The* Lightning *met her end by fire at Geelong, Australia.*

Opposite previous page: The Cutty Sark *in her dry-dock at Greenwich. 'Earth will not see such ships as these again.'*

famous for their speed. At New York between 1850 and 1853 William H. Webb built the *Celestial* of 810 tons; the *Challenge* of 2,006 tons; the *Comet* of 1,836; the *Sword Fish* of 1,034 tons; and the *Young America* of 1,962.

At East Boston in 1850 Donald McKay, who had already made his name as a builder of packet ships, launched the 1,534-ton *Stag Hound*, his first clipper. He had contracted to build her in 60 days. The launching from his yard at the bottom of Border Street drew a crowd estimated at over 10,000 in December weather so cold that everyone feared the tallow on the slipway would freeze. Far from sticking, the *Stag Hound* moved so fast that the foreman just managed to smash his bottle of Medford rum on her forefoot, shouting 'Stag Hound – your name's Stag Hound!' and losing his hat. She had a long, sharp bow and a light elliptical stern and her greatest breadth was amidships. New York was as much

surprised as Boston when the ship arrived there. On 1 February 1851, in a strong westerly breeze, she left the Battery, to pass Sandy Hook at ten knots.

From Valparaiso, where she spent five days, she made a passage of 42 days to San Francisco. Her time at sea was 108 days and her best day's run was 358 nautical miles. Donald McKay had no need to worry about his future as a builder of clipper ships. The *Stag Hound* provided a bold and successful illustration of the theory put forward by his friend John Willis Griffiths, the designer of the *Rainbow*. 'This daring innovator', wrote Richard McKay, grandson of the master builder, 'proposed a model of a knifelike, concave entrance, melting into an easy run to the midship section, where, instead of forward, he located the extreme breadth of beam. Thence this fullness of breadth melted again into the after end in lines almost as fine as those forward. In place of the codfish underbody, he gave his innovation a dead rise amidships.' Richard McKay added: 'The superior excellence of our ships was obtained wholly by the use of the waterline model in the designing of them!'

Such was the formula of McKay ships to come. Soon after the *Stag Hound* proved herself, Georges Frances Train, a famous Boston Shipowner, told her creator that he wanted a vessel of 2,000 tons.

broken – by Donald McKay. In the *Sovereign of the Seas,* he produced a ship of 2,420 tons which outsailed the *Flying Cloud.* She measured 265ft in extreme length and 44ft in beam. Her mainmast rose 92ft 9in. and her bowsprit, of hard pine, extended 20ft outboard and was 34in. in diameter. As no merchant in New England would buy such a vessel, McKay ran her himself with his brother Lauchlan in command. She left for San Francisco loaded with 2,950 tons of

Later the *Boston Daily Atlas* reported: 'If great length, sharpness of ends, with proportionate breadth and depth, conduce to speed, the *Flying Cloud* must be uncommonly swift, for in all these she is great. Her length on the keel is 208ft, on deck 225, and over all, from the knight heads to the taffrail, 235 – extreme breadth of beam 41ft, depth of hold 21½, including 7 feet 8 inches height of between-decks, dead-rise at half floor 20 inches, rounding of sides 6 inches, and sheer about 3ft.'

On 3 June 1851, in a westerly breeze which soon freshened to a gale, she ran past Sandy Hook under three skysails, royals, topgallant, to topmast and square lower studding sails. Her destination was California, and she swept through the Golden Gate at 11.30 on the morning of 30 August, having made the passage in the record time of 89 days 21 hours from Sandy Hook. However McKay records were made to be

Above: The three-masted barque Rapido, *built at the little Cumberland port of Harrington (now part of Workington) in 1855.*

Left: Among the ships well-known at Hong Kong in the last great era of sail was the 814-ton Maiden Queen, *shown here in a painting of 1860.*

merchandise, the largest cargo ever despatched from the port of New York and arrived at the Golden Gate in 103 days. It was said that she had beaten every vessel that sailed within a month of her. She certainly beat the steamship *Canada* across the Atlantic. The *Canada* put in at Liverpool to be greeted by a large canvas sign telling all on board that the *Sovereign of the Seas* had already arrived, in 13 days 22 hours.

Thanks to the master builder from Nova

before the trade winds of the Indian Ocean, running down to the Cape of Good Hope. They sailed by Flores in the Azores, where the *Revenge* had fought her last battle, on the same day. For the greater part of Sunday, 5 September, the *Ariel* and *Taeping* were in sight of each other as they headed up the Channel at fourteen knots. The *Ariel* signalled her number off Deal at eight o'clock on the Monday morning and the *Taeping* followed suit in ten minutes. Later that day both of them reached London, where the *Serica* also arrived, shortly before the dock gates closed. The *Taeping* was in the London Docks at 9.45 pm, the *Ariel* in the East India Docks at 10.15, and the *Serica* in the West Indies Docks

at 11.30. They had crossed 16,000 miles of sea in 99 days. The *Fiery Cross* and *Taitsing* put in two days later. Also rans though they were, they had nevertheless beaten the previous record by six days.

The *Taeping, Ariel, Sir Lancelot, Titania, Lahloo* and *Kaisow,* all built by Robert Steele and Sons, made some of the fastest passages ever recorded on the China run. In 1866–7 the *Ariel* was only 80 days, between pilots, from London to Hong Kong; in 1869 the *Sir Lancelot* passed the Lizard 84 days after leaving Foochow; and in 1871 the *Titania* completed the passage in 93 days.

In 1868 the magnificent *Thermopylae,* built

more quickly. Wooden ships in the China trade were copper-sheathed until 'composite construction' came to be used from about 1863. Inspired by the iron ships on the Australian run, shipbuilders gave their tea clippers interior frameworks of iron and then planked the hull with wood, to which a sheathing of copper or yellow metal was added below the waterline. Between 1839 and 1860 the British Patent Office received more than thirty applications relating to composite construction.

The British clippers were helped by ill-winds in the United States, the depression of 1857 and then the Civil War from 1861 to 1865. American shipbuilding declined, and the British tea-trade prospered in answer to an increasing demand. Every year at the end of May the Pagoda

New Seas and New Lands

ST PAUL

The Phoenicians circumnavigated Africa as early as 700 BC; Hanno of Carthage voyaged to Sierra Leone *circa* 470 BC; Pytheas of Greece sailed around Britain in 330 BC; and Alexander the Great's seamen penetrated by way of the Red Sea into the Indian Ocean in 325 BC. But the earliest significant voyage of which we have a contemporary record was Julius Caesar's in 55 BC from Gaul across the Channel to conquer England.

A much longer voyage, of which we also have a contemporary record, was made a century later. In AD 55 Paul, 'a Jew, a Tarsian of Cilicia, a citizen of no mean city', and a rabid convert to Christianity, was brought before Felix, the Roman Governor, and charged by the High Priest with preaching a seditious doctrine. Felix was so undecided how to deal with the case that he held Paul in custody for all of two years. But Festus, his successor, lost no time before he tackled it, whereupon Paul exercized his right as a citizen of a province under Roman domination: 'I', he said, 'appeal to Caesar' to which Festus answered: 'To Caesar you shall go'.

Whether Paul was wise to make this appeal is questionable, since King Agrippa judged that 'this man is doing nothing that deserves death or imprisonment. The fellow could have been discharged if he had not appealed to the Emperor'. As it was, Paul was handed over to a centurion, with whom he embarked in 'a ship bound for ports in the province of Asia'. They voyaged from Israel along the southern coast of what is now Turkey before transferring to 'an Alexandrian vessel bound for Italy' which carried 276 passengers and crew. (Since ships were then so small they must have been herded in her like cattle.) Adverse winds delayed her progress along the south coast of Crete until a 'northeaster . . . caught the ship and we had to run

Opposite: The French brig Brésilien, *leaving Le Havre, painted in 1882 by Ed. Adam.*

before it', with the consequence that for 'four days on end there was no sign of either sun or stars, a great storm was raging, and our last hopes of coming through alive began to fade'.

However, on 'the fourteenth night . . . the sailors felt that land was getting near. . . . Fearing that they might be cast ashore on a rugged coast they dropped four anchors.' The crew then proposed to abandon ship, but Paul advised them against this. And 'when day broke they could not recognize the land but noticed a bay with a sandy beach', so they weighed anchor, and allowed the wind to drive the ship on shore. 'And thus it was that all came safely to . . . the island of Malta' – in the haven now known as St Paul's Bay.

The Maltese treated Paul and his guards 'with uncommon kindness' throughout the three months that they were obliged to stay there before they could 'set sail in a ship which had wintered in the island. She was the *Castor and Pollux* of Alexandria' (the first vessel in all history of which we know the name). They sailed to Putcoli, in the Gulf of Naples, in only two days, whence Paul completed his journey over land to Rome in AD 58. There he was allowed to live and preach the Gospel for all of two years before being brought to trial. Moreover, not until AD 64 did Nero condemn him to death, by which time Christianity was so firmly rooted in Mediterranean countries that less than three centuries elapsed before, around AD 320, the Emperor Constantine I was himself converted.

Thenceforward Christianity spread across Europe, St Columba voyaging as far as the island of Iona to begin converting the Picts in AD 563, and St Augustine crossed the Channel to Thanet to do likewise with the Anglo-Saxons in AD 597.

COLUMBUS

As the Roman Empire declined, one of its last Emperors, Justinian, sent emissaries overseas to China to obtain silk worms (AD 500). In the subsequent thousand years of the Dark and

Middle Ages (c.550 to c.1500) the Norsemen of Scandinavia carried out their seaborne raids; the Danes founded Dublin and Limerick (AD 840) and a few years later colonized much of England. This was also the period in which the Vikings circumnavigated Iceland in their longships (880), and went on to Greenland (982), and Leif Ericsson discovered Nova Scotia (1000).

This, too, was the era in which William of Normandy crossed the Channel to conquer England (1066), and King Richard I of England voyaged to Palestine to take part in the Crusades (1191). The Genoese captured Rhodes (1248), Haco of Norway attempted the last Scandinavian invasion of Scotland (1263) and, half the world away, Kublai Khan made an abortive attempt to invade Japan (1274). The Normans voyaged as far south as Senegal (1364), and a Dane, Dietrich Pining, claimed to have discovered Newfoundland (1472), though a better claimant is the Venetian John Cabot (1497).

The available records of most of these voyages are, however, so scanty that it is impracticable to do more than mention them. Not until the last century of the Middle Ages can one write in any detail about voyages of discovery of which the first and most important was made by Christopher Columbus. Born into a Genoese family of woolweavers in 1451, he went to sea as an illiterate youth in vessels sailing within the Mediterranean. The first ship in which he sailed out through the Straits of Gibraltar was sunk by a French squadron off Lagos in 1476. However, Columbus managed to escape being taken prisoner by swimming ashore, whence he made his way to Lisbon to join a Portuguese vessel.

As a result of wide reading he overcame his illiteracy, and this made him too ambitious to be content with such an ordinary career. He knew something of the much-sought-after spices and other riches which came from the [East] Indies. He knew, too, of the difficulties involved in bringing them to Europe by way of the Red Sea, with the need for transhipment across the Isthmus of Suez. He was not unaware that there might be an all-sea route around Africa. But having joined those who now believed the world to be spherical in shape – not a flat plane over whose edge you might sail into oblivion – he was convinced that there was a much shorter route across the Atlantic to the west.

Unfortunately, he grossly underestimated the distance as being only 2,400 miles from the Canaries, which compares with the reality of more than 10,000. Moreover, when he sought backers for a voyage to prove his 'Enterprise of the Indies', he made exorbitant demands. He not only required three vessels with their crews but, should he be successful, promotion to the nobility, jurisdiction over any new lands he found, and a ten per cent share of all trade.

Not surprisingly Portugal's King John II,

England's King Henry VII and France's King Charles VIII successively turned him down. Eventually, after 'a terrible, continued, painful and prolonged battle' lasting for more than ten years, Columbus persuaded King Ferdinand and Queen Isabella of Spain – chiefly the latter because Ferdinand never really liked him – to meet all his demands and to give him the support he needed. The *Santa Maria*, a caravel of 100 tons, was chartered as his 'flagship' in 1492 and manned by a crew of 40. The rest of the squadron comprised the 90-tons *Niña*, and the 50-tons *Pinta*, each with a crew of 18. Together the three vessels sailed from Palos, within the Río Tinto river, on 3 August.

Columbus planned to call first at the Canaries and thence to allow the easterly trade winds to take his ships to the west until, according to the geographical ideas of that time, he came to Japan, where he expected to set up a profitable trading post. At first all went well. Leaving Las Palmas on 6 September, this tiny squadron of ships not much larger than 'cockleshells' made good 1,163 nautical miles in ten days. Thereafter, however, they lay becalmed so that their crews began grumbling and proposed to return to Spain. On 2 October the easterly trade wind blew again. But the crews were not satisfied; on the 10th they threatened mutiny. Columbus pacified them by promising to turn back if no land was sighted within three days. In half that time, at 2.0 am on the 12th, he made a landfall; by the light of the moon he saw the cliffs of one of the islands in the Bahamas.

Having named this San Salvador and taken possession of it for Spain, Columbus, believing that he had reached an island off the eastern seaboard of Asia, took his squadron south expecting to find Japan. Instead, on 28 October, he discovered Cuba, an island whose appearance was so unlike the Japan described by the great overland explorer and disciple of Kublai Khan, Marco Polo, that he decided that it must be part of China.

Columbus next found Hispaniola (which now comprises Haiti and the Dominican Republic) on 5 December where the *Santa Maria* was wrecked on an offshore reef. Having built a fort by Caracol Bay and left a party of volunteers to man it, he set sail again on 4 January 1493, this time in the *Niña* with the *Pinta* in company, and headed for home. After an exceptionally stormy voyage these two ships reached the Azores on 18 February, where an over-zealous captain of the port supposed them to be poachers and arrested their crews. Once this misunderstanding had been overcome, Columbus continued his easterly voyage on 24 February, to ride out another fierce gales under bare poles before reaching the safety of the Tagus on 4 March. When he had convinced the King of Portugal that he had discovered the westerly route to the [East] Indies,

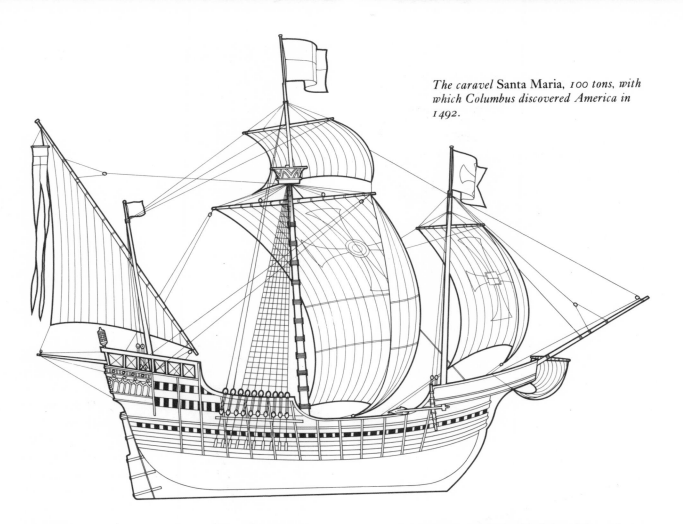

The caravel Santa Maria, *100 tons, with which Columbus discovered America in 1492.*

Columbus took his two ships back to Palos from where they had sailed nine months before.

There followed his hour of triumph. Summoning him to Barcelona, King Ferdinand and Queen Isabella not only confirmed the titles and privileges for which Columbus had undertaken his voyage, but authorized him to prepare another, larger expedition to exploit these new-found Indies. On 25 September 1493, Columbus left Cadiz at the head of a fleet of 17 ships, including the *Niña*, carrying nearly 1,500 prospective colonists. Six weeks later they anchored off an island which Columbus named Guadeloupe, and he went on to discover the rest of what we know as the Leeward Islands, before making for Hispaniola where Columbus found that the natives had killed all the Spaniards he had left in Fort Caracol.

This grim discovery was followed by an exciting one: large nuggets of gold. Columbus sent these home to Spain in 12 of his ships. With the other five he cruised to the west in the hope of confirming that Cuba was part of China – not surprisingly without success. By way of compensation he found Jamaica.

By the time that Columbus returned to Isabella, the base which he had established on the north coast of Cuba, he found that his younger brother, Diego, whom he had left in charge, had been unable to maintain order among the greedy, gold-seeking Spanish colonists. Moreover, the once-friendly natives were now so openly hostile that Columbus had to spend all of 1495 sub-

duing them, at the end of which he shipped 500 back to Spain as slaves.

Leaving his elder brother, Bartholomew, in charge, he set sail again on 10 March 1496 in the *Niña* for what proved to be a long and tedious voyage. Not until 11 June did this small, overcrowded vessel – she carried 225 Spaniards and slaves, in addition to her crew of 18 – reach an anchorage off Cadiz.

Two years later, Ferdinand and Isabella were persuaded to allow him to make a third voyage. In the *Santa Maria de Guia*, with two caravels in company, he sailed on 30 May 1498, and took his departure from the Cape Verde Islands on 4 July. Nearly four weeks later, the squadron made a landfall on a large island which Columbus named Trinidad. He went on to explore a part of what is now Venezuela. Here, in *South America*, Columbus was the first European to land, if one discounts the already mentioned earlier discoveries of Newfoundland and Nova Scotia.

From the great quantity of water coming down the Orinoco River, Columbus realized that he had found a continent (which was to gain its name from Amerigo Vespucci who landed in Venezuela in 1499) but supposed it to lie close off Asia. Still believing that he was in the [East] Indies, he sailed north across the Caribbean to reach Hispaniola on 31 August 1498. He found that the Spanish colonists had by now established Santo Domingo as the island's capital. He learned also that the natives had again raised the

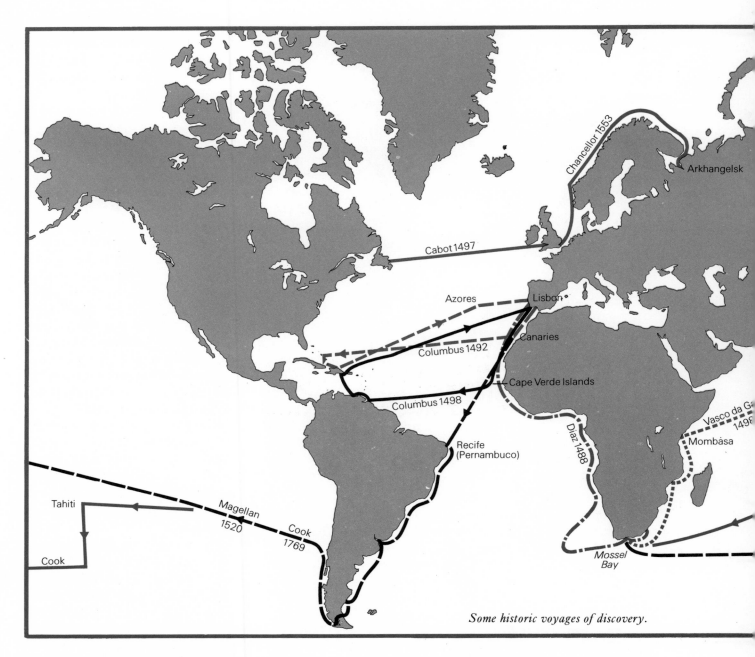

Some historic voyages of discovery.

flag of rebellion. And although Columbus managed to suppress this, he did it at such cost in lives, with a consequent reduction in shipments of gold, that the Spanish sovereigns sent Francisco de Bobadilla to take over the island's rule.

Bobadilla's first action was to seize Christopher Columbus and his brothers, Bartholomew and Diego, as prisoners and to ship them back to Spain in chains. King Ferdinand and Queen Isabella were more merciful. The brothers Columbus were soon released and, although Christopher was stripped of his titles and of further sovereignty over the Indies, he was authorized to make another voyage. Sailing from Cadiz in the *La Capitana*, with three smaller vessels in company, he aimed to find a way through what we know as the Gulf of Mexico into the Indian Ocean.

The squadron reached Martinique after a quick passage on 15 June. Thence, after weathering a hurricane, Columbus proceeded to Honduras, near where the city of Trujillo was later built. He went on to explore the coasts of Nicaragua and Costa Rica in the vain hope of finding a strait leading into the Indian Ocean. Learning from the natives that there was another ocean not very far away, he turned south, voyaging as far as what is now the northern entrance to the Panama Canal by 6 January 1503. There the squadron stayed until April, never suspecting how close they were to the Pacific (which was actually discovered in 1513 by Vasco Balboa when he crossed the Isthmus of Panama), before attempting to return to Spain. With his force reduced to two ships by the evil activities of the toredo worm, Columbus reached Jamaica on 25 June, where both vessels went aground and were wrecked. There he and his companions had to stay for more than a year before a vessel came to their rescue, and they finally reached Spain in November 1504.

Eighteen months later Columbus died at the age of 54, stricken with arthritis, frustrated by his failure to find the western route through to the East Indies, and furious with Ferdinand (Isabella was now dead) for ignoring his claims

132

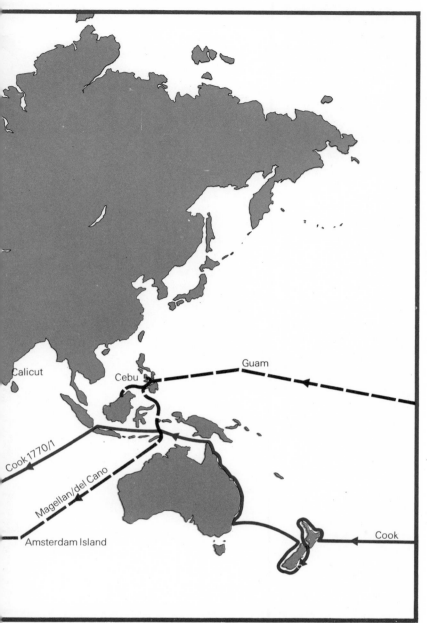

Gulf of Guinea (1471), and discovered the island of Fernando Po (1472). Diego Cam found the Congo (1484) and went on south to Angola (1486). From there it was but a short step to the Cape of Good Hope, the credit for whose discovery goes to Bartholomew Diaz.

Born in 1455 he achieved distinction as a navigator by commanding an expedition to the Gold Coast in 1481. Six years later he led a squadron of three ships to explore the African coast further south than this. After reaching south-west Africa, his ships were swept far to the south by strong gales that lasted for almost a fortnight. When these moderated, and they were able to turn north again, they made a landfall at Mossel Bay, to the east of the Cape of Good Hope, in February 1488. From there Diaz coasted up to the mouth of the Great Fish River before his crews became sufficiently alarmed by their venturing so far into the un-known that they compelled him to return – but not before it had become clear that they had rounded the southernmost point of Africa.

The honour of following up this discovery fell to Vasco da Gama. Some ten years younger, he started his career as a soldier before becoming a seaman. In 1497 he was chosen to command a squadron of four ships to find whether the way round the Cape led into the Indian Ocean – as indeed he did by going as far as Calicut on the Malabar coast which he claimed for Portugal in 1498. He was, however, unable to establish a trading post because the Arabs, already settled there, incited the natives to rise against him. However, the rich cargo which he brought home to Lisbon in 1499, whereby his voyage showed a 600 per cent profit, ensured that he was pro-fusely honoured and rewarded by King Manuel.

Pedro Cabral was ordered to exploit da Gama's discoveries with an expedition of 14 ships which left Portugal in March 1500, with Diaz as second-in-command. Because Cabral began by sailing further to the west across the Atlantic than previous navigators, he accidentally discovered Brazil and claimed it for Portugal. His ships subsequently encountered a fierce storm while rounding the Cape, in which Diaz perished. This tragedy did not, however, deter the squadron from going on to Calicut where Cabral successfully established a trading post Its occupants were, however, subsequently killed at Arab instigation. When news of this slaughter reached Lisbon, da Gama, with the rank of 'Admiral of India', was given a fleet of ten ships and ordered to seek revenge. Arriving off Calicut in 1502, he bombarded the town, destroying much of it, and killed many of the inhabitants. From there he sailed on to Cochin to load his ships with spices before returning home.

Created Count of Vidigueira, da Gama retired to enjoy his wealth until 1524. King John then

to be rewarded for discovering so many rich new colonies for Spain. The world now ranks him among the greatest of navigators. He explored virtually the whole of the Caribbean, except for the east coast of Mexico and what is now the southern seaboard of the U.S.A., and on his third voyage discovered, despite his mistaken identification, the American continent. Unhappily, he was no administrator; an Italian trying to rule over Spaniards was foredoomed to failure. But as a seaman, no one (with the possible exception of Magellan) made ocean voyages which, in their outcome, were of greater importance to mankind.

DIAZ AND DA GAMA

Straddling the years of Columbus's journeys were those in which the Portuguese discovered the eastern all-sea route to the Indies. In 1419 they colonized Madeira. Gonzalo Cabral found the Azores (1432). Cadamosto of Venice dis-covered the Cape Verde Islands (1456). Pedro de Cintra founded Sierra Leone (1462). Others worked along the west coast of Africa into the nominated him as viceroy, and charged him with remedying the many abuses by now common in Portugal's administration of her Indian colonies. But although he reached Goa in September, da Gama was taken ill before he could begin work, and died in Cochin on 24 December. His body was brought home and buried at Vidigueira. More than three centuries later, in 1880, his country signified its appreciation of his principal discovery, the all-sea route to the east, by his reburial in the church of Santa Maria de Belém in Lisbon.

MAGELLAN
Other voyages of this era included those by which Portuguese navigators discovered Ascension Island (1501), St Helena and the Seychelles (1502), Ceylon and Mauritius (1505). But these pale into insignificance when compared with one undertaken by Ferdinand Magellan.

Born in 1480, Magellan first voyaged overseas, to India in 1505, in the retinue of Portugal's first Viceroy of the East. Four years later he went as far as Cochin and the Spice Islands. Next he joined the expedition under Alfonso d'Albuquerque which discovered Malacca (1511). On returning to Portugal he was ennobled, only to be so angered by an accusation of trading with the enemy during an attack on the Moroccan town of Azamur, that he renounced his Portuguese nationality and moved to Spain. There he persuaded King Charles V to subsidize a voyage designed to find a westward route to the Indies round to the south of the continent of America.

With his flag in the *Trinidad*, and with four other vessels in company, Magellan crossed the Atlantic in September 1519, to near Pernambuco from where he coasted south to Port St Julian in Patagonia by March 1520. There he had to suppress a mutiny led by one of his pilots, Juan Sebastian del Cano, before sailing into the long, winding straight through the archipelago of Tierra del Fuego which today bears his name. The passage against contrary winds through these treacherous waters took them all of 38 days before they reached their goal, the calmer waters which Magellan justly called the Pacific Ocean.

He took his ships to the north and west for many thousands of miles, his crews suffering great hardships from starvation and scurvy before they at last made a landfall on Guam after a voyage lasting 98 days. The squadron sailed on to reach the Philippines in March 1521. Believing in the friendship of the native ruler of Cebu, especially after converting him to Christianity, Magellan was persuaded to lead an expedition to conquer the neighbouring island of Mactan. And there, in a fight against the inhabitants, he met his death.

The ruler of Cebu then tried to murder Magellan's comrades, but two of his ships

escaped to Borneo. From there, for lack of sufficient men to crew two vessels, only the 85-tons *Vittoria* sailed on under the former mutineer del Cano. With her crew again suffering from starvation and scurvy, which reduced their numbers to only 31 out of the total of 270 who had left Spain nearly three years before, the *Vittoria* struggled round the Cape of Good Hope to reach Seville at the end of July 1522, the first ship in all history to circumnavigate the globe.

CARTIER
In 1505 England's King Henry VII followed up Cabot's discovery of Nova Scotia by granting a charter to the trading company of Merchant Adventurers. By 1510 its members had voyaged down the eastern seaboard of North America as far as Charleston, before Ponce de León discovered and claimed Florida for Spain (1513) and William Hawkins made the first of three voyages to Brazil (1530). The English were, however, slow to take advantage of their finds; they were forestalled by the French, notably by Jacques Cartier.

Born in 1491, he was one of those who believed that there must be a way to the Indies round to the north of the American continent. John Rut made an unsuccessful voyage in search of this North-West Passage in 1527. Cartier decided to follow up his expedition by undertaking a voyage with two ships in 1534. Having reached Newfoundland he entered the Belle Isle Strait, but found this so uninviting that he reversed course to round Newfoundland and enter the St Lawrence River.

Two years later Cartier sailed up the St Lawrence as far as the Ile d'Orleans, whence he continued his voyage in longboats to the site on which the city of Montreal was later built. After returning to St Malo in 1537, he set out for his third voyage in 1541, the year after Spanish navigators worked up the west coast of North America as far as California. This time he led five ships with orders to escort a convoy of transports carrying troops to conquer the supposedly rich territory of 'Sagwenay', whom he landed well up the St Lawrence in the spring of 1542.

In the next year Cartier made his last voyage to bring back these troops whose mission had proved a failure because 'Sagwenay' did not, in fact, exist. Thereafter he lived quietly in St Malo until his death in 1557, since when history has remembered him as the man who not only discovered and explored the St Lawrence, but paved the way for French colonization of what is now the Canadian province of Quebec.

CHANCELLOR AND BARENTS
Cartier's voyages were followed by important ones in the opposite direction. In 1527 an

Englishman, Robert Thorn, suggested that the best way of reaching China might be by what came to be called the North-East Passage – along the north of Russia. But not until 1553 was Sir Hugh Willoughby chosen to lead an expedition to find it; this comprised the 120-tons *Bona Esperanza*, the 160-tons *Edward Bonaventure*, carrying his chief pilot, Richard Chancellor, and the 90-tons *Bona Confidentia*. This squadron left the Thames in July. A month later Willoughby and Chancellor reached the Lofoten Islands, from where they headed for Norway's North Cape, but before they could round it a severe gale separated the *Bonaventure* from the other two vessels.

Willoughby went on to sight land before the end of August but contrary winds delayed his further progress. Not for another month did he anchor the *Esperanza* and the *Confidentia* in Lapland's Arzinca Bay. Here, according to his journal, they saw 'very evill weather, snow and haile', and chose 'to winter there', which was to prove a tragic decision. Chancellor, in the *Bonaventure*, reached the White Sea, where he disembarked to travel overland to Moscow, to be received by Ivan the Terrible, and to found the Muscovy Company, which for several centuries did much to further trade between Britain and Russia.

On returning to the White Sea in 1555, Chancellor called en route at Arzinca Bay, and discovered Willoughby's journal, and other evidence that, for want of adequate clothing and other necessities with which to face an Arctic

winter, he and the crews of his two ships had perished in January 1554.

At the end of a third voyage to the White Sea in 1556, Chancellor brought back a ship-load of gifts from Ivan for Elizabeth, and Russia's first ambassador to the Court of St James, who was charged with conveying a proposal of marriage between England's Queen and Russia's Tsar. Unhappily the ship was wrecked off the east coast of Scotland, near Aberdeen, where more than Ivan's princely gifts were lost: the few survivors included neither Chancellor nor the Russian ambassador.

Stephen Brough (1556), and Henry Hudson (1607 and 1608) were just two among other Englishmen who later tried to find the North-East Passage. So, more importantly, did Willem Barents. Born around 1550, this resolute Dutch explorer set out from Amsterdam with two ships in 1594 to reach the coast of Novaya Zemlya. In the next year he tried to go further with seven ships but was prevented by ice off Vayjack Island. Two years later Barents tried again with two ships which sighted Spitzbergen and Bear Island. There they separated, Barents heading for Novaya Zemlya and this time sailing right round it. But before he could head for home his ship was trapped in ice and he was obliged to winter in the Arctic. Alas, the spring thaw did not spread far enough to the north; their ship was still held fast. So Barents made the momentous decision to abandon her, he and his crew sailing to the west in two open boats, in one of which Barents himself died of cold and exposure

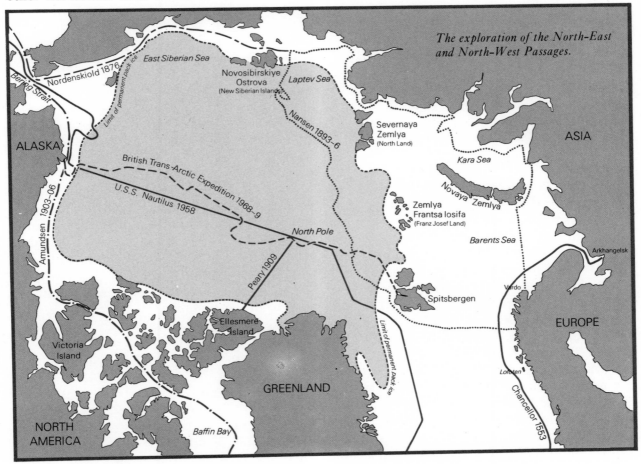

The exploration of the North-East and North-West Passages.

in June 1597, as did all but three of his men who eventually returned to Amsterdam.

As a matter of subsequent interest, Barent's winter quarters on Novaya Zemlya were not found until as late as 1871. Long before this, however, his name had been given to the sea to the east of North Cape, by which he is today remembered. But although his voyage and others of around this time made notable discoveries, none came near to finding a way through from the White Sea to the Bering Strait. So interest in the North-East Passage waned and did not revive until the nineteenth century.

Long before this a number of English explorers followed up Cabot's and Cartier's attempts to discover a North-West Passage. Martin Frobisher made three voyages (1576–78), to get as far as the bay named after him. John Davis also made three voyages (1585–87) and discovered the strait that bears his name. (Later (1592) he voyaged south and discovered the Falkland Islands.) And the already-mentioned Hudson made four voyages on which he discovered Jan Mayen Island and subsequently Canada's Hudson Bay. There his ship, the 55-tons *Discovery*, was frozen in for the winter (1610–11), which provoked his crew to mutiny and to set him adrift, with his son, and the few who remained loyal to him. Henry Greene, leader of the mutiny, was subsequently killed by Eskimos; others died before the *Discovery* reached England, where the rest were imprisoned. But of Hudson and his companions nothing more was seen or heard.

William Baffin made five voyages (1612–16), penetrating the North-West Passage as far as the bay that bears his name. And Luke Fox and Thomas James explored even further (1631). But whether there was, in truth, a North-West Passage, eluded them, just as it did those who tried to find one to the north-east. So, as with the latter, interest in discovering it waned and was not renewed until the nineteenth century.

DAMPIER

As Spanish and Portuguese power and influence declined in the seventeenth century and Britain began to acquire an empire, so in the eighteenth century were the most famous voyages made by Englishmen. This is not to decry those made by such navigators as Vitus Bering, the Dane who discovered the sea named after him which divides Siberia from Alaska (1728), and later found the Aleutian Islands and Alaska itself (1741), and by Chivikov, the first Russian to cross the north Pacific to California (1741).

Born in Somerset in 1652, William Dampier was first apprenticed at 18 for a voyage to the Newfoundland fisheries. A subsequent one to Java in an East Indiaman aroused his lasting interest in that part of the world. Many years elapsed, however, before he could pursue it.

He served in the Royal Navy during the Third Dutch War, then worked on a sugar plantation in Jamaica, followed by logwood cutting near the Bay of Campeachey. This being the nursery of many an English buccaneer, he was drawn to their type of life. Joining a band led by Captain Bartholomew Sharp, he marched across the central American isthmus to attack the town of Panama. There they seized a Spanish ship and went on to pillage Spain's outposts along the coast of Peru.

In 1680 Dampier quarrelled with Sharp and, with 50 others, left him and returned to Panama and back to the Gulf of Mexico. There he followed a buccaneering career until he joined a new band led by Captain Cook (*not* the famous explorer of that name to be mentioned shortly) who in 1683 set out on a piratical voyage to the South Seas. This proved to be a combination of great hardships at sea, when the starving men went so far as to propose killing and eating their officers, and drunkenness and debauchery at the islands at which they called. Nonetheless, Dampier managed to keep a journal, in which he recorded many useful observations of the winds and tides, flora and fauna.

However, Dampier wearied of the life favoured by many of his companions to such an extent that he and some of the crew deserted while they were in the Philippines. They began a fresh voyage of their own to the Spice Islands and, in 1685, they went as far south as the Australian mainland. The existence of a continent in this part of the world, long suspected, was first appreciated by Luis Torres, a Portuguese navigator who, in Spain's employment, discovered as early as 1606 the strait that bears his name between New Guinea and northern Australia. But not until 1642 did Abel Tasman, a navigator employed by the Dutch East Indies Company, set out to discover whether such a continent existed. He not only circumnavigated it, calling it New Holland, but he also found the large island that bears his name, followed by New Zealand and several lesser south Pacific islands. Nonetheless, the whole area remained uncharted, so that it was supposed that Tasmania was a part of the Australian mainland. That it was in reality an island had to await *its* circumnavigation by George Bass and Matthew Flinders in 1798. Dampier returned to England in 1691. There, in 1699, he persuaded the Admiralty to appoint him in command of HMS *Roebuck*, with orders to survey Australian waters. This he did down much of the west coast, until the need to refit and reprovision his ship obliged him to head for Timor. Not long after he again set out to continue his work by way of New Guinea, his crew mutinied against his harsh discipline and compelled him to sail for home. En route the *Roebuck* was wrecked on Ascension Island, where her crew's distress signals were seen by

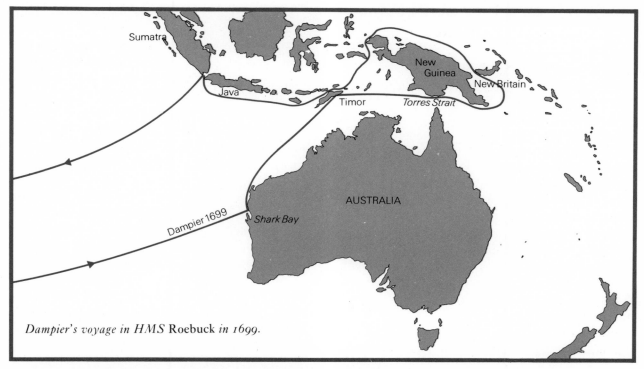

Dampier's voyage in HMS Roebuck *in 1699.*

an East Indiaman which took them on to England in 1701. Dampier was subsequently convicted by a court martial for his conduct in the *Roebuck*, heavily fined and dismissed from the Service.

Notwithstanding this proof of his unfitness for command, Dampier's enviable reputation as a navigator remained unsullied. In 1703 he obtained command of two privateers which were being sent to the Pacific. This voyage was, however, an unmitigated disaster. The captain of the ship accompanying the *St George*, in which Dampier sailed, soon tired of his autocratic ways and parted company. Next, the crew of the *St George* mutinied, most of them leaving her in a captured vessel in which they returned home. Left with only 27 men in the *St George*, Dampier had to abandon all ideas of loading her with captured treasure, and sailed instead for England. But in the Gulf of Panama the *St George*'s timbers proved so rotten that her bottom fell out. Only because they had recently captured a Spanish ship were Dampier and his handful of companions able to return home in 1707 by way of the Cape of Good Hope. This his second circumnavigation of the globe was, incidentally, the one on which Alexander Selkirk was, at his own request, marooned on one of the Juan Fernández islands in the Pacific.

A year later Dampier set out on his third and last voyage around the world, not this time in command but as navigator to Captain Woodes Rogers. En route they rescued Selkirk after he had lived all alone for four years and brought him back to England, which inspired Daniel Defoe to write the immortal story of *Robinson Crusoe*. More important, in another way, through Rogers's skill and initiative they brought home in 1711 a shipload of treasure. Dampier did not, however, live to enjoy his share of the profits for very long for he died in 1715.

COOK

More than half a century elapsed before anyone made a serious attempt to follow up the discoveries of Tasman and Dampier. Not until 1768 did James Cook make his first voyage to the Antipodes. But before dealing with his discoveries we must mention George Anson's circumnavigation of the globe.

After nearly 30 years of service in the Royal Navy, Anson was appointed commodore at the age of 40 of a squadron of six ships sent to the Pacific on the outbreak of the War of the Austrian Succession in 1740. With orders to do as much damage as possible to Spanish interests, he rounded the Horn to spend the next three years capturing Spanish ships and raiding their ports. During this time various mishaps reduced his force to no more than his flagship, the *Centurion*, and the large majority of his men fell victims of scurvy. Yet in June 1743, while cruising through the Philippines, he seized treasure valued at £500,000 from a Spanish vessel.

After his promotion to flag rank in 1745, Anson became well known for his victory over the French Admiral de la Jonquière off Cape Finisterre in 1747. And having been created a peer, he was one of Britain's most successful First Lords of the Admiralty from 1751 (except for one brief interval) until his death in 1762. Those fourteen years are notable on the one hand for the highly successful strategy with which he and the Elder Pitt pursued the Seven Years War which gained for England both Canada and India, and on the other for his numerous administrative reforms. Best remembered of these are his classification of ships-of-the-line into six different rates according to the number of guns they mounted, and the introduction of a standard uniform for officers whose colour was subsequently adopted by other navies world wide.

Born in 1728, Cook was the son of a Yorkshire labourer. Largely self-educated, he became a skilful navigator and mate of a ship within six years of becoming a sea-apprentice. Deciding that the merchant service offered little scope for his ambitions, he joined the Royal Navy in 1755 as an able-seaman. That Service quickly recognized Cook's exceptional qualities; he was promoted to boatswain and then to be master (*i.e.* navigator) of HMS *Solebay*, followed by HMS *Pembroke*. The latter ship accompanied the fleet with which Admiral Boscawen and General Amhurst captured Louisburg (1758), and with which Admiral Saunders and General Wolfe captured Quebec (1759), when Cook's skill in surveying the St Lawrence River attracted considerable attention.

He was next master of the British flagship in North American waters, until after the end of the Seven Years War, when he spent five years surveying the coast of Newfoundland. His work having by now come to the notice of the influential Royal Society, he was chosen to be one of their observers to go to Tahiti to record the transit of Venus across the face of the sun. But the Admiralty trumped this ace by vetoing a civilian commander, Alexander Dalrymple, for the expedition and appointing Cook to lead it. Moreover, he was ordered to go on from Tahiti to search for the legendary Terra Australis Incognita, and to confirm Tasman's discovery of New Zealand, before returning to England via the Cape of Good Hope.

Cook sailed from Plymouth in August 1768 in command of HMS *Endeavour*, to round Cape Horn and reach Tahiti in April 1769. Having duly observed the transit of Venus, Cook headed the *Endeavour* south from Tahiti in July. Having gone as far as latitude 40° S, where the heavy swell convinced him that there could be nothing but open sea in that direction, he turned west. In October he not only sighted New Zealand but discovered the strait that bears his name between the North and South Islands.

Next Cook decided to explore the east coast of New Holland (Australia), where he anchored in Botany Bay, six miles to the south of where the city of Sydney was later to be built, and became the first European to encounter the implacably hostile, primitive aborigines. Continuing northwards, inside the Great Barrier Reef, Cook had the misfortune to run the *Endeavour* on to a coral reef. However, he managed to get his ship off this obstacle, and to take her for repairs into the estuary of the river which now bears her name.

Sailing again early in August 1770, Cook coasted north to Cape York, then passed through the strait bearing de Torres's name to confirm that New Guinea was not a part of Australia, before heading for Batavia in October. There the *Endeavour*'s crew was tragically decimated by malaria and dysentry before Cook could sail her round the Cape of Good Hope to reach English waters in July 1771.

The barque Endeavour, *366 tons, in which Captain Cook circumnavigated the globe during 1768–71.*

Because he remained convinced that the legendary Terra Australis Incognita must exist, and fearing that it would be discovered and claimed by the French, Cook decided to try again. For this expedition he sailed in HMS *Resolution* with HMS *Adventure* in company in July 1772, this time by way of the Cape, to head south-east into the unknown. And in January 1773 he became the first navigator to cross the Antarctic Circle. Ice then obliged him to turn north so that he reached New Zealand's Queen Charlotte Sound in March, having this time clearly established that, at least in the eastern hemisphere, there was no large undiscovered continent. Having refitted his ships, he went on to obtain similar proof for an area as far as the meridian of Pitcairn Island before turning north-west to reach Tahiti in July.

Soon after sailing again from this island, intending another visit to the Antarctic, Cook's two ships lost touch with each other. Unable to find the *Resolution* again, Commander Tobias Furneaux took the *Adventure* home by way of Cape Horn, thereby becoming the first commander to circumnavigate the globe from west to east. The *Resolution* went on from Queen Charlotte's Sound to cross the Antarctic Circle twice, as far as latitude 71°70′ S on 30 January 1774, before being turned back by ice. Next Cook explored more of the Pacific. Although he made no fresh discoveries, he charted the Marquesas, the Friendly Isles, New Caledonia and much more, before returning to Queen Charlotte's Sound in the autumn of 1774 for a final refit. He sailed for home in November, taking the *Resolution* far to the south across the Pacific before rounding the Horn to visit South Georgia. Only there did he turn north to reach Portsmouth in July 1775, when he was promoted to post-captain and elected a Fellow of the Royal Society.

A year later, at the age of 48, Cook sailed again in the *Resolution*, this time with HMS *Discovery* in company. He was ordered to go via the Cape and the French Indian Ocean islands, notably Kerguelen, to Tahiti. Thence he was to head for the west coast of North America and try to find that elusive North-West Passage. All went reasonably well as far as Tahiti. Thence Cook sailed to discover, in January 1778, the Sandwich Islands, now known as the Hawaiian Islands, before sighting the North American coast in March. From Nootka Sound the two ships coasted north, then west along the southern shore of Alaska, and north through the Bering Strait, until ice barred their way in latitude 70°30′ N.

Having accomplished so much – and the North-West Passage itself was to elude discovery for more than another century – Cook took his ships back to the Sandwich Islands to refit them in Hawaii's Kealakekua Bay. Two days after his departure in February, the *Resolution* sprang her foremast, and Cook was obliged to return. Hostility arose when one of the *Resolution*'s boats was stolen by some of the islanders, and Cook went ashore to take a hostage for the boat's return. He was met by a mob, one of whom attacked him, whereupon Cook fired one barrel of his shotgun in self-defence which provoked a general assault in which he was stabbed to death.

DE BOUGAINVILLE

Cook's voyages straddled a notable one by a Frenchman. Born in 1729 Louis Antoine Bougainville began his career as a lawyer. In 1752 he gained the distinction of a fellowship of Britain's Royal Society for a treatise on the integral calculus, after which he was a secretary in the French Embassy in London. Following the outbreak of the Seven Years War, he served with distinction under General Montcalm in Canada, first as his A.D.C., later in command of a corps.

Having by now become something of a Jack of all trades, he followed the Peace of Paris by turning his attention to the sea at the late age of 34. He financed an expedition which colonized the Falkland Islands. But Spain raised such strong objections to this that, in 1766, the French Government appointed Bougainville in command of the frigate *Boudeuse*, with orders to evacuate the settlement. The rapidity with which he achieved post-rank in the French navy is noteworthy.

From the Falklands Bougainville took the *Boudeuse* through the Straits of Magellan and across the south Pacific, where he took possession of Tahiti for his country, Britain's Captain Samuel Wallis, another circumnavigator, who discovered the island eight months earlier, having neglected to stake any such claim. Continuing westward Bougainville found his way barred by the Great Barrier Reef off Australia's eastern seaboard. So he headed north to weather New Guinea, by way of the Solomon Islands, the Moluccas and Batavia. Thence he crossed the Indian Ocean to round the Cape of Good Hope and to reach St Malo in 1769. He was thus the first Frenchman to circumnavigate the globe.

Bougainville subsequently gained flag rank, to fight in the War of American Independence under Admiral de Grasse, and to command the van of the French fleet in the battle fought off The Saints on 12 April 1782 at which Admiral Rodney won a decisive British victory. Bougainville later gained favour with Napoleon who created him the Comte de Bougainville, and appointed him a senator and a member of the Legion of Honour. He died in 1811, and is now best remembered by the flamboyant scarlet creeper which he discovered in South America, now widely known as Bougainvillea.

PERRY

In the whole of the nineteenth century no voyage had greater consequences than one undertaken by Matthew Calbraith Perry. Born at Newport, Rhode Island, in 1794, Perry entered the United States Navy in time to fight for his country against Britain during the War of 1812. After subsequent service on various overseas stations, he attained the rank of commodore, then the highest in his navy, with a reputation for being a strict disciplinarian which, coupled with his gruff voice, led to him being known as 'Old Bruin'. From 1843–45 Perry was in command of his country's Africa Squadron, when he played a substantial part in the foundation of the Republic of Liberia. But his chief claim to fame rests on the voyages which he made while in command of the U.S. East India Squadron.

By fighting the First Opium War (1839–42), Britain compelled China to open five, and later more, of her ports (known as Treaty Ports) to foreign trade – specifically for India's opium crop. Because the U.S.A. also required new outlets for her products, Congress decided to persuade Japan, whose rulers had kept their country closed to all foreigners for more than two centuries, to open their ports. In 1853 Perry was ordered to take the steam frigate *Mississippi*, with the similar *Susquehanna* in company, into Japan's Sagami Bay, bearing a letter from the President to the Emperor to this effect. The Japanese were hostile, but eventually accepted the letter. Perry then sailed for Okinawa in the Ryukyus which did not come under Japanese domination until 1879, and which in 1945 was the scene of some of the fiercest fighting that took place during the Second World War. Since 'colonialism' and 'imperialism' were not yet ugly words in America, he hoisted the Stars and Stripes on Mount Shuri, and forced the King of the Ryukyus to sign a treaty guaranteeing favourable treatment for American merchant ships visiting this group of islands.

In February 1854 Perry returned to Japan, anchoring this time off Yokosuka. Satisfied that conquest was not his purpose, the Emperor's representatives signed the Treaty of Kanagawa on 31 March. This opened Shimoda and Hakodate as Treaty Ports, provided for the return of imprisoned shipwrecked American seamen, and allowed for the establishment of a U.S. consulate.

This notable success ended Perry's active career. On his death in 1858 he was accorded a state funeral. And the U.S.A. was not alone in appreciating his achievements: Japan erected several monuments to him.

ROSS, PARRY AND FRANKLIN

Most of the world's oceans were effectively surveyed in the nineteenth century. The young British naturalist Charles Darwin sailed in HM sloop *Beagle* to the Pacific (1831–36), which led him to write several classic books including his highly controversial *Origin of Species*; and the American Joshua Slocum became the first man to circumnavigate the globe single-handed (1895–98). More significant, however, were the renewed attempts to open up the North-West and North-East Passages.

Not satisfied with the progress which had been made towards finding the north-west route to the Indies, Parliament as early as 1714 offered a reward of £20,000 to the first British subject to discover a way from the Atlantic to the Pacific round the north of Canada. But this Act excepted naval vessels, and for all of a century produced nothing. It required a fresh law in 1817, removing the exception, to spur the Admiralty into organizing an expedition under Commodore (later Sir) John Ross, comprised of HM ships *Isabella* and *Alexander*, with William Edward Parry as his second-in-command. They penetrated Davis Strait and Baffin Bay as far as Lancaster Sound in 1818 before being confronted with what Ross believed to be mountains.

A famous Secretary of the Admiralty, Sir John Barrow, so far doubted the existence of this barrier that, in the next year, a second naval expedition was sent to Lancaster Sound, this time under Parry's command. Sailing in HMS *Hecla* and *Griper* in 1819, these two vessels did not return to England until the autumn of 1820, which made them the first to winter in this part of the Arctic. But this was far from being Parry's only achievement: he not only showed that Ross's mountain barrier did not exist, but penetrated through Lancaster Sound, Barrow Strait and Melville Sound as far as Melville Island. This encouraged the Admiralty to instruct him to lead a second expedition, of HMS *Fury* and *Hecla*, in 1821, and a third with the same vessels in 1824–25, which was marred by the loss of the *Fury*. Parry was subsequently knighted and promoted to flag rank. Neither of these voyages was, however, more successful than those undertaken in the same year by Captain George Lyon in HMS *Griper*, and by Captain (later Rear-Admiral) Frederick Beechey in HMS *Blossom*, both of whom tried to find an eastward route from the Bering Strait.

Ross was next back on the scene, this time with a privately financed expedition which sailed in 1829 and did not return until 1833. He was compelled to spend all of four winters on the Boothia Peninsula after his ship, the *Victory*, had been wrecked, during which his nephew and second-in-command, (later Sir) James Clark Ross, discovered the magnetic Pole. Three years after Ross's return, Captain (later Sir) George Back sought the North-West Passage as unsuccessfully in HMS *Terror* in which he spent one winter in the Arctic.

There followed the tragedy of Sir John

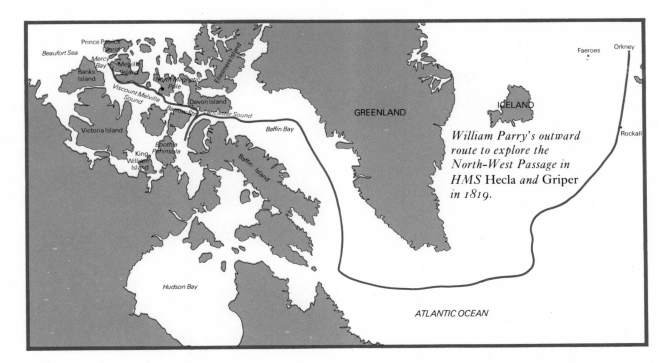

William Parry's outward route to explore the North-West Passage in HMS Hecla *and* Griper *in 1819.*

Franklin. Born in 1786, Franklin served in HMS *Polyphemus* at the battle of Copenhagen, and in HMS *Bellerophon* at Trafalgar, before becoming a notable surveyor and explorer. After being promoted to post-captain, elected a Fellow of the Royal Society, honoured with a knighthood, and serving for seven years as Governor of Tasmania, he was chosen to command HMS *Erebus* which, with HMS *Terror*, was ordered to find the North-West Passage in 1845.

These two vessels crossed the Atlantic, to be sighted at the head of Baffin Bay on 26 July. Nothing more was heard or seen of them. Not until 1857 did Captain (later Admiral Sir) Francis McClintock, in the yacht *Fox*, discover a cairn containing the log of the expedition up to April 1848. From this it became clear that, when the *Erebus* and *Terror* were near to finding a passage through Peel Sound, both ships were trapped in the ice off King William Island. Eighteen months later Franklin decided to abandon his ships and to march south with his crews, but none of them survived the rigours of this hazardous overland journey.

Ironically enough, well before McClintock made this find, another British naval officer, Captain (later Admiral Sir) Robert McClure, who set out in HMS *Investigator* in 1850, had actually discovered the North-West Passage. His ship was subsequently wrecked in Mercy Bay and had to be abandoned in June 1853. But, more fortunate than Franklin and his companions, McClure and his crew, after suffering much from scurvy, were rescued by HMS *Resolute*, Captain (later Admiral Sir) Henry Kellett, in 1854. But although the North-West Passage had thus been found, it was clearly not a practicable route for navigation even in the summer months – at least not with the ships then available. Indeed, not until the next century was any further attempt made to use it. During the years

1903–06 the Norwegian, Roald Amundsen, in the 50-ton fishing smack *Gjøa*, explored the whole route. But this success was not again challenged until 1940, when the Royal Canadian Patrol boat *St Roch* accomplished the voyage, and repeated it in 1944.

Since then the North-West Passage has been used occasionally in summer by specially-designed icebreaking vessels, notably those under the Canadian Captains O.C. Robertson in 1954 and C. Pullen in 1956 and 1957. More recently it has been navigated by U.S. nuclear submarines, the first being the *Nautilus*, Commander W.R. Anderson, USN, in 1958. But, except for freighters proceeding as far as Hudson Bay, no regular use has yet been found for this route which joins the Atlantic to the Pacific despite all the efforts of so many distinguished explorers to locate it.

NORDENSKIÖLD

The opposite is true of the North-East Passage, although the distance along the north of Russia, in Europe and in Asia, is much greater. The extent to which various English and other navigators penetrated it in the sixteenth and seventeenth centuries has already been mentioned. The next notable progress was made by the Russian Great Northern Expedition between 1733 and 1743. Comprised of a number of separate parties which travelled overland to the sea at various points, this succeeded in mapping the whole of the north Russian seaboard. Not, however, until the first half of the nineteenth century were any attempts made to follow up this work.

Several Russian expeditions, mostly naval, then clarified particular regions. But the honour of making the first voyage right through from west to east fell to a Swedish Finn. Born in 1832, to become a professor of geology, Nils A.E.

Nordenskiöld took part in a number of expeditions to Spitzbergen and Greenland. Then, in the early summer of 1875, he began one in the *Vega*. With the advantage of an auxiliary steam engine as well as a full rig of sails, this 300-tons barque voyaged to within 100 miles of the Bering Strait before, in September, ice prevented further progress. There, almost in sight of reaching his goal in a single season, Nordenskiöld had to pass the winter. Not until the summer of 1876 was he able to complete his circumnavigation of the continents of Europe and Asia. Although Nordenskiöld made other voyages before his death in 1901, this initial penetration of the North-East Passage, for which he was created a baron, remained the feat for which his name is now remembered.

The *Vega*'s success was soon followed by others, although not all the subsequent explorers of this desolate part of the world aimed to pass along the whole route. The American G.N. de Long in the *Jeanette* was trapped in the ice while trying to find the North Pole by way of the Bering Strait. She drifted across the East Siberian Sea for nearly two years before being crushed and sunk (1879–81). The Norwegian Fridtjof Nansen explored the Kara and Laptev Seas before allowing his 402-tons *Fram* to be frozen in and to drift across the Arctic Ocean (1893–96). And the Russian Baron E. Toll in the yacht *Zarya* followed Nansen's route as far as Novosibirskiye Ostrova (1900–1902). Nansen was, however, the only one of this trio to survive such hazardous voyages.

The next significant attempt to make the full journey was undertaken in 1912 by two Russians, G.L. Bruschov in the *St Anna* and V.A. Rusanov in the *Gerkulis*, but this expedition met disaster in the Kara Sea. B.A. Vilkitskiy in the *Taymyr* and *Vaygach* was more successful in 1914–15, achieving the first recorded voyage through from east to west. Four years later the whole route was again successfully explored from west to east (1918–20) by Roald Amundsen. But not until 1932 was the complete voyage first achieved in a single season, by the Russian explorer Otto Schmidt in the Soviet icebreaker *Sibiryakov*.

During the Second World War the Northern Route was used by at least one German disguised armed merchant raider, the *Komet*, to reach the Pacific without risking an encounter with Allied warships in the Atlantic; by the Soviet icebreaker *Joseph Stalin* which was the first vessel to complete the double journey in a single season; and by ships of the Soviet Pacific fleet reinforcing their Atlantic fleet after the Nazi assault on the U.S.S.R. in 1941.

Helped by a dozen large, modern icebreakers, notably the nuclear-powered, 16,500-tons *Lenin*, the Northern Sea Route is now used regularly each summer by between 200 and 300 Soviet freighters.

PEARY AND AMUNDSEN

Born in 1856 at Cresson, Pennsylvania, Robert Peary joined the U.S. Navy's civil engineer corps in 1881. He first explored Greenland in 1881, then did so again ten years later, when, with a Norwegian companion, he crossed the ice-cap to prove that Greenland is an island. In 1908, Peary returned to Greenland in the *Roosevelt* and, accompanied only by his negro servant and four Eskimos, he travelled north by sledge and succeeded in becoming the first man to reach the North Pole on 6 April 1909. There he stayed for 30 hours, sounding through a fracture in the ice to find no bottom at 1,500 fathoms. Peary received the thanks of Congress for his achievement and was promoted to rear-admiral on the retired list before he died in 1920.

Since Peary's triumph the North Pole has been reached entirely by sea. The nuclear-powered submarine USS *Skate* travelled under the ice-cap, to break through it and surface at the Pole on 17 March 1959, a feat subsequently repeated by British as well as by other U.S. submarines, and no doubt by ones from the U.S.S.R. Moreover, one cannot go on to deal with the discovery of the South Pole without mentioning a British Trans-Arctic Expedition under W. Herbert, which sledged all the way across the ice-cap from Alaska to Spitzbergen by way of the North Pole as recently as 1968–69.

Unlike the North Pole, which is in the centre of an ice-capped ocean, the South Pole is in the middle of the ice-bound continent of Antarctica. Of this, as already mentioned, the outlying island of South Georgia was discovered by Captain Cook on his second great voyage of exploration (1775). The South Shetland Isles were found by another Englishman, William Smith (1819). The mainland was first sighted by an Englishman, Edward Branfield, and an American, Nathaniel Palmer (1820). And this last continent to be discovered was first circumnavigated by the Russian Thaddeus von Bellingshausen (1821–22). Other voyages to open up these profitable sealing and whaling waters followed, notably those by an Englishman, James Weddell, who entered the sea that bears his name and achieved the record latitude of 74° 15′ S. (1823), by another Englishman, John Biscoe (1830), and by Peter Kemp (1833–34).

A Frenchman, Jules Dumont d'Urville, failed to penetrate the Weddell Sea as far south as Weddell had done (1838), but subsequently discovered Terre Adélie (1840). Lieutenant Charles Wilkes, USN, reached latitude 70° S. (1839) and Ross (discoverer of the north magnetic Pole) with HMS *Erebus* and *Terror* penetrated as far as latitude 78° 4′ S. (1842). Half a century elapsed before anyone made another significant voyage in this region; but those which were then made by explorers of many nations – from HMS *Challenger*, the first steam vessel to cross the Antarctic Circle (1874) to Sir Ernest Shackleton's vain attempt to reach the South Pole (1908) – are too numerous to mention here if we are to record the achievements of Robert Falcon Scott and Roald Amundsen.

Born in 1868, Scott followed a normal career in the Royal Navy until 1899, when he was chosen to command the specially designed polar exploration vessel *Discovery* of 485 tons. In her he explored Victoria Land, in the New Zealand sector of Antarctica, reaching latitude 82° 17′ S. (1901–1904), before returning to normal naval service and being promoted to captain. Then, in 1910, he sailed in the 749-tons barque *Terra Nova* with the announced intention of achieving the ultimate goal that had eluded Shackleton, that of reaching the South Pole.

Amundsen, a Norwegian and four years the younger man, devoted his life to polar exploration from as early as 1897. Most of his initial years were spent in the Arctic, using the 50-tons *Gjøa*. But in 1910 he equipped the 402-tons schooner *Fram*, which had been used by Nansen to explore the Arctic, for an attempt to reach the South Pole. Scott only learned of this on his arrival in New Zealand. Thenceforward the race was on.

Scott took the *Terra Nova* as far south as the ice would allow; then on 1 November set out at the head of a sledge party for the Pole. By 4 January 1912 he had reached the foot of the Beardmore Glacier, and all his support parties had turned back. With only four companions, Scott pressed on to reach the Pole on the 18th – but did not achieve his aim. The Norwegian flag was already flying there because, by avoiding the Beardmore Glacier, Amundsen and his four companions had already reached the Pole on 14 December. How ironic the fact that, after so many years, this exceptionally difficult feat should be accomplished by one distinguished explorer, a Norwegian, just four weeks before another, an Englishman.

There was tragedy in it too. Amundsen's return journey was accomplished without incident; but Scott's was marred by a series of disasters, and shortage of food and fuel. After two members of his party had died, the remaining three were caught by a blizzard in which they, too, perished when only eleven miles from safety, their bodies being found eight months later. But though they failed in their purpose, the names of Dr E.A. Wilson, Captain L.E.G. Oates, Lieutenant H.R. Bowers and Petty Officer Edgar Evans, as well as that of Scott himself, will always be remembered as those of five

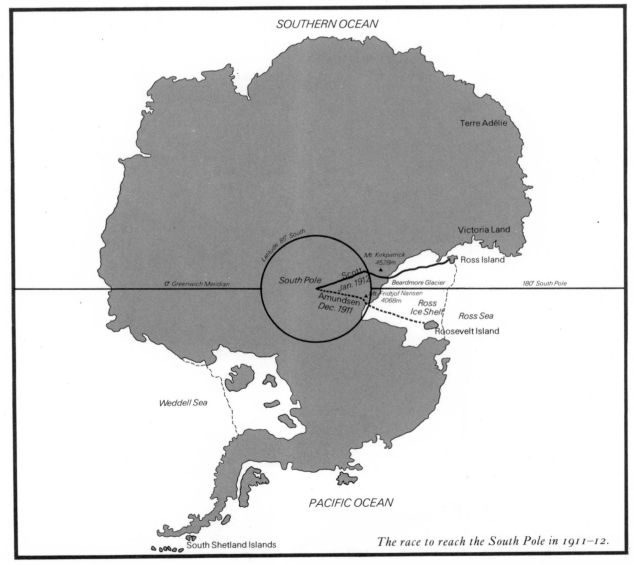

The race to reach the South Pole in 1911–12.

Englishmen who, by their courage, endurance and self-sacrifice, set for all time a supreme example.

Amundsen resumed his exploration of the Arctic after the First World War, at first in the polar ship *Maud* (1919–21), and subsequently by air. He met his death in 1928 when, in an attempt to rescue the crew of the airship *Italia*, wrecked off Spitzbergen, his seaplane vanished without trace.

It might be thought that since both Poles had been reached, there would be no opportunity for man to make further famous voyages. Yet there have already been the following, to mention just a few. In the First World War the German Admiral Graf von Spee's East Asiatic Squadron accomplished the exceptionally difficult eastwards voyage across the Pacific – exceptionally difficult because these ships had no bases at which to coal – to win the battle of Coronel on 1 November 1914, the first defeat inflicted on the British Navy for more than a hundred years. In the Second World War the Polish submarine *Orzel* escaped from internment in an Estonian port in September 1939, to travel out of the Baltic and across the North Sea to Rosyth, *without charts* to find the way – a unique feat of navigation. Again in the Second World War, German armed merchant raiders sometimes stayed at sea for as long as a year. And in more recent times a U.S. nuclear submarine circumnavigated the globe submerged throughout; the Norwegian Dr Thor Heyerdahl travelled 3,800 miles from South America to Polynesia on the *Kon-tiki*, a raft of balsa wood (1947); Sir Francis Chichester circumnavigated the world single-handed in the yacht *Gipsy Moth IV* (1966) in only 274 days, a tenth of the time taken by Joshua Slocum, and Sir Alec Rose did likewise in the yacht *Lively Lady* (1967–68).

In short, the navigators and explorers of the past may, by their exploits, have opened up all the world for mankind, but of the making of famous voyages there is no end.

Of the ships mentioned in this chapter the following are today preserved as 'museums':

Name	Type	Place	Country
Discovery	Research ship	London	England
Fram	Topsail schooner	Oslo	Norway
Gjøa	Sloop	San Francisco	U.S.A.
Gipsy Moth IV	Yacht	London	England
Kon-tiki	Raft	Oslo	Norway
Mayflower II	Replica of original	Plymouth, Mass.	U.S.A.
Santa Maria	Replica of original	Barcelona	Spain

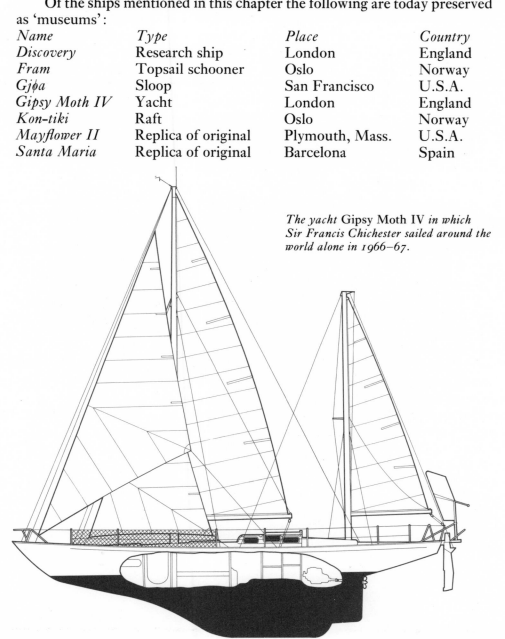

The yacht Gipsy Moth IV *in which Sir Francis Chichester sailed around the world alone in 1966–67.*

Cargo and Container Ships

DURING THE MIDDLE AGES the English ranged the seas of Europe. They carried wool to France and cloth to the Low Countries; they passed through the Straits of Gibraltar, between the Pillars of Hercules which once had marked the limits of the known world; they sailed to Venice and the Greek islands and called at the busy ports of the Levant, sometimes on voyages lasting a year.

Not until the reign of Elizabeth did the English devote any serious thought to making a settlement in the New World. Most voyagers – the Pilgrim Fathers were among the great exceptions – intended to come back again bringing something with them unless they were looking, like Cabot, for the way to richer cargoes. Men dreamed of finding the North-West Passage or – somewhere near Mozambique perhaps – the mysterious Land of Prester John.

Valuable cargoes were indeed brought home from afar. On 31 December 1600 the British East India Company came into existence, and traded until 1 June 1874. In the course of that long period, two and three-quarter centuries, it became a vast trading empire with powers resembling those of a sovereign state – for 'John Company' had its own army and navy, civil service and mercantile marine, and even a college (Haileybury in Hertfordshire). It was formed by London merchants who had petitioned the Queen for a charter granting them the monopoly of the trade. Before they had received this document, they bought four vessels, the *Dragon* (formerly a privateer), and the *Hector*, *Ascension* and *Susan*. Accompanied by a supply ship, the *Guest*, the four left the Thames in February 1600 carrying trade goods together with presents for the Indian princes. Calm weather in the Channel delayed them, and it was April when they put out from Dartmouth. They reached the Canary Islands in May, crossed the Equator in June and were then held back by more calms. When they came to the site of Cape Town in September all on board were suffering from scurvy except those who had been given three spoonsful of lemon juice every morning. They voyaged for a little more than a year before anchoring off Sumatra where they were welcomed by a royal procession of elephants.

Marco Polo had evidently told the truth. But what the English most needed from the wealth of the Indies was pepper. They filled their holds with it in the islands and then set out for England. They had been away nearly three years, and when they returned after many trials and tragedies the Queen was dead, London was stricken by the plague and the market already had more pepper than the public needed for a time. However the voyage eventually brought in a large profit.

At first the East India Company was concerned with the spices of the islands off the south-eastern corner of Asia. It showed little interest in India itself until the Dutch, who had had their own East India Company since 1602, fought them successfully for the Spice Islands trade and compelled them to find other cargoes on the Indian subcontinent. The new venture had immense consequences, the creation of Britain's Indian Empire.

After leasing the Deptford yard for 20 years, John Company decided that it would be less costly to hire ships. Nearly all the later East Indiamen came from the yard at Blackwall, where a whole community derived its livelihood from shipbuilding and seafaring. The vessels looked very much like the warships of their time and were sometimes mistaken for them. At night they snugged down; unlike the clippers which succeeded them, they had no need to hurry. Life on board was comfortable by the standards of the time within a stern naval-style discipline and the company took care of its men at sea and on shore. One of its many rules laid down the complement to be carried; 101 for a ship of 750 to 800 tons, 110 for one of 900 tons, and so on.

History of Ship Design

EARLY TIMES

The genesis of the ship is lost in the mists of antiquity. We know, however, that primitive man carried his goods across water on logs bound together in the form of a RAFT. There is, indeed, evidence that by this means he crossed not only seas but oceans. It was not long, however, before man realized that he could make better progress in a desired direction if he used the hollowed-out trunk of a tree. But aversion to the labour which building such a craft involved, with the elementary tools then available, led him to devise a circular skeleton (*frame*) of strips of wood lashed together, which he covered with skins or hides. (This very early type of vessel, called a CORACLE [or currach], is still used by fishermen in Wales and Ireland.) American Indians likewise used birch bark to cover a frame of the shape known as a CANOE.

Neither of these craft, which were of a size which we should term generically a BOAT, could carry many passengers, nor more than a small quantity of goods. To remedy this deficiency man began to build larger vessels using the same basic principle. The frame of a SHIP comprised a longitudinal *keel* (backbone) – with *stem-* and *stern-posts*, and athwartships *ribs* – which was transformed into a watertight vessel by covering it with a *skin*, initially of bundles of reeds, later of planks coated with pitch. These might overlap (*clinker built*) or be flush (*carvel built*), the latter becoming the more usual form. Iron nails replaced the wooden pegs with which a ship's *scantlings* were secured as soon as they became available. Otherwise, except for the addition of longitudinal members (*stringers*) to give the frame greater strength, ships were built in this way for so long as wood reigned supreme.

Moreover, when iron came into general use early in the nineteenth century, this principle was adapted to it. Iron scantlings secured by

Opposite: The USS Bainbridge, *a nuclear-powered guided-missile frigate.*

rivets replaced timbers secured by nails. So, too, with the later use of steel; indeed, as may be seen today in any shipyard where a vessel is under construction on a launching slipway, this idea is still the basic principle of almost all ship design.

The oldest ship of which we have definite knowledge was built for the funeral of the Pharaoh Cheops (3960–3908 BC). Found in a trench near his tomb and covered with sand, this was 133 feet in length and had a maximum beam of 26 feet. Constructed of some 600 separate pieces of wood, the largest being 75 feet long, the probability is that it was used only for Cheops's funeral and never went to sea nor floated on the Nile. But there is plenty of evidence in contemporary rock carvings and paintings from which we can deduce that the Egyptians employed ships very like it for trading across the Mediterranean.

The same source tells us that, while such ships were normally propelled by *oars* manned by slaves, the Egyptians also harnessed the natural power of the wind by hoisting a rectangular *sail* of papyrus or cotton, hung from a *yard* which was hoisted on a *mast* stepped amidships. So, too, do we know that such a ship was steered by an extra large oar slung over her quarter from which the word *steerboard* was coined (hence 'starboard' for the right-hand side of a ship).

The Phoenicians, who ruled much of the Mediterranean littoral from about 1000 to 250 BC, improved on the Egyptian design. They built small vessels with which to trade within that sea, and larger TARSHISH SHIPS with which they ventured out through the Straits of Gibraltar, up to the Scilly Isles and, if Herodotus is to be believed, around Africa into the Indian Ocean.

From wall paintings found in tombs near Rome it appears that from about 450 BC, a ship's carrying capacity was increased by building up her *bulwarks*. The same source tells us that by this time some ships stepped two masts with a sail hoisted on each. Because they were so broad-beamed, such trading vessels were known as

161

ROUNDSHIPS. The Greeks increased their size. The Romans introduced the idea of partly *decking* them to give their crews shelter from the elements. They also appreciated that, by adjusting the angle of her sail, or sails, a ship could be steered on a course other than one with the wind blowing from right aft. In more northern waters the Scandinavians evolved a different form of hull better suited to weather Atlantic waves: their ships had a high bow and stern, both

box with a bow. Its stern was built up so that it would remain dry in a following sea. Inside, on the centre line, a second, vertical, watertight box contained the steering oar, which was thus near to the form which came to be known as a *rudder* when it was adopted in the West.

The Chinese decked these JUNKS; more importantly, they divided them into separate compartments by *transverse bulkheads*, an improvement which was not introduced in the

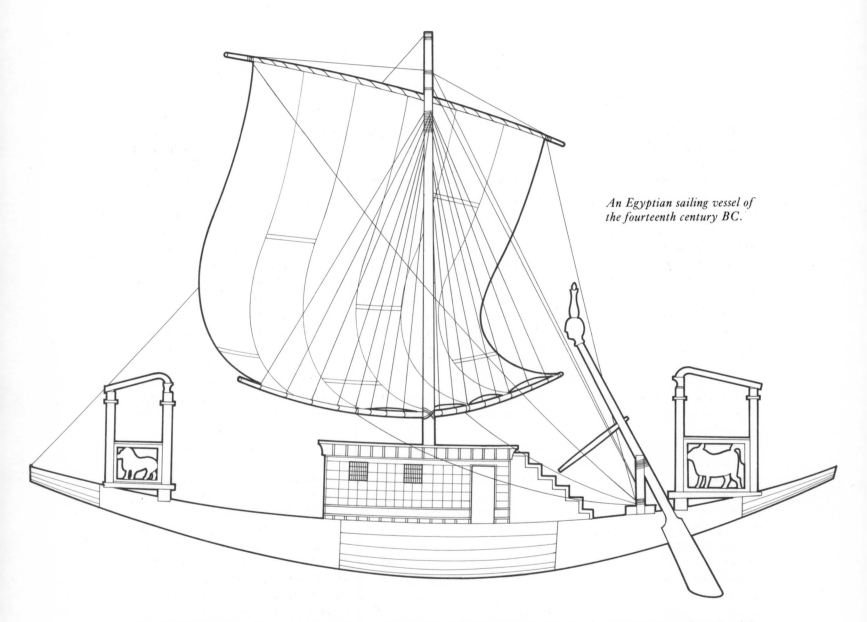

An Egyptian sailing vessel of the fourteenth century BC.

sharply pointed, with a well-rounded midships section, a design still used today for lifeboats.

The Arabs discovered the better sailing qualities of a large triangular sail over a rectangular one. Their *lateen* rigged DHOWS are still to be seen in, for example, the Red Sea. This innovation was subsequently adopted by the Egyptians for their FELUCCAS, which remain in use today on the Nile. But in the Far East the Chinese evolved an entirely different design of vessel. They joined two dugout canoes together with planking, then built up the sides, bow and stern to form a flat-bottomed wooden box (i.e. one without a keel). A wedge-shaped addition provided this

West until much later. They were rigged with one or two rectangular sails comprised of many narrow panels of straw matting, with which they could steer a course *close-hauled*. Junks were, indeed, considerably superior to any Western vessel built before the eighteenth century, in that they were more seaworthy and able to sail closer to the wind, which is one reason why such, to us, primitive craft are still to be seen carrying passengers and cargo off the Chinese coast and on the Yangtse and other Chinese rivers.

The Japanese also built junks, but theirs were squat and heavy and were not rigged with panelled sails. They were, therefore, never as

162

well suited for their purpose as the Chinese variety, for which reason they are seldom seen today.

In war the Egyptians and Phoenicians *armed* their trading ships with *soldiers* (hence the term WARSHIPS). These, when they came close to an enemy vessel, first hurled their spears at her, then tried to take her by *boarding* and then by hand-to-hand fighting with sword and shield (hence the term MAN-OF-WAR as an alternative to warship).

Appreciating the tactical advantage of speed in naval warfare, the Greeks evolved GALLEYS up to 100 feet in length with a beam of only 15 feet. BIREMES had two banks of oars; TRIREMES had three. To these they added two new weapons. One was *Greek Fire* (made chiefly of naphtha) with which they endeavoured to set an enemy vessel's masts and sails alight. The other was the *ram*, a massive wedge-shaped forefoot which, in a deliberate collision with an opponent, could hole and possibly sink her. With such ships and weapons the earliest of recorded naval actions, the battle of Salamis, was fought in 480 BC.

Larger galleys were later built. QUINQUEREMES, 150 feet in length, were propelled by five banks of oars, each being manned by four slaves. The Romans added a *corvus* to their galleys, a raised structure in the bow from which soldiers could more easily hurl their spears and javelins at the enemy and board more quickly. The Chinese and the Japanese likewise used their trading junks in war by 'arming' them with fighting men, when they became WAR JUNKS.

THE MIDDLE AGES

The seventh century AD introduced a new phase in ship design. From remains such as the Nydam boat found near Flensburg in 1863 and another discovered more recently in a burial mound at Sutton Hoo in England, we know that the vessels with which the Vikings carried out their overseas raids were long and narrow, and of shallow draught, with only a rudimentary keel so that they could easily be beached. Sometimes propelled by oars, these were more usually driven by a large cloth sail, either a plain blood red in colour or striped in red and blue.

A century later, as we learned from remains found at Gokstad in Norway in 1880, these Viking LONGSHIPS were clinker-built of oak, around 80 feet in length, and double ended, bow and stern rearing up in a graceful sweep, the former having a carved *figurehead*. Each *gunwhale* was pierced with holes for 16 oars. Outboard on each side was a rack in which the crew placed their shields, for ceremonial display in harbour rather than for protection at sea. A mast stepped amidships carried a single large rectangular sail. A short *tiller* fitted at right angles to the steerboard made steering easier.

The ships which Alfred the Great (849–901) built for England's first navy were similar to, but larger than those of the Vikings, some having as many as 60 oars. To judge from the Bayeux Tapestry, those used by William of Normandy to invade Britain in 1066 were of this design except for being partially decked and for having a corvus at the stern as well as in the bows, from which soldiers used their bows and arrows against the enemy before they came close enough to board.

By the thirteenth century the COG was the most common type of vessel in northern waters. A broad beam and deep draught gave these a greater carrying capacity than ships of the Norman era. They were, moreover, the first ships for which sails were the normal method of propulsion, oars being rarely used. For this reason the number of sails was increased and in some sails were hoisted on two masts. Cogs were also steered by rudders. For war the English erected temporary castles (a more elaborate version of the corvus) forward and aft in their cogs (hence the later term *forecastle* which is still in use).

In the next century the cog was superseded by the first vessels to which the term *ship* was actually applied. These were of as much as 500 tons burden (or burthen) and stepped two masts. Those required for war had *castles* built as a part of them, the aftercastle having a 'roof' which became the *poop deck* (so that the term 'aftercastle' has not survived). Each of these warships had a crew of 90 seamen, and carried 60 spearmen and 130 archers for whom 'loopholes' were cut in their bulwarks.

Countries bordering the Mediterranean evolved their own type of sailing vessel, the CARAVEL. Initially lateen rigged on two masts, these later stepped three, with square sails on the forward two, and a lateen sail on the mizen (after mast). Intended for relatively calm waters, they could nonetheless be used for longer journeys, as Columbus proved when he used the *Santa Maria*. The much larger CARRACK was evolved out of the caravel around 1450.

By the fourteenth century *guns* (cannons) had become available. Initially, those mounted in ships, which could be as large as 1,000 tons burden, were light enough to be mounted on their castles. But in the next century the natural desire to employ larger ones led to a vital development. By fitting a *lower deck* below the *upper deck* and by cutting *square ports* in a ship's side at this level, a *broadside armament* of 'great guns' was mounted.

The best known, and possibly the first fighting ship to be so designed, was built for England's King Henry VIII. Launched in 1514, the *Henry Grâce à Dieu* (or *Great Harry*) mounted 21 bronze muzzle-loaders as well as numerous smaller weapons. The largest ship in the world of her time, she was of more than 1,500 tons burden, stepped four masts, two with square

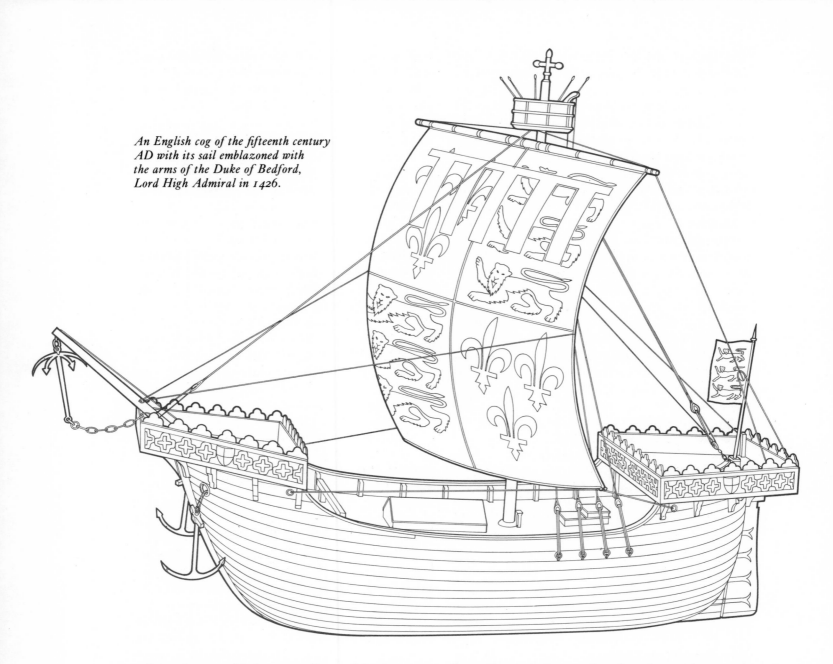

An English cog of the fifteenth century AD with its sail emblazoned with the arms of the Duke of Bedford, Lord High Admiral in 1426.

sails and two with lateen sails, and had a complement of 700 men.

Caravels and carracks were similarly transformed, although the Mediterranean countries in this area continued to use large, oared galleys, known as GALLEASSES, until well into the eighteenth century.

By 1570 England's Sir John Hawkins had realized that the high forecastles of northern warships caught the wind and made it difficult to sail to windward. More weatherly and manoeuvrable vessels, known as *galleons*, were therefore built without this excrescence, both by northern European countries and in the Mediterranean where they superseded carracks. The Spanish Armada of 1588 was composed of carracks and galleons, and galleasses which proved unmanageable in the wild Atlantic seas. The English fleet included galleons as well as ships of the earlier, high-forecastle design.

Hawkins's idea was carried further in the next century. A ship's bow was dropped below the forecastle level, in the beaked form which can still be seen in Nelson's preserved flagship, HMS *Victory*, whose crew numbered more than

850 officers and men. Another sixteenth-century innovation was the *wheel*, for turning the rudder. Though it often had to be manned by several men, this made steering easier.

SHIPS-OF-THE-LINE
The supreme example of a seventeenth-century warship was England's *Sovereign of the Seas* (later renamed *Royal Sovereign*), designed by Phineas Pett for King Charles I. Launched in the Thames in 1637, she mounted 100 guns on three decks: lower, main and upper. The carved and gilded *galleries* to her stern would have been no discredit to Grinling Gibbons. Her bow carried an ornately painted figurehead, as most ships were to do until the end of the sailing era. Her rig included a long *bowsprit* on which *spritsails* were set, in addition to three masts – not the four favoured for the *Great Harry*. Very few warships were, however, as large as this and most carried fewer guns, the average number being between 60 and 80.

The Dutch designed similar warships with which they fought the Anglo-Dutch Wars in many of whose battles the *Sovereign* played her part. Indeed, her career lasted until 1696, and only ended then because she was accidentally destroyed by fire while lying at Chatham. (Forty to sixty years was by no means an unusual life for a wooden sailing ship, so stout were her oak timbers.) By this date the difference between warships used by Mediterranean countries and those of northern Europe was so slight that those of France and Spain differed from Britain's only in minor details.

Merchant ships of the seventeenth and eighteenth centuries were very similar in size, design and rig to contemporary warships. Because piracy was rife they were armed, but with fewer guns. The space saved allowed *cabins* to be provided for passengers, and for *holds* roomy enough for freight. The finest merchant ships were built by the British and Dutch East Indies Companies for trading with that rich part of the world. Known as EAST INDIAMEN, they were so magnificently equipped, not least to enhance the prestige of their owners, that they were much admired by all who knew them.

By the seventeenth century several standard rigs had been evolved for sailing vessels. The most common was the *square-rigged* SHIP. Each of her three *lower masts* was surmounted by a *topmast* and a *topgallant mast*. The bowsprit, which had carried square spritsails, was now used for triangular *jibs* stayed to the *foremast*. This hoisted a *fore course, fore topsail* and *fore topgallantsail*, all of them square in shape, each from its own yard by which it could be braced at the angle needed to steer a course 'close-hauled', which was now possible with the wind only 45 degrees on the bow. So, likewise, were three square sails hoisted on the mainmast. The lowest sail on the mizen was a fore-and-aft *driver* or *spanker* (rather than a course), with square topsail and topgallant above it. Triangular *staysails*, similar to jibs, were hoisted between the masts. Some ships carried *royals* above their topgallants and, exceptionally, *skysails* above these. And, when running before the wind, their yards were extended with booms from which square *studding sails* were set. With all this sail area ships could make good eight knots, sometimes more.

Vessels too small to carry so much sail, such as SLOOPS, stepped only two masts, while CUTTERS stepped only one. The former was said to be *brig rigged* if she hoisted square sails, *schooner rigged* if she hoisted fore-and-aft sails. The latter hoisted a couple of jibs and a fore-and-aft mainsail and topsail (a rig still to be seen occasionally on the few remaining Thames sailing barges).

The admirals who fought the Anglo-Dutch Wars concluded that naval battles were best fought in the formation known as line ahead. It was, consequently, necessary to decide which ships were large enough, and sufficiently well armed, to form such a line against an enemy fleet.

First termed *line-of-battle ships*, these soon became better known as SHIPS-OF-THE-LINE.

Britain's First Lord of the Admiralty in the mid-eighteenth century, Admiral Anson, decided to classify all ships-of-the-line according to their size and armament, a practice followed by other countries. The largest, mounting 100 or more guns (mostly 24- and 32-pounders, i.e. the weight of the solid iron ball which they fired – the calibre of a 32-pounder was about 6 inches) were *first rates*; those with 90–98 guns were *second rates*, and those with 64–84 guns were *third rates*. Those with 90 guns or more had them distributed between three decks, hence the term *three-decker*. The rest were *two-deckers*, the most common class in any navy being *third rates* with 64 or 74 guns. Ships 'below the line' (i.e. not fit to lie in a line of battle) were likewise classified. Two-deckers with 50–60 guns were *fourth rates*; two-deckers with 32–44 guns were *fifth rates*, and those with 20–28 guns mounted on a single deck, which needed no ports cut in their sides, were *sixth rates*.

The keel length of these ships ranged from around 190 feet for a first rate down to 110 feet for a sixth rate, their beam from 50 feet down to 30, and their burden from 2,200 down to 500 tons. Because warships were evolved out of trading ships the tonnage of the former was calculated according to their theoretical cargo-carrying capacity in tons (length of keel multiplied by greatest beam multiplied by maximum draught, all measured in feet, and divided by 100) until the more realistic displacement (i.e. actual weight) method was introduced in the mid-nineteenth century. For a rough comparison a first rate of 2,200 tons burden displaced about 3,500 tons.

An admirable word picture of one of these instruments of maritime power, which the English writer John Ruskin described as 'take it all in all...the most honourable thing that man... has ever produced', is to be found in Michael Scott's *Tom Cringle's Log* (here abridged):

She had just tacked, and was close aboard on our lee quarter, within musket shot, bowling along upon a wind, with the green sea surging along her sides. The press of canvas laid her over until her copper sheathing [introduced to combat the destructive toredo worm] was high above the water. Above it rose the jet black bands and chrome yellow streaks of her sides, broken at regular intervals by ports from which cannon grinned, open-mouthed. Clean, well stowed hammocks filled the nettings above the bulwarks from taffrail to cat-head. Aloft a cloud of white sail swelled to the breeze, bending the masts like willow-wands, straining shrouds and backstays as taut as the strings of a violin, and tearing her bows out of the long swell until ten yards of her keel were clear of the sea, into which she plunged again burying everything up to the hawse holes. We were so near that I could see the faces of the men at their quarters in their clean white frocks [i.e. canvas jumpers] and trousers, the officers and the marines clearly distinguishable by their blue and red coats. High overhead, the red cross of St. George blew out from the peak, like a sheet of flickering flame, while from the main truck her captain's pendant streamed into the azure heavens like a ray of silver light.

All this of a British ship-of-the-line is as true of other countries, with three significant exceptions. Those built by the Dutch had to be of shallow draught so that they would enter the Texel. Spain built the largest: the first-rate *Santísima Trinidad*, which fought at Trafalgar, was a four-decker mounting 140 guns. And those built by France were the best designed, especially those laid down during the regime of King Louis XIV's distinguished Minister of Marine, Jean Baptiste Colbert. 'How fortunate has it been that when they [the French] have built their ships they do not know how to navigate them', wrote the Royal Navy's Captain J.F. Fremantle with some feeling after seeing many of them during the British occupation of Toulon in 1793.

The French were the first to evolve a fifth rate of a kind which they called a *frégate*, whose lighter scantlings and finer lines enabled her to outsail other ships, which improved her chances of avoiding an unequal fight with a ship-of-the-line. Other countries followed their example: the first British FRIGATE, the *Constant Warwick*, was built in 1649. Similar sixth rates, also evolved by the French, were called CORVETTES.

Ships 'below the line' were chiefly employed capturing enemy merchant vessels and escorting convoys. But the British recognized the special value of frigates as scouts and for repeating signals, duties for which Nelson complained that he had not half enough. (He had none with the fleet with which he fought the battle of the Nile when his opponent had five, and only four at Trafalgar, though these served him well enough under Captain Blackwood's skilful direction.) But for the War of 1812 a fledgling U.S.A. built frigates with the armament of a fourth rate, with the consequence that just six of them were able to control the sea off America's east coast until Britain, heavily involved in war with Napoleonic France, could send a fleet of ships-of-the-line across the Atlantic.

Two other types of warship must briefly be mentioned. FIRESHIPS were vessels of little fighting value that were filled with tar and other

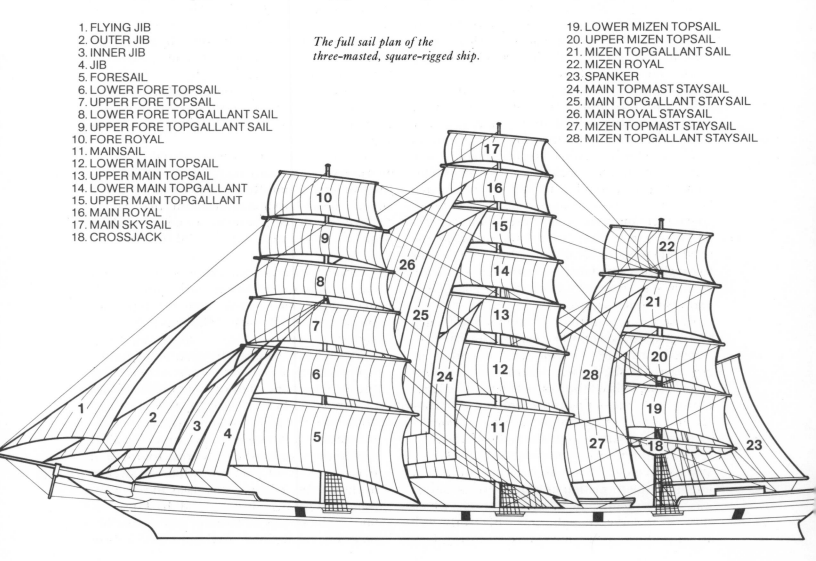

1. FLYING JIB
2. OUTER JIB
3. INNER JIB
4. JIB
5. FORESAIL
6. LOWER FORE TOPSAIL
7. UPPER FORE TOPSAIL
8. LOWER FORE TOPGALLANT SAIL
9. UPPER FORE TOPGALLANT SAIL
10. FORE ROYAL
11. MAINSAIL
12. LOWER MAIN TOPSAIL
13. UPPER MAIN TOPSAIL
14. LOWER MAIN TOPGALLANT
15. UPPER MAIN TOPGALLANT
16. MAIN ROYAL
17. MAIN SKYSAIL
18. CROSSJACK

The full sail plan of the three-masted, square-rigged ship.

19. LOWER MIZEN TOPSAIL
20. UPPER MIZEN TOPSAIL
21. MIZEN TOPGALLANT SAIL
22. MIZEN ROYAL
23. SPANKER
24. MAIN TOPMAST STAYSAIL
25. MAIN TOPGALLANT STAYSAIL
26. MAIN ROYAL STAYSAIL
27. MIZEN TOPMAST STAYSAIL
28. MIZEN TOPGALLANT STAYSAIL

166

combustible substances and sailed into an enemy fleet as it lay at anchor, when they were set alight. They were the chief weapon with which Britain decimated the Spanish Armada off Calais in 1588, and destroyed a French squadron in the Basque Roads in 1811. BOMBS were small vessels armed with a *mortar* (a short-barrelled gun with a high elevation) firing fused explosive *shells* for bombarding shore defences.

The Napoleonic Wars were the greatest days of fighting sail. At the battle of Cape St Vincent in 1797 Britain's Admiral Sir John Jervis, with 15 ships-of-the-line, captured four of Spain's 27 and put the rest to flight. Eight years later, off Cape Trafalgar, Nelson's 27 captured or destroyed more than half of the 33 which formed the Combined Fleets of France and Spain. Thereafter the use of wood for ships' hulls, and sails for driving them, steadily declined. But before dealing with how both were eclipsed, three notable developments must be recorded. First, ships-of-the-line grew larger, mounting more and bigger guns. The British three-decker *Duke of Wellington*, laid down in 1849, was of 3,771 tons burden and mounted 130 guns. HMS *Victoria*, launched ten years later, was not only considerably larger than this – her displacement was twice that of Nelson's *Victory* – but mounted sixty-two 8-inch guns in addition to fifty-eight 32-pounders.

Secondly, new sail plans were evolved, chiefly for merchant ships, which combined the best features of the square and fore-and-aft rigs. The larger ships became BARQUES, with from three up to seven masts (named after the days of the week) or BARQUENTINES, and the smaller ones were BRIGS or BRIGANTINES. Training ships excepted, the last sailing vessels regularly employed were the large barques which continued to carry Chilean nitrate round Cape Horn until the Panama Canal was opened in 1914.

The third innovation was the CLIPPER. These were sailing ships designed to make very fast passages. Their hulls were long and low, with a draught deeper aft than forward, and with a sharply raked stem and a counter stern. The first, built in the U.S.A. around 1812, were two-masted schooners for the West African slave trade. But by 1832 they were being built as fully rigged, three-masted ships, to meet the demand for speedy passages to and from Australia and California for those who wanted to take advantage of the discovery of gold in these regions. The American *Sovereign of the Seas* made the fastest Atlantic crossing under sail on record: she reached Liverpool from New York in 13 days 14 hours, sometimes making good as much as 22 knots.

The success attending these American vessels spurred British shipbuilders to emulate them and, taking advantage of the American Civil War (1861–65), to improve on them for the profitable China tea trade. In 1866 five British clippers left south China ports between 29 and 31 May, each determined to be the first to dock in London. The *Taiping* completed the 16,000 miles journey via the Cape of Good Hope in 14 weeks. The next two to arrive in this historic race docked the same morning, and the others only two days later.

With the opening of the Suez Canal in 1869, the tea clippers were transferred to the Australian wool trade for so long as this now obsolescent method of carrying freight remained profitable. One of the more famous British clippers, the *Cutty Sark*, completed in 1869 and famous for her 1872 race home from Foochow against the *Thermopylae* (in which they were lying level until the *Cutty Sark* lost her rudder in a gale off the South African coast), is preserved in dry dock at Greenwich.

STEAM, IRON AND STEEL

These developments were, however, as nothing beside two other innovations which, by the end of the nineteenth century, produced a wholesale transformation in the design of both warships and merchant ships. In 1802, in the wake of the Industrial Revolution in Britain, William Symington built the world's first *steam*-driven craft on Scotland's River Clyde. A year later the American inventor, Robert Fulton, produced a similar vessel for use on France's River Seine. And in 1807, having returned to his own country, he built a larger one which completed the journey of 150 miles from New York to Albany in 32 hours.

The early steam engines were, however, of small horsepower and, inevitably, were unreliable. More important their boilers were heavy consumers of coal, when bunkering facilities on the world's trade routes were scarce. So, for the best part of half a century, except for tugs, river craft and despatch vessels (or MAIL PACKETS) for short sea routes (e.g. across the English Channel), steam was only an auxiliary to sail. Although engines and boilers were installed in many warships and merchant ships from around 1830 onwards, Oscar Wilde's lines
And in the throbbing engine room
Leap the long rods of polished steel
usually applied only when there was insufficient wind to fill their sails.

To this there were, however, exceptions. In 1838 Isambard Kingdom Brunel completed his wooden-hulled steamship *Great Western*. Of 1,321 tons burden, and driven by *paddle-wheels*, she completed her maiden voyage from Bristol to New York in 1838 in 15 days, with 24 first-class passengers on board. She thus became the initiator of a regular trans-Atlantic steamer service.

Paddle-wheels had, however, several disadvantages. They were too easily damaged in bad weather; and in warships they not only

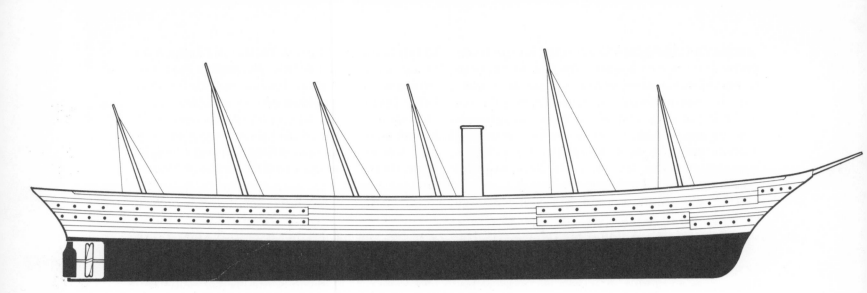

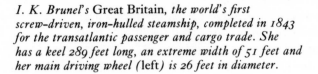

I. K. Brunel's Great Britain, *the world's first screw-driven, iron-hulled steamship, completed in 1843 for the transatlantic passenger and cargo trade. She has a keel 289 feet long, an extreme width of 51 feet and her main driving wheel (*left*) is 26 feet in diameter.*

occupied a part of each broadside, reducing the number of guns that could be mounted there, but were very vulnerable to enemy fire. Shipbuilders were, however, reluctant to adopt *screw* propulsion until the British Admiralty carried out comparative trials between two very similar frigates in 1845. Having been secured by a hawser stern to stern, HMS *Rattler*, fitted with a screw, managed to tow HMS *Alecto* stern first at 2.7 knots, despite the fact that the latter's paddle-wheels were going full speed ahead.

Thenceforward most steamships were driven by screws. Moreover, as more powerful reciprocating engines and higher-pressure boilers became available during the second half of the nineteenth century, steam steadily supplanted sails as the principal method of ship propulsion.

The other important innovation of this century of technological change was the use of iron for ships' hulls, followed around 1860 by a much stronger metal, steel. Both allowed larger ships to be built. To the basic conception of a frame for a ship's hull, hallowed by more than 2,000 years of sea experience, Brunel added stringers for longitudinal strength, and transverse watertight bulkheads which improved a vessel's chances of surviving should she be holed below the waterline (e.g. in collision with another ship), the whole being covered with iron plates secured with rivets. His second passenger and cargo ship, the *Great Britain* of 3,270 tons (now preserved at Bristol) was thus completed in 1843 with screw propulsion and ship rig.

There were, nonetheless, plenty of 'dismal Jimmys' who denied that an iron hull could float and who therefore built *composite ships*. They conceded the advantages of iron for a ship's keel and frames but planked her hull with wood instead of with iron plates.

Brunel's third ship was, unhappily, an historic failure. Launched in 1858 and built entirely of iron, the *Great Eastern* was nearly 700 feet in length and had a designed tonnage of nearly 19,000. Propelled by both paddle-wheels and a screw, as well as by sails, she was supposed to be able to carry as many as 4,000 passengers (or 10,000 troops) to India or Australia, plus 6,000 tons of cargo at a speed of 15 knots. But with this vessel Brunel over-reached himself: she was far too large for her time; her engines were underpowered; and since there was no possibility of finding so many passengers, she was never financially viable. She did, however, perform the useful service of helping to lay four telegraph cables across the Atlantic before she was broken up in 1888. The *Great Eastern* was, incidentally, the first ship with a cellular double bottom, to improve her chances of surviving a grounding. She was also the first to have a steam steering engine. These two innovations soon became common features of ship design.

FREIGHTERS AND LINERS

It is of incidental interest, but more important in its implications, that the *Great Eastern* and her contemporaries mounted no guns. In the years following the Napoleonic Wars, and the British bombardment of Algiers in 1816 which settled the pretensions of the Barbary States, piracy on the high seas was so far reduced (except in Chinese waters where it survived into the twentieth century) that it was no longer necessary for merchant ships to be armed for their own protection in peace-time. At the same time technological progress stemming from the Industrial Revolution made it possible to produce much larger guns than those with which navies had fought their battles for some four centuries. The consequent need to mount these larger weapons in ships led to a complete divorce, around the middle of the nineteenth century, between the design of merchant ships and of warships. We must, therefore, henceforward consider how these developed separately.

A merchant ship's prime purpose was to carry freight, hence the generic term FREIGHTER (though many were also known as TRAMPS). By the end of the nineteenth century the greater part of such a steel-framed and plated ship of around 4,000 tons comprised two holds forward, separated by a transverse watertight bulkhead, each with several decks for the stowage of general cargo, and two similar holds aft. The ship's midships section contained coal-fired boilers and a vertical, triple-expansion, steam reciprocating engine driving a single screw giving a best speed of ten knots. The machinery was placed amidships, even though this involved a long propeller shaft, in part because it was of necessity sited there during the brief paddle-wheel era, and in part because here was the best position for the coal bunkers outboard of the boiler room.

The crew were accommodated below the forecastle and below the poop. The officers' cabins were in a superstructure surrounding a single funnel rising out of the boiler-room, and ventilators for the engine-room. Here, too, was the bridge and wheelhouse, steam propulsion having allowed these to be moved to where the captain and officer of the watch could keep a better look out for other shipping (moved, that is, from the poop, where they had to be in a sailing ship in order that the sails could be seen, and where of necessity the wheel had to be in relation to the rudder until steam steering gear became available). And there were only two masts, one forward and one aft, retained chiefly to support derricks for working the cargo holds. (A few had heavy derricks able to lift a load of 100 tons or more, such as a railway locomotive, notably those of the British Bel line.) There were, of course, also larger freighters with more than four holds, and smaller ones with fewer.

The superstructure of some ships included accommodation for passengers. In many this was kept to a maximum of twelve for which the regulations did not require a doctor to be carried. But a rising demand for passages to and from Europe and the East, Australasia and South Africa, and above all across the Atlantic, led to the design of passenger LINERS. In these, cabins and saloons for hundreds of passengers occupied so much space that little, if any, remained for cargo holds. Their size and tonnage grew to be larger than freighters, a figure of 15,000 tons being the norm, because passengers required both space and comfort. So, too, were they faster, being propelled by twin screws at a best speed of around 18 knots, for which the increased numbers of boilers required two, three or even four funnels, because passengers expected to reach their destination in a shorter time than it took for freight.

In the same era the old sailing packets with auxiliary steam engines, for short sea voyages, were superseded by, in effect, miniature liners of around 1,500 tons with a speed of 20 knots. These FERRIES could be kept small because few passengers required sleeping accommodation. They had twin screws and sometimes a bow rudder for ease of manoeuvre in such harbours as Dover and Calais.

By the first decade of the twentieth century, the demand for rapid passages across the Atlantic led to the design of very large liners (which during the Second World War were not inappropriately termed 'monsters'). Among the earliest of these was the British *Lusitania* of 31,500 tons. Completed in 1906 with accommodation for more than a thousand passengers, she was propelled by four screws at a best speed of 24 knots until she was sunk by a German U-boat in 1915.

Between the two World Wars, and immediately after the Second, the size and speed of liners increased. Some of those built for the routes to the Far East and Australia exceeded 20,000 tons and could sustain more than 20 knots. Transatlantic 'monsters' included luxury liners as large as the *France* of more than 60,500 tons, the British *Queen Mary* of some 80,000 tons, and the *United States* of more than 50,000 tons, all with best speeds of over 30 knots. The luxury with which these carried some 2,000 passengers across the Atlantic in less than five days in peace-time is well demonstrated by the fact that during the Second World War each accommodated as many as 35,000 troops.

To requisition liners to carry troops overseas has for long been normal practice in war. But for transporting them in peace-time, e.g. between Britain and India, a number of TROOPSHIPS were built. These were similar to medium-sized liners but with Other Ranks in accommodation comparable with the barrack rooms to which they were accustomed ashore, which allowed a larger number to be carried than was possible with paying passengers who expected cabins. For many years troopships had their holds suitably equipped to accommodate cavalry horses.

HOSPITAL SHIPS, being seldom required except in war, are usually requisitioned liners suitably converted with wards for sick and wounded, operating theatres, and accommodation for medical and nursing staff. In accordance with the Geneva Convention they are painted white with a broad green band and red crosses and are floodlit at night.

Since the end of the Second World War, air travel has largely superseded passages by sea so that a journey which once took a matter of days, not to mention weeks, can now be accomplished in a matter of hours. The liner, in its old guise of a ship maintaining a regular passenger service between, for example, Southampton and New York or between London and Hong Kong, is virtually obsolete. Those that remain, including the last 'monster' to be built, the British *Queen Elizabeth II*, are now employed as cruise liners for which there is a continuing demand.

In sharp contrast, although planes are now used to carry some kinds of cargo, the total amount, in bulk and weight, which has to be moved about the modern world is such that it must still be transported by sea in freighters. The design of these has, however, been improved. Many are now larger and faster than earlier vessels: the norm is around 8,000 tons with a speed of 12 knots, but a sizeable number are larger than this and have a speed of 17 knots.

In addition to freighters and liners various specialized types of merchant ships have been evolved. The oldest is the YACHT. Of Dutch origin, and intended to bring pleasure sailing within the means of individual owners, their concept and design was brought to England by King Charles II on his accession and spread later to other countries. By the middle of the nineteenth century yachts had been divided into two types: those with fine lines and the largest possible sail plan which were for racing, and those able to weather an ocean gale which were

for cruising. Most were of boat size, but larger ones were built, notably those designed to gain the America's Cup. Won first in 1851 by the 170-ton schooner *America*, no challenger has yet succeeded in wresting that trophy from the U.S.A.

By the end of the nineteenth century the larger cruising yachts were steam driven, notable examples of ship size being Queen Victoria's graceful *Victoria and Albert*, Kaiser William II's *Hohenzollern* which was large enough to become the cruise liner *Stella Maris*, and the U.S. millionaire J. Pierrepont Morgan's 4,000-tons *Corsair*. Today there is none to compare with the British Royal Yacht *Britannia*, built in the 1950s and so designed that she can be used as a hospital ship in the unhappy event of war.

In the 1850s, well before the Forth Bridge was built, an Englishman, Thomas Bouch devised a vessel with a through deck to which two lines of rails were fixed. This first TRAIN FERRY carried laden goods wagons across the Firth of Forth from Granton to Burntisland. Much improved, with the train deck under cover, with access to it by stern doors, and with four rail tracks, train ferries able to carry passenger coaches as well as goods vehicles were later introduced and are still in service on such routes as across the English Channel and between Sweden and Germany.

A post-World War Two adaptation of this type of ship is the CAR FERRY, a very similar vessel, usually with two clear, through decks for cars and lorries. Those used for a service such as

1. PASSENGER ACCOMMODATION
2. GARAGE
3. LAUNDRY ROOM
4. ENGINE ROOM
5. BOILER ROOM
6. TURBO-ALTERNATOR ROOM
7. HOSPITAL
8. PRINTING SHOP
9. REFRIGERATED STOREROOMS
10. BOW THRUSTERS (PROPELLERS WHICH THRUST WATER OUT OF EITHER SIDE TO HELP STEERING AT LOW SPEEDS)

11. BRIDGE AND CHARTROOM
12. RESTAURANTS
13. THEATRE
14. MAIN LOUNGE
15. DANCE FLOOR – WITH BALCONY (THE LARGEST ROOM AFLOAT)
16. LIDO DECKS

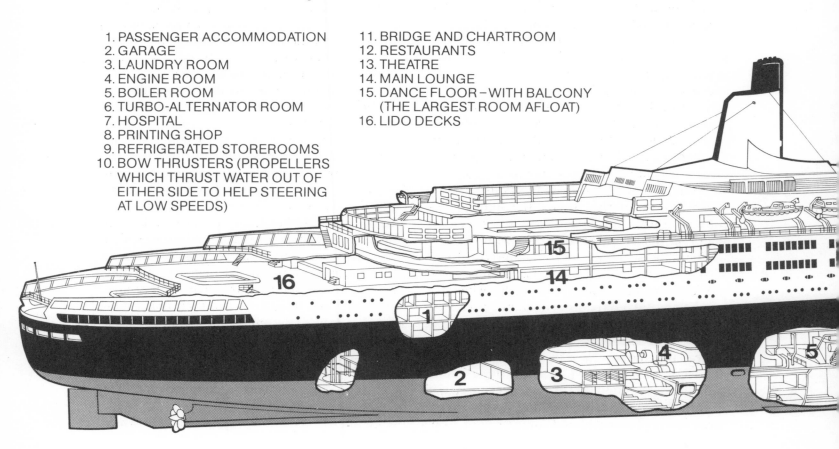

that between Southampton and Spain, a 36-hour run, are of a considerable size compared with those employed on the short crossing between Dover and Calais. Also post-World War Two, ROLL-ON-ROLL-OFF SHIPS have been evolved, chiefly for ferrying laden lorries. These are very similar to car ferries but have bow doors instead of doors at the stern.

CONTAINER SHIPS are another innovation. These are designed to carry freight overseas, pre-packed in large aluminium containers which are brought to a port by rail or by truck and there hoisted on board, without disturbing their contents, into suitably arranged holds. Similarly, at the port of arrival the containers are unloaded directly on to lorries or rail wagons which take them to their destination. This method effects considerable economies because it reduces the number of dockers required to handle the cargo, cuts the time taken to load and unload a ship, and lessens the risk of pilfering en route and so brings down the insurance costs. Comparable ships have been designed to carry fully laden barges to bridge the ocean gap between one country's inland waterway system and that of another without having to disturb their cargoes.

Other specialized types of merchant ship include ICEBREAKERS, employed in the Baltic, on the Northern Sea Route (to the north of the U.S.S.R.) and in Canadian Arctic waters; WHALE FACTORY SHIPS, vessels of more than 20,000 tons equipped to process whales immediately after they have been caught; and REFRIGERATED SHIPS, whose holds are designed to carry such cargoes as frozen meat. Most important of all, however, is the BULK CARRIER. But since the majority of these are OIL TANKERS, their design is best described in the next section of this chapter.

The British Queen Elizabeth II, *built post-World War Two, now the world's largest passenger liner.*

First, however, we must make a passing reference to the most recent innovations in ship design – if indeed they can be called ships. The hulls of HYDROFOILS are designed to skim through the water at 40 knots or more. HOVERCRAFT, which have proved more successful, are carried a few feet above the sea on a self-produced cushion of air which allows aircraft engines and propellers to drive them at much higher speeds than have been achieved by conventional types of ship.

TURBINES AND OIL

The first notable improvement in ship propulsion, after the steam reciprocating engine finally replaced sail, came around the end of the nineteenth century. With the three-drum *watertube boiler*, steam could be raised more quickly, and be produced in greater volume at higher pressure, than with the simple cylindrical firetube type. *Superheaters* followed, so did larger boilers, with the consequence that steam pressures were raised from the early figure of less than 50 lbf/in^2 to above 500 lbf/in^2. Moreover, while 42 boilers were needed to produce 120,000 horsepower in a ship completed in 1916, only eight were needed for 130,000 horsepower in a ship built in 1946, which had the additional advantage of requiring many fewer men to tend them.

More significant, however, was the introduction of the *steam turbine*. The speed which could be achieved with large reciprocating engines, which occupied much space, was limited to about 24 knots. First demonstrated by Charles Parsons in his yacht *Turbinia* at Queen Victoria's Diamond Jubilee Review, a turbine not only occupied less space but drove a ship much faster. Turbines were, therefore, initially installed only in ships required to achieve 20 knots or more. But a subsequent development, *reduction gearing*, made it possible to install them in such ships as freighters whose propellors turned slowly.

More important than these innovations was

171

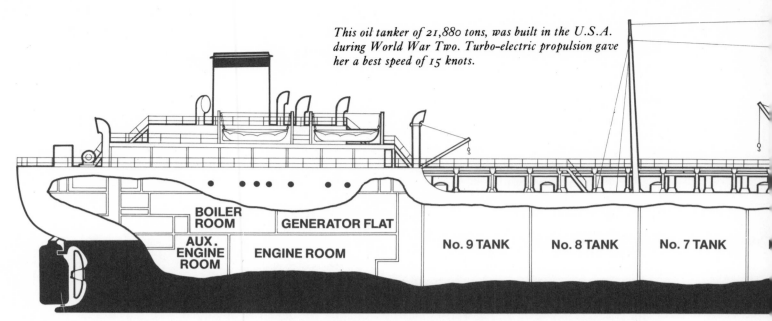

This oil tanker of 21,880 tons, was built in the U.S.A. during World War Two. Turbo-electric propulsion gave her a best speed of 15 knots.

BOILER ROOM | GENERATOR FLAT

AUX. ENGINE ROOM | ENGINE ROOM | No. 9 TANK | No. 8 TANK | No. 7 TANK

the change from coal to *oil* for firing ships' boilers. First introduced around 1910, oil has now supplanted coal in all but a few old vessels. Fuel tanks could be incorporated much more easily than coal bunkers in a ship's design, while replenishment became a simple operation needing only a handful of men instead of hundreds. It was no longer necessary, in addition, to install a ship's engines and boilers amidships; they, and crew accommodation, could be sited right aft, leaving the whole of the rest of the vessel available for cargo holds or passengers. The British liner *Queen Elizabeth II* was so built after the Second World War.

This practice has, however, only been adopted generally for one specialized type of merchant vessel, the BULK CARRIER. Some of these were designed to carry such cargoes as iron ore or grain. The majority have, however, been built as OIL TANKERS to meet the need to transport this product in quantity all over the world from such oil-rich regions as the Persian Gulf and Texas, not only for fuelling ships but for many industrial purposes, and to supply the great increase in road transport made possible by the internal combustion engine.

Most of an oil tanker's hull contains a number of large fuel tanks which are separated by transverse bulkheads, all of these being forward of the engine room and boiler room, above which rises a superstructure containing officers' and crew's quarters, a single funnel and the bridge and wheelhouse. The early tankers were relatively small, carrying no more than 5,000 tons of oil, but in the post-World War One decades this grew to around 25,000 tons. And their capacity might well have stayed around this figure but for the closure of the Suez Canal following the Anglo-French attack on Egypt in 1956, and again after the Arab-Israeli War of 1967.

This impelled the construction of SUPER-TANKERS. The first were designed to carry 100,000 tons, but this figure was soon exceeded. Many are now more than 1,000 feet long and

carry as much as 400,000 tons of oil, and even larger ones are projected notwithstanding the very limited number of ports at which they can discharge. Such ships have to end a voyage at an isolated anchorage, such as Ireland's Bantry Bay, where they discharge their oil into smaller tankers which carry it to ports such as Thames Haven and Amsterdam.

As early as 1910 ship designers saw potential advantages in the *internal combustion engine*, in its *diesel* form, for ship propulsion. The first MOTORSHIPS were easy to distinguish for they had no funnels, but in later ones this feature was restored. More often than not, however, these vessels proved unreliable, so this method of propulsion has not succeeded steam. Indeed, after a number of years in service, several liners had their diesel engines replaced by boilers and turbines.

The U.S.A. has tried *electric propulsion*, using boilers and turbines to run dynamos which produce the current to drive electric motors coupled through gearing to the propellor shafts, but the results achieved have not been encouraging.

A recent development is the use of *nuclear propulsion*, using a nuclear reactor to produce heat which generates steam to drive conventional turbines. For warships and, above all, submarines this has major advantages: fuel replenishment is only necessary after some years in service, and submarines can remain submerged for almost indefinite periods. But for merchant ships, a notable example being the U.S. liner *Savannah*, completed in 1959, nuclear propulsion has proved uneconomic. It also suffers the serious disadvantage that, for fear of radioactive pollution, few countries are willing to allow such ships to enter their ports.

For the smaller types of warship, for which the high cost of installing a nuclear reactor is not justified, *gas-turbine propulsion* is now popular. A by-product of aircraft-engine development, this has two advantages: high speed from an

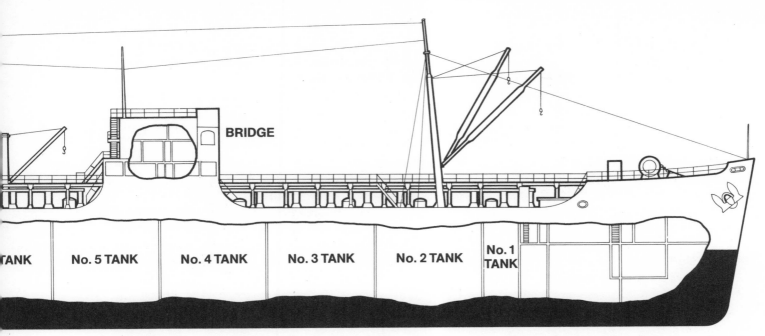

BRIDGE

TANK | No. 5 TANK | No. 4 TANK | No. 3 TANK | No. 2 TANK | No. 1 TANK

engine occupying little space, and the ability to proceed to sea in little more time than is needed to weigh anchor. It is, however, unlikely that this form of propulsion will be installed in merchant ships because there is, now, no demand for these to have a speed in excess of 20 knots.

Other significant innovations in ship design can be mentioned only briefly. *Electricity* was first provided in ships around 1880 for lighting, but its use was soon extended to driving auxiliary machinery, such as ventilating fans, derrick winches and cable windlasses, because it obviated the need to run steam pipes throughout a ship, especially through her living accommodation.

In the 1930s *welding* began to replace rivetting for securing scantlings, whereby it became possible to prefabricate sections of a ship before welding them together on a slipway. This enabled the U.S.A. to mass-produce freighters by the thousand (*Liberty ships*) during the Second World War to replace those lost by the Allies to U-boat attack.

In more recent years *air-conditioning* has been installed in liners, which has greatly improved their habitability in the tropics. Such ships are also now fitted with *stabilizers* – large, power-operated horizontal fins below water, which do much to reduce rolling in a seaway.

BATTLESHIPS, CRUISERS AND DESTROYERS

Legend has it that Korea's Admiral Yisunsin built the world's first iron-hulled warships, with which he destroyed Japan's Admiral Hideyoshi's wooden war junks as far back as 1598. Be this as it may, history credits France with producing the first IRONCLAD in 1858, a frigate with an *auxiliary steam engine*, named *La Gloire*. Britain was quick to follow with the *Warrior* in 1860.

Crimean War experience having shown that neither the 18-inch oak sides of the old 'wooden-walls', nor 2-inch iron plates, were sufficient to keep out the explosive-filled shells that had succeeded solid iron cannon balls, ships of either type were protected by backing their iron plates with teak. But this form of *armour* was soon succeeded by $4\frac{1}{2}$ inches of iron which, before the end of the century, was replaced by much thicker and stronger slabs of steel.

The most difficult problem facing naval architects in this era of great changes in warship design was, however, where to mount the larger guns that were now available. Their size and weight meant, for example, that HMS *Achilles*, completed in 1864, could mount only twenty 100-pounders and six 68-pounders. The initial solution was to place half of them on each broadside as before, but all on a single deck. When, however, later ships carried no more than sixteen 7-inch guns, or eight 8-inch, these were concentrated amidships in what became known as *central battery ships*.

This, however, was no solution for those who wanted to equip their ironclads with yet larger weapons. As early as 1858 Britain's Captain Cowper Coles pointed the way with an armoured, centre-line, pivoted mounting, which would allow a gun to fire on either broadside. Four years later, during the American Civil War, the USS *Monitor*, with only two guns, proved the value of this *barbette*, or *turret*, mounting by her destruction of two wooden frigates and a successful duel with an armoured vessel in Hampton Roads. And notwithstanding the disaster suffered by HMS *Captain*, which mounted four 10-inch in two twin turrets – she capsized in a gale in 1870, with the loss of almost all on board, including Captain Coles who had misguidedly designed her with a freeboard of only $6\frac{1}{2}$ feet – this method came into its own. HMS *Sultan*, completed in 1871, mounted eight 10-inch and four 9-inch in a central battery but HMS *Devastation*, completed two years later, mounted four larger weapons in two centre-line turrets. The latter was, moreover, the first British BATTLESHIP (the type name by which armoured ships-of-the-line became known) to be built without sails, steam being her only form of propulsion.

The ease with which steam-driven warships could be manoeuvred in action prompted a return to a weapon which had become obsolete when sailing ships supplanted oared galleys. Ironclads were equipped with rams. These had one notable success: at the battle of Lissa fought in 1866, the Austrian Admiral Tegetthoff thus sank his opponent's flagship. Otherwise the ram proved a liability, as when HMS *Camperdown* sank HMS *Victoria* in 1893. By the end of the century it had become obsolete for the second time.

The completion of HMS *Devastation* and her sister ship, the *Thunderer*, by no means settled the controversy between those who favoured a few large guns in turrets and those who argued for more smaller weapons in central batteries. Nor were those who wanted to retain sails in addition to steam as yet vanquished. This was, indeed, an era of experiment in which it was rare for more than one battleship to be completed to the same design. Whereas France laid down the *Admiral Duperré* in 1879 to mount four 13.4-inch guns in single turrets, plus two broadside batteries each of six 5.5-inch, Britain, only two years later, laid down the *Conqueror* and *Hero* with two 12-inch in a single turret forward, plus four 6-inch in casemates aft.

Indeed, not until 1890 were Admiralties sufficiently certain of their ideas to build homogeneous battleship squadrons. Thenceforward, however, all proceeded to build what became the standard battleship of the end of the century. The nine British 'Majestics', completed in 1895–98, displaced 14,900 tons, had a best speed of 17 knots, and mounted four 12-inch guns in twin turrets forward and aft, plus six 6-inch in two broadside batteries amidships. Their turrets were of steel armour 14 inches thick; their machinery spaces and magazines were protected by a 9-inch belt of side armour; and each ship required a crew of 672 officers and men.

During the same half century naval architects sought to provide steam-driven, iron- (later steel-) hulled vessels to replace the old sailing frigates. Their solution was the CRUISER, of which two types were evolved, *armoured* and *protected*. The former included the British 'Cressy' class, of 12,000 tons, with two 9.2-inch and twelve 6-inch, a 6-inch belt, a best speed of 21 knots, and required a crew of 760. The latter were of around 5,000 tons, armed with ten 6-inch, and with no more than a 3-inch protective deck, but with the same speed of some 4–5 knots more than a battleship, for which they needed a crew of around 500.

Meantime, before the end of the century, came a new weapon that was greatly to influence naval warfare, the Whitehead *torpedo*. Initially these self-propelled, underwater weapons were launched from small vessels of no more than 20 tons, which were carried to their point of attack by battleships or specially-designed mother ships. But TORPEDOBOATS soon grew into vessels of several hundred tons with the ability to keep the sea on their own. Against attack by these, battleships depended initially on their secondary armaments (i.e. their 6-inch quick-firing guns) but the need for something more effective led to the design of TORPEDOBOAT-DESTROYERS, which were small gunvessels with a torpedoboat's high speed. But the provision of both these types was so uneconomic that the latter soon mounted torpedo-tubes in addition to guns, and were able to fulfil both roles, their type name being shortened to DESTROYER. Typical of these was HMS *Havock*, completed in 1893: displacing 250 tons, and with a best speed of 26½ knots, she mounted one 12-pounder and three 6-pounder guns, plus three torpedo-tubes, and had a crew of around 50 officers and men.

The range of the first torpedoes was no more than 2,000 yards but by the beginning of the twentieth century improvements had more than doubled this figure. The threat which these weapons then presented to battleships in action impelled admirals to realize that they must fight their guns at greater ranges than those which they had believed possible – which were, indeed, not much more than those at which the old sailing ships-of-the-line had fought. This confronted them with the difficulty that whereas a mixed armament of 12-inch, 9.2-inch and 6-inch guns (which the latest battleships mounted) could be aimed, fired and spotted by individual gunlayers on to a target distant 4,000 yards, at greater ranges it was necessary for a ship to fire controlled *salvoes*, spotting these as 'short', 'over' or 'straddle' (i.e. some 'over', some 'short', plus, with luck, a hit). To do this and to apply the range correction needed to obtain a straddle was found to be impracticable. It also became apparent (and this was demonstrated in the Russo-Japanese War) that the argument that 6-inch quick-firing weapons were needed to compensate for the slow rate of fire of 12-inch guns was no longer valid: the damage done by the latter against an armoured vessel was out of all proportion to that done by the smaller weapons.

Britain's Admiral Lord Fisher provided the solution in 1906. Displacing 18,000 tons and protected by 8–11 inches of armour, HMS *Dreadnought* mounted a single-calibre armament of ten 12-inch in five twin turrets (plus batteries of 12-pounders to counter torpedoboat attacks), for which she needed a crew of 860. She was, moreover, the first battleship to be driven by turbines at a speed as high as 21 knots, and the first to have a *tripod mast* to support her gunnery control position. It being very clear that a PRE-DREADNOUGHT was no match for a DREADNOUGHT, all navies were obliged to build the latter type, though the U.S.A. opted for *lattice cage masts* instead of tripods, until both types were succeeded in the 1920s by the massive bridge structure first seen in HMS *Nelson* and *Rodney*.

For the same reasons Fisher produced all-big-gun armoured cruisers, which he called BATTLE-CRUISERS. The first was HMS *Invincible*, completed in 1908. Of about the same displacement as the *Dreadnought*, she mounted only eight 12-inch guns and was protected by only six inches of armour, so that she could have a best speed of 26 knots, with a complement of about 800 officers and men.

The First World War proved to be the heyday of the dreadnought. At Jutland in 1916 Britain's Grand Fleet numbered 28, some with eight 15-inch guns plus a secondary armament increased to twelve 6-inch, and a best speed of 24 knots. Germany, with only 16, had to make up her High Seas Fleet with six pre-dreadnoughts. The disastrous loss of three British battlecruisers in this controversial action demonstrated the inadequacy of their armour and thereafter few were built. Instead navies designed, in time for completion during the Second World War, fast battleships of which the largest were the Japanese *Musashi* and *Yamato* of 64,170 tons, armed with nine 18-inch guns plus a multiplicity of anti-aircraft weapons, with armour as thick as 16 inches, and a best speed of $27\frac{1}{2}$ knots. Each of these needed a crew of 2,500 officers and men.

But they were almost the last of their kind. Only Britain's *Vanguard*, of 44,500 tons, armed with eight 15-inch and with a best speed of 30 knots, and France's *Jean Bart* of 43,293 tons, with the same main armament and best speed, were completed after the end of hostilities in 1945. By this time air power had demonstrated that the battleship was no longer the queen of the maritime chessboard. The last to fire her guns in anger was an American vessel during the war in Vietnam. All have since been scrapped or are preserved as museums.

As battlecruisers succeeded armoured cruisers during the first two decades of the twentieth century, so did LIGHT CRUISERS succeed the protected type. These displaced around 4,000 tons, were armed with five 6-inch guns, had a best speed of 28 knots, and a crew of 350. In between the two World Wars the generic term CRUISER was brought back into use, both for vessels as large as 10,000 tons armed with eight 8-inch guns, and for smaller ones of around 6,000 tons armed with six 6-inch.

A typical First World War destroyer displaced 1,300 tons, was armed with four 4-inch guns and six torpedo tubes, had a best speed around 30 knots, and needed a crew of 110. During the Second World War many displaced 2,000 tons, were armed with up to eight 5-inch guns, and twelve torpedo tubes, had a best speed of 36 knots, and required 350 officers and men.

Only brief mention can be made of the specialized types of warship designed and built during both World Wars, notably those for the anti-submarine role, for which the old-type names FRIGATE and CORVETTE were revived; and those with bow doors for landing armoured vehicles (LANDING SHIPS) on beaches for combined (amphibious) operations. But this chapter would be incomplete if it omitted to describe the development of two very significant types of warship, both of which have been evolved during the present century.

AIRCRAFT-CARRIERS AND SUBMARINES

To enable *aircraft* to operate with her fleet, Britain developed SEAPLANE CARRIERS in the early years of the First World War by adding a small hangar and crane to a number of requisitioned cross-Channel steamers. But conditions in the North Sea seldom allowed floatplanes to take off or land, so there arose a demand for a ship which could operate wheeled planes. In 1917 the large cruiser *Furious* was fitted with a *flight deck* and a *hangar* below it. This first

The world's largest warship, the U.S. nuclear-powered aircraft-carrier Enterprise *of 75,700 tons, built post-World War Two to operate 100 planes.*

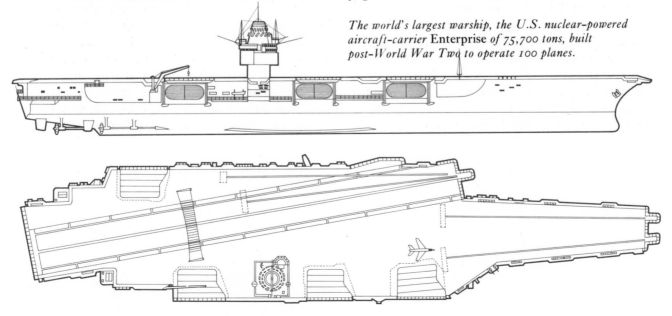

AIRCRAFT-CARRIER begat a whole generation of these vessels in all the principal navies between the wars. A typical one displaced 20,000 tons, and had a best speed of 34 knots. A hangar below its long flight deck, which was reached by three large lifts, served 100 planes. The bridge, mast and funnel were combined in an island structure at the starboard edge of the flight deck. Her crew numbered 2,200.

When, during the Second World War, it became apparent that air power would play the predominant role and that large numbers of aircraft-carriers were urgently needed, three different types were designed. The *fleet carrier*, of around 45,000 tons, often with the flight deck armoured, carried nearly 140 planes. The *light fleet carrier*, of around 12,000 tons, stowed some 40 planes. The *escort carrier* was of around the same tonnage but able to operate only 20 planes.

Since the end of the Second World War the smaller types have become obsolete and the generic term *aircraft-carrier* has been used for ships of more than 50,000 tons, with a best speed of 30 knots, a hangar large enough to service upwards of 120 planes, and with a crew of more than 4,000. Steam-operated *catapults* assist the heavier types of machine to take off, and an *angled flight deck* allows planes to land and provides a parking area.

A warship able to approach an enemy *submerged* has such obvious advantages that it is not surprising that as early as the Napoleonic Wars the American inventor Robert Fulton tried to interest first France and then Britain in a SUBMARINE of his own design. But neither Fulton's vessel, nor those of subsequent nineteenth-century inventors, met with any significant success, chiefly for lack of any adequate method of underwater propulsion. Not until the internal-combustion engine became available at the turn of the century were submarines added to the world's fleets.

These comprised a cylindrical, watertight and pressure-tight hull, which was sub-divided by transverse bulkheads into compartments containing torpedo-tubes, propulsion machinery and living accommodation. This was surrounded by an outer hull sub-divided into tanks, into which the sea could be admitted to give the craft negative buoyancy for submerging, and expelled by compressed air to give it positive buoyancy for surfacing. The whole was surmounted by a structure containing the *conning tower*, periscopes, radio mast and a gun for surface action. Propulsion was by battery-supplied *electric motors* when submerged and by *diesel engines* on the surface, the latter also driving dynamos for battery charging.

By 1920 a typical submarine displaced around 1,000 tons, had a surface speed of 17 knots and a submerged speed of 10 knots, was armed with six torpedo-tubes and a single 4-inch gun, and had a crew of 40. Submarines of around this size were built during the Second World War, but there were also larger ones of 1,500 tons or more, with speeds of 20 knots on the surface and 10 knots when submerged, armed with ten torpedo-tubes and a 5-inch gun, and having a crew of 70.

A notable Second World War development was the German use of a Dutch invention, the *Schnorkel* (*anglice* Snort), a device which has since come into universal use, by which a submarine can be driven by her diesel engines while remaining below the surface, except for the head of a pipe containing a watertight valve through which air is drawn and exhaust fumes expelled.

More recently *nuclear propulsion* has made it possible to build *true* submarines, i.e. craft which can remain submerged almost indefinitely. This, and the need to carry long-range *guided missiles* with nuclear warheads, has impelled the design of submarines displacing more than 5,000 tons, with better streamlined hulls which allow much higher underwater speeds.

In the principal navies today, the most important warships are aircraft-carriers and nuclear-propelled submarines, some of these being armed with nuclear-warhead guided missiles, others with the latest in torpedoes. Both of these types are supported by cruisers, destroyers and frigates which differ from those with which the Second World War was fought chiefly in that, instead of guns and torpedo-tubes, they are armed with surface-to-surface and surface-to-air guided missiles, and with anti-submarine *helicopters*. All incorporate such other mid-twentieth-century innovations as welded hulls, air-conditioning, and gas-turbine propulsion as have been mentioned earlier in this chapter in connection with merchant-ship design. Their appearance has also been much changed by the need to fit structures akin to small towers, instead of masts, to support their massive radar aerials.

A typical nuclear-powered submarine carrying sixteen long-range guided missiles with nuclear warheads amidships, plus torpedoes forward.

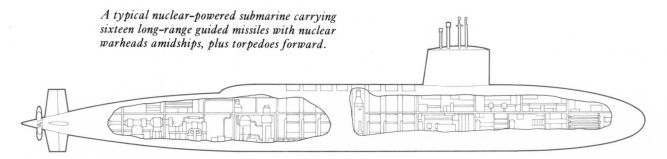

Voyages of Adventure

ON SUNDAY 9 AUGUST 1573, at sermon time, the thunder of guns in Plymouth Sound startled the worshippers at St Andrew's Church and sent most of them rushing out, untroubled at missing the rest of the discourse. Francis Drake was back from the Spanish Main. 'The news of his return', we are told, 'did so speedily pass over all the church, and surpassed their minds with desire and delight to see him, that very few or none remained with the preacher, all hastening to see the evidence of God's love and blessing towards our gracious Queen and country.'

The evidence was a glittering haul of silver and gold captured from the Spanish mule trains at Nombre de Dios on the Isthmus of Panama. Four years later Drake was off on another raiding expedition. On 15 November 1577, he sailed proudly out of Sutton Pool, with a little fleet of 'ships and barks'. Everyone in Plymouth had heard that he was on his way to Alexandria for currants, but there were some who guessed that sooner or later he would arrive in the Indies. The Spanish knew better; one of their agents in London had reported the 'pirate Drake' was planning to kidnap 'the prince of Scotland'.

The civilized luxuries of Drake's cabin in the flagship *Pelican* were almost weirdly remote from the perils and discomforts, the great tempests and barren shores, that lay ahead. Drake was not looking for currants. On the Panama expedition he had gazed out to the Pacific, like Cortez or Balboa 'silent upon a peak in Darien', from a platform in the branches of a very tall tree; and there, high up in a fair wind, he had asked God 'to give him life and leave to sail once in his life upon that sea'.

He sailed into it in the late summer of 1578 through the straits which Ferdinand Magellan had discovered 58 years before.

Besides holding a service of thanksgiving, he changed the name of his flagship to the *Golden Hind*, at the same time placing on her poop the crest of Sir Christopher Hatton, a *hind trippant or*.

Hatton was the Queen's Captain of the Guard and an important shareholder in the venture. As Thomas Doughty, his representative on the voyage, had been beheaded for behaviour tending to 'contention or mutiny, or some other disorder', the change of name was a shrewd stroke on Drake's part. Whatever Hatton might make of the Doughty affair, he could hardly fail to be pleased that the flagship was now called after the hind on his crest. Off the west coast of Africa Drake had acquired a pinnace and named her the *Christopher*, obviously in honour of Hatton, but he had afterwards let her drift.

He entered the Pacific on 6 September, to find, as he said at the time, that 'Mare Pacificum' would have been better named 'Mare Furiosum'. After 70 leagues of ocean wilderness, the *Golden Hind* and her consorts ran into a gale. On 15 September, at six in the evening, an eclipse of the moon began, and while the sea was darkened the *Marigold* vanished for ever with all on board her. From the *Golden Hind* Francis Fletcher, the chaplain, heard their cries blown towards him from 'the mountains of the sea'. The voyagers called these waters 'the Bay of the Severing of Friends'. Not long afterwards the *Golden Hind* and the *Elizabeth* lost sight of each other. Returning through the Straits of Magellan, Wynter's *Elizabeth* reached England a year before the flagship, but the crews of both ships grieved until they met again. Wynter's voyage scotched for ever the belief that no ship which sailed through the Straits of Magellan could ever sail back again.

Early in 1577 a number of meetings had been held in Mortlake, at the home of Dr John Dee, Fellow of Trinity College, Cambridge, the geographer, mathematician, astrologer and inventor of the British Empire. Dee was convinced that ships could reach Cathay by sailing west-about round North America through the Straits of Anian, once the entrance to those straits had been discovered. Beyond lay the unknown Southland, 'Terra Australis Incognita'; for surely Providence

The new fonde londe quhar men goeth a fisching

The greet occeane sey

Of the entillas

espagnolla

the cost of pezon

The Indis of occident quhar the spanyazurg douth occupy

Lucatan

Couba

Londe of Flozida

perform the voyage. She must also be of a construction that will bear to take the ground, and of a size which, in case of necessity, may be safely and conveniently laid on shore to repair any accidental damage or defect. These properties are not to be found in ships of war of forty guns, nor in frigates, nor in East India Company's ships, nor in large three-decked West India ships, nor indeed in any other but North-country ships such as are built for the coal trade, which are peculiarly adapted for this purpose.

James Cook knew all about Whitby colliers. At eighteen he had gone to sea as an apprentice and served in small vessels touching along the coast between the coal ports and London. In 1768, when he set out as Lieutenant Cook on his first voyage of discovery, he was experienced in coastal and deep-water navigation. He had served under Wolfe and had attracted favourable attention with his survey work in the St Lawrence and on the coast of Newfoundland: sailing directions for Newfoundland waters are still largely based on his observations.

Long before the crew of the *Endeavour* had their goose pie Christmas dinner among the Three Kings Islands in 1770, Abel Janszoon Tasman of the Dutch East India Company had abruptly sailed away from those waters, leaving a great question still unanswered: 'We trust that this is the mainland coast of the unknown Southland?' The question had been asked ever since ancient times. Could an inaccessible part of the earth be inhabited? James Cook was determined to settle the problem for ever. At six o'clock on the morning of 19 April 1770 those on board the *Endeavour* (she had left England with five officers and 88 men) saw land extending from north-east to west.

We continued standing to the westward [Cook wrote] with the wind at south-south-west until eight, at which time we got top-gallant yards across, made all sail, and bore away alongshore north-east for the easternmost land we had in sight, being at this time in the latitude of 37 degrees 58 minutes south, and longitude of 210 degrees 39 minutes west. The southernmost point of land we had in sight, which bore from us west one-quarter south, I judged to be in the latitude of 38 degrees south, and in the longitude of 211 degrees 7 minutes west from the meridian of Greenwich. I have named it Point Hicks, because Lieutenant Hicks was the first who discovered this land.

The first Briton to set foot in New Holland, the land that would be called Australia, was Isaac Smith, a midshipman and a cousin of the commander.

After returning home in 1771, Cook said that another voyage was needed to settle the question of the Great Southland. On his second expedi-

Extreme left: The Resolution beating through the ice, with the Discovery in the most imminent danger in the distance *by John Webber.*

Below: Reconstructions at Jamestown Festival Park, Virginia, of the Susan Constant, Godspeed, *and* Discovery, *which carried the colonists who founded the first permanent English settlement in America in 1607.*

Left: A model of the Endeavour Bark, *made in 1969 by craftsmen at the National Maritime Museum.*

tion, which began in 1772, he had two ships, the *Resolution* and the *Adventure.* The *Endeavour Bark*, after sailing into history, returned to her unromantic duties, but her commander thought so highly of her that he was given two similar vessels. The 462-ton *Resolution* and 336-ton *Adventure* were Whitby colliers, nearly new when the Admiralty bought them. They were carrying a total of thirteen officers and 171 men when they left Plymouth in July. On the first voyage Cook had taken with him, besides the equipment needed for observing the transit of Venus, a pocket watch, the *Nautical Almanac* and Hadley reflecting quadrants and a sextant, two recent inventions. He now had a copy of Harrison's perfected chronometer; both 'watch machines' are still ticking away at the National Maritime Museum.

On his return in 1775, he wrote to a friend at Whitby: 'I was now fully satisfied that there was no Southern Continent.' Hardly less important was his discovery of how scurvy could be prevented by strict attention to diet and cleanliness; the ships themselves were constantly 'cured with fires' or 'smoked with gunpowder mixed with vinegar'. In three years he had not lost a single man from scurvy.

Having satisfied himself that 'Terra Australis' did not exist, the great navigator directed his attention to that other centuries-old puzzle, the existence of the North-West Passage. He chose the *Resolution* again, and left in company with Captain Charles Clerke on board the *Discovery*. She, too, was a Whitby collier, the smallest of the four at just under 300 tons. Unfortunately she was badly fitted out in the royal dockyard at Deptford where incompetence, indifference and corruption reigned. Cook said that the second-hand gear left over from coal carrying always lasted longer in his vessels than the new material from the dockyards.

Altogether the two ships had thirteen officers and 163 men. They carried such a collection of cattle, sheep, horses and goats that Cook described the *Resolution* as resembling Noah's Ark. Her master was William Bligh, later to command a ship called the *Bounty*.

Sailing northwards from the Sandwich Islands, the mariners entered the North Pacific and came to 'the longed-for coast of New Albion'. They had arrived off Drake's shore almost exactly two centuries after the *Golden Hind*. It is strange to reflect that while they were travelling, like Drake, past lonely shores, and meeting only occasional Indians, the American colonists were fighting a war to free themselves from British rule.

The Indians at Nootka Sound proved to be experts at helping themselves. 'Before we left the place,' says Cook, 'hardly a bit of brass was left in the ship.' They departed on 26 April. On 9 August they reached the westernmost point of North America, which they called Cape Prince

of Wales, and to the sea which they entered they gave the name Bering after the Dane from Petersburg who had explored it half a century earlier. The great inlet on the American side they mapped as Norton Sound, in honour of the Speaker of the House of Commons.

Cook had been told to investigate the North American coast as far as 65 degrees and then search for the passage leading towards Hudson Bay, or Baffin Bay between Greenland and America. If he could not complete the exploration in the first season, he was to winter at a convenient place and try again in the summer. In the event, having too little time left, he decided to retire south and winter in the Sandwich Islands. He did not return. 'It is with the

utmost concern,' announced the *London Gazette* in January 1780,

> that we inform the public that the celebrated circumnavigator, Captain Cook, was killed by the inhabitants of a new-discover'd island in the South Seas. The Captain and crew were first treated as deities, but, upon visiting that island, hostilities ensued and the above melancholy scene was the consequence. This account is come from Kamchatka by letters from Captain Clerke and others. But the crews of the ships were in a very good state of health, and all in the most desirable condition. His successful attempts to preserve the healths of his crews are well known, and his discoveries will be an everlasting honour to his country.

The news that the great explorer had been stabbed in Hawaii travelled to London from Siberia, Captain Clerke having sailed back to northern waters and made contact with the Russians at the harbour of St Peter and St Paul (now Petropavlosk). A month after turning south again he died of tuberculosis. Captain John Gore, who served on all Cook's voyages and had been in the Pacific with John Byron (the poet's grandfather) and Samuel Wallis before him, took the ships home by way of China. When they arrived in the Thames they had been away for over four years.

No one could detect an entrance to the North-West Passage, but the attempts to find it added to man's knowledge of his own planet. John Ross and William Edward Parry, for example, made important contributions in 1818 when they explored the Baffin Bay area in the *Isabella* of 385 tons and the *Alexander* of 252. In the following year Parry continued the search in the 375-ton *Hecla*, accompanied by the brig *Griper* of 180 tons. Hecla and Griper Bay was one of his discoveries.

In 1820 Parry set out again. He was to search from the east towards the west, while John Franklin explored from the other direction. The two did not meet. Parry later made a Polar voyage in the *Hecla* and Franklin, after many further adventures, himself became the object of a great search when his ships, the *Erebus* and *Terror*, disappeared on a quest of the Passage in 1845. They anchored near the island of Disco on the west coast of Greenland, and no more was seen of them. Sir James Ross, and then Sir John Richardson, looked for them in vain. The Government offered a reward of £20,000 to which Lady Franklin added £3,000, for news of the party. In the autumn of 1850 fifteen ships were searching.

After years of continuing silence, Sir Francis McClintock put out in the *Fox*, a steam yacht of 170 tons. Led by various clues, such as a naval button worn by an Eskimo, McClintock discovered a cairn on the north-west coast of King William's Island. A blue ship's paper left by one of Franklin's officers related the fate of the expedition. The vessels had been abandoned on 22 April 1848, after being locked in ice since September 1846, and Sir John Franklin had died on 11 June 1847. Other relics were found, some to be preserved at the United Service Institution in London. While Franklin was credited with 'the priority of discovery' of the North-West Passage, an award of £10,000 for finding it went to Sir Robert McLure and the men who had sailed with him in the *Investigator* on one of the searches for Franklin.

Reading of Franklin's adventures, a boy called Roald Amundsen, born on 16 July 1872 at Borge in south-east Norway, decided to become a Polar explorer. He served as mate with the Belgic Antarctic Expedition of 1897, gained his captain's ticket, studied terrestrial magnetism in Germany, and then left in a 47-ton smack to explore the waters around Norway and Greenland. For a second voyage he acquired the *Gjøa*, a fishing vessel 69ft long and 20.6ft in breadth, with a 7.7ft draught and a 3ft freeboard. She had been built at the Rosendal yard in Hardanger Fjord, Norway, in 1872 and for 28 years had been employed in the herring fishery. Amundsen gave her a thirteen-horsepower two-cylinder engine and had her hull and decks strengthened against ice.

She took him through the North-West Passage.

Left: The Fram *in the ice. After taking Nansen deep into the Arctic, she carried Amundsen to the South Pole – and now enjoys a happy retirement in Oslo, Norway.*

Above: Scott's Discovery. *Since 1937 she has been moored in the Thames at London, off the Victoria Embankment.*

Right: Parry's Fury *and* Hecla *which joined the long search for the North-West Passage.*

triple-expansion engine of 220 indicated horse-power.

In 1896, at the end of amazing journeys by sea and land, he reached home, to be honoured as the man who had been further north than anyone before him. The little *Fram* had not ended her career. After the North-West Passage expedition, Amundsen took her over for a new expedition which he was planning. He had set his heart on being first at the North Pole. In 1909 all was ready for his departure when the world learnt that the Pole had been reached on 6 April by Robert Edwin Peary from Pennsylvania who traced his interest in the North Pole to Norden-skiöld's *Exploration of Greenland*. Leaving the ship *Roosevelt* in the ice, a party of six – Peary, his Negro companion Matthew Henson, and four Eskimos – had completed a sledge journey of 140 miles. From Newfoundland the explorer sent the message which ruined Amundsen's plans: 'Stars and Stripes nailed to the Pole – Peary!'

The Norwegian immediately turned the prow of the *Fram* in the other direction. On 14 December 1911 he arrived at the South Pole, to be followed on 17 January 1912 by Robert Falcon Scott who had made the sea voyage in the *Terra Nova*.

There is a model of the barque-rigged *Terra Nova* at the London Science Museum. She was built as an auxiliary whaler of 744 tons gross, 187ft between perpendiculars and 31ft in breadth. She was built of wood in 1884 for Arctic whaling and her engines developed 140 nominal horse-power. After her Antarctic service she joined the Newfoundland sealing fleet and in September 1943 was lost off South Greenland.

The *Gjøa* and the *Fram* still exist. After Amundsen's voyage through the North-West Passage, the *Gjøa* battled her way to San Francisco through the fierce storm of October 1906. In April the city had been almost destroyed by the earthquake, but the explorers received a tremendous welcome. It was arranged that their

He left with a selected crew on 16 June 1903. Sailing through Coronation Gulf, the voyagers reached the mouth of the Mackenzie River.

Nearly a quarter of a century earlier an American expedition had tried to reach the North Pole by way of the Bering Strait. Its ship, the *Jeannette*, was wrecked in 1881, off the coast of Siberia, and in 1884 articles from the wreck were found on the south-west coast of Greenland. On reading of this discovery in a Norwegian newspaper, Fridtjof Nansen realized that they must have drifted on a floe right across the Polar Sea. 'It immediately occurred to me,' he wrote, 'that here lay the route to the Pole, ready to hand.' On 26 June 1893 he put out from Rækvik with eleven companions in the 400-ton *Fram*, a three-masted schooner which could also use a

ship should stay at the Mare Island naval base until the opening of the Panama Canal, when she would be the first ship through; but a little while afterwards she was bought by the Norwegian colony in San Francisco and presented to the city. She was there for 66 years. In 1971, just before the Amundsen centenary, the Gjøa Foundation asked for her return, and she was sent home on board the Norwegian *Star Billabong* to be restored and placed on permanent display at the National Maritime Museum in Oslo. The *Fram* has a home of her own in the same city: at the end of her active life she was hauled up a specially-constructed slipway and an attractive building was erected around her.

No Polar expedition ship is more famous than Captain Scott's *Discovery*, a Dundee-built wooden vessel of 1,620 tons, 198ft long and 34ft in beam. She took Scott to the Antarctic in 1901 and was away a little over four years. The Hudson's Bay Company acquired her in 1905. She took munitions to Russia in 1915 and performed various other duties. When Shackleton and his party were stranded on Elephant Island, the *Endurance* having been crushed in the ice, she left with a rescue party, only to discover at Port Stanley that the help was not required. She then sailed for Montevideo and loaded grain for France, where she was kept in coastal service, carrying grain to the smaller French ports, until 1920. The rest of her active career was spent on exploration and survey work, in the Falklands area and Antarctica, and by the time of her return to England she had steamed nearly 150,000 nautical miles. In 1936 she was taken over as a memorial to Captain Scott and a training ship for Sea Scouts but her upkeep proved difficult until the Admiralty had her refitted as HMS *Discovery*, flagship to the Admiral Commanding Reserves. She lies in the Thames, not far from the Houses of Parliament and Westminster Abbey.

Exploration in the Pacific did not end when Captain Cook sailed northward. His own work in southern waters was completed by Matthew Flinders. In the sloop *Norfolk*, of 25 tons, Flinders and his Lincolnshire friend George Bass proved that Tasmania was an island by sailing right round it. The Admiralty then sent him off in the *Investigator*, a vessel of the same breed as Captain Cook's, to find out if the eastern part of New Holland was separated from the rest by a big strait. He sailed until his vessel was beyond repair and then left for England to get another. The wreck of the ship in which he was sailing as a passenger led to a series of adventures and to his being imprisoned as a spy when he put in at Mauritius. The French held him for six years. He gave some of his familiar Lincolnshire names to the places he discovered without knowing that one day they would be joined by such names as Flinders Island, Flinders River and

Flinders University. It was he who suggested that New Holland should be known as Australia.

In the great age of Pacific exploration the Dutch, British, Spanish, Portuguese, and French – one of whom, Louis Antoine de Bougainville, has an island called after him as well as the bougainvillea – helped to complete the map of the world. The Dutch were active from an early date. Christopher Newport was at sea with the *Susan Constant*, *Godspeed* and *Discovery* in 1606, and in that same year Willem Janszoon sailed the yacht *Duyfken* out of Bantam to explore the whole of New Guinea. He reached the gulf of Carpentaria, as it would be known, and Cape Turnagain (Cape Keerweer). Ten years afterwards Dirk Hartog, on his way from the Cape of Good Hope to Java in the *De Eendracht*, went ashore on an unknown coast and set up a pole with a plate engraved by one of the sailors: 'On October 25, AD 1616, the ship *Eendracht* arrived here.' In 1696 Willem de Vlamingh, master of the *Geelvinck*, found the plate – it is now in the Rijksmuseum in Amsterdam – and took it with him to Batavia, leaving an inscription of his own. There are almost as many Dutch names in the history of Pacific discovery as there are in the history of art.

Modern exploration is largely concerned with surveying and research in the spirit pioneered by Captain Cook. Two especially notable research voyages were made in the nineteenth century,

Previous pages: Ra I, *a carefully constructed facsimile of an ancient Egyptian vessel of papyrus reeds, in which Thor Heyerdahl and a small international crew set out from Morocco in 1969 to sail across the Atlantic Ocean. They got to within 600 miles from Central America before the boat broke up in heavy seas.*

the first of them by Charles Darwin and Captain Robert Fitzroy in the *Beagle* and the second by Captain George Nares and his companions in the *Challenger*. The giant turtles and iguana lizards in the Galapagos Islands awakened young Darwin to 'that mystery of mysteries – the first appearance of new beings upon this earth'. He was 22 at the time; at 50 he published *The Origin of Species*.

HMS *Beagle* was a ten-gun brig of 242 tons burden, only 100ft long. Officially HMS *Challenger* was described as a steam corvette – she had an engine of rather more than 1,200 horsepower – but for most of the time she depended on wind and canvas. She was a three-masted, square-rigged wooden ship of 2,300 tons dis-

great navigators'. There was a day when he passed through the Torres Strait on a voyage from Sydney to Mauritius, 'commanding very likely the first, and certainly the last, merchant ship that carried a cargo that way'. He came out of the strait – before dusk fell:

Just as a clear sun sank ahead of my ship I took a bearing of a little island for a fresh departure, an insignificant crumb of dark earth, lonely, like an advanced sentinel of that mass of broken land and water, to watch the approaches from the side of Arafura Sea. But to me it was a hallowed spot, for I knew that the *Endeavour* had been hove to off it in the year 1762 for her captain, whose name was James Cook, to go ashore for half an hour. . . .

Left: Darwin's Beagle *at Sydney Harbour in 1841. The future author of* The Descent of Man *and* The Origin of Species *was 22 when his friend J.S. Henslow, Professor of Botany at Cambridge, invited him to join HMS* Beagle *as naturalist on an expedition to South America and the Pacific.*

Below left: Erebus and Terror in a storm *by Beechey. They left England in May 1845 on an ill-fated quest for the North-West Passage.*

placement, about 200ft long overall. Sailing from Portsmouth in 1872, she circumnavigated the world, logging over 68,000 nautical miles on a voyage that lasted 1,000 days.

Endeavour, Resolution, Adventure and *Discovery* – the names of James Cook's ships sum up a great era on the oceans. One word is missing: courage. In the achievement of the discoverers and explorers by sea there is inspiration for us all. Joseph Conrad said that he was never lonely at sea because he had with him 'the company of

Thus the sea has been for me a hallowed ground, thanks to those books of travel and discovery which have peopled it with unforgettable shades of the masters in the calling which, in a humble way, was to be mine, too; men great in their endeavour and in hard-won successes of militant geography; men who went forth each according to his lights and with varied motives, laudable or sinful, but each bearing in his breast a spark of the sacred fire.

Above: A Cautious Landing *by W. Hodges. Captain Cook arrives at Tana, New Hebrides, in 1744.*

Index